MURDER IN THE MOUNTAINS

MURDER IN THE MOUNTAINS

Historic True Crime in Western North Carolina

NADIA DEAN

VALLEY RIVER PRESS

Published by Valley River Press, P.O. Box 369, Cherokee, North Carolina 28719

ISBN: 978-0-9831133-5-5 (paperback)
ISBN: 978-0-9831133-6-2 (ebook)

Library of Congress Control Number: 2021913396

Cover and interior design: MediaNeighbours.com

This book narrates true murder stories. While the author has written with compassion and respect, it may yet be troubling for some readers. Discretion is advised.

This book is dedicated to my "papaw," D. D. York,
who told me the family history
that inspired this collection of stories.

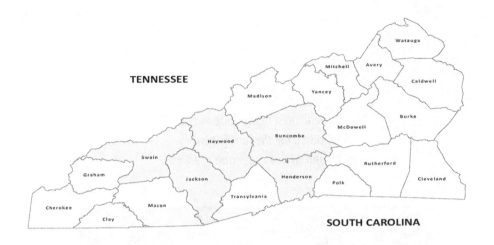

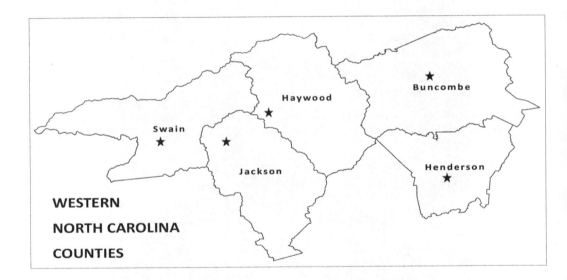

WESTERN
NORTH CAROLINA
COUNTIES

BUNCOMBE COUNTY
Buncombe's Boasted Bastille Busted
Anderson & Ray jailed & escaped, 1885

The Lynching of Bob Brackett
Arrested, jailed, seized & hanged, 1897

The Hanging of Jack Lambert
Jailed for murder, 1885

JACKSON COUNTY
The Hanging of Jack Lambert
The murder of Dick Wilson, 1884

SWAIN COUNTY
The Hanging of Jack Lambert
Trial & execution, 1885-1886

HENDERSON COUNTY
Buncombe's Boasted Bastille Busted
Anderson & Ray jailed, 1884

HAYWOOD COUNTY
Murder in Big Bend
Murders of Scott Brown and Mims White, 1930

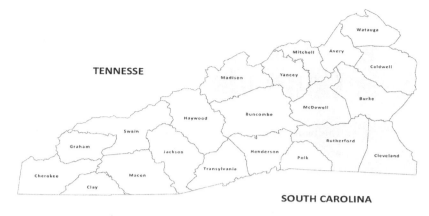

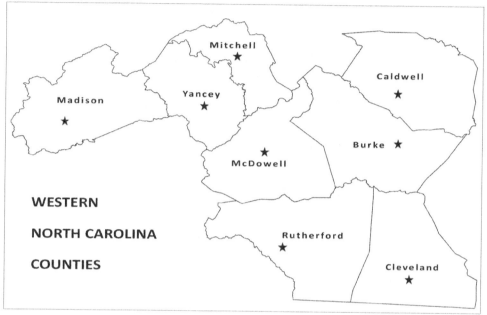

WESTERN

NORTH CAROLINA

COUNTIES

BURKE COUNTY
Emotional Insanity
Murder of Fleming, trial of Avery, 1851

CALDWELL COUNTY
Buncombe's Boasted Bastille Busted
Anderson & Ray jailed & trials, 1884-1885

MADISON COUNTY
Bloody Madison
The murders of Drury Norton & his three sons,
1854, 1864

YANCEY COUNTY
The Tragedy of Montraville Ray
The murder of A. J. Brown & trial of Mont Ray,
1870, 1882

RUTHERFORD COUNTY
The Weston Family Massacre
Adair trials and hangings, 1871-1872

The Whipping of Aaron Biggerstaff
1st attack by the KKK, 1871

CLEVELAND COUNTY
The Whipping of Aaron Biggerstaff
2nd attack by the KKK, 1871

MCDOWELL COUNTY
Emotional Insanity
The bullwhipping of W. W. Avery, 1851

MITCHELL COUNTY
Buncombe's Boasted Bastille Busted
The murders of Horton, Burleson & Miller, 1884

Contents

This book narrates true murder stories. While the author has written with compassion and respect, it may yet be troubling for some readers. Discretion is advised.

Acknowledgments .... **x**

Author's Note .... **xii**

1. Emotional Insanity **1**

A lawyer who in broad daylight is bullwhipped by his opponent takes the law into his own hands, committing an act of insanity in the presence of a judge (1851).

2. Bloody Madison **12**

A Union sympathizer in the heart of southern Appalachia becomes an efficient spy after Confederates rain hell and terror on her Madison County farm (1864).

3. The Tragedy of Montraville Ray **27**

A Confederate deserter turned Union sympathizer directs a daring raid on the town of Burnsville, and the hatred that ensues leads to murder and a fugitive from justice (1870, 1882).

4. The Weston Family Massacre **40**

Claiming allegiance to the KKK, two brothers slaughter a mixed-race family and fittingly get fitted for a noose (1872).

5. The Whipping of Aaron Biggerstaff **53**

Two brothers with different mothers carry on a feud. Their animosity ignites violence that rises to the national level when Congress investigates KKK atrocities in North Carolina (1871).

6. The Hanging of Jack Lambert **65**

A restless miner, a revenue officer, a night of drinking, and pistols. What could go wrong (1884-1886)?

7. "Buncombe's Boasted Bastille Busted" 83
A US Deputy Marshal convicted of murder and sentenced to hang gets help from his powerful father-in-law before his fateful day on the gallows (1884-1885).

8. The Lynching of Bob Brackett 109
Hundreds of angry men storm the county jail to seize a Black man accused of raping a White woman, only to find the prisoner gone (1897).

9. Murder in Big Bend 121
A femme fatale sparks the disappearance of her first two husbands, but a vacationing Chicago detective pops the lid on the whole thing (1931).

10. Fugitive Justice 135
A revenue officer with a dark past reinvents himself as a lawman, hoping to win a governor's pardon so he can return home (1885-1913).

Appendices
  1. Forty Women Indicted..165
  2. Map Detail of Charley Hood's Adventures 166
  3. Rutherford County Ku Klux Klan, aka the White
     Brotherhood and the Invisible Empire 167
  4. Those Who Testified before Congress in 1871
     Who'd Also Been Indicted in the Biggerstaff Case.......170
  5. Cases of Execution by Hanging in North Carolina......173
  6. Transcription of the Sentencing of John M. Williams ...175

End Notes...180

Sources 200

Illustration Credits 207

Index..211

About the Author 231

Acknowledgments

I THANK THE CREATOR, WHO AWAKENS our sense of story and its importance in our lives. I'm thankful for my parents, who gave me a never-ending curiosity of the world. I'm grateful for my grandfather, D. D. York, who told me the story that led to the making of this book—the story of my 2nd great-grandfather being murdered by fratricide. Thanks to my husband, Hugh Lambert III, whose love and support makes my work possible. Thanks to Evelyn Duffy, whose excellent editorial assistance for legendary journalist Bob Woodward carried over into four stories in this chronicle of a fascinating, yet overlooked time in American history. Thanks Dr. Lloyd Bailey for sharing Yancey County research. Special thanks to Marshal Trimble, Arizona's premier state historian, for help in sorting out the train robberies. Thanks Charles Miller for introducing me to the story of Oma Hicks. Thank you, Sheila Kay Adams, for inspiring talks about your extraordinary ancestor Nancy Franklin. Thanks, Dan Slagle, for sharing research about Nancy Franklin and for urging me to write the story of Montraville Ray. Thanks to Susan Sloate for great story insights and editorial assistance on four stories. Thanks to Robert Ryals for helpful editorial assistance. Thanks to Bryan Koontz for creating lovely depictions of our beautiful Smoky Mountains. Thanks, Sonnet Fitzgerald, for insightful editing. Thanks, Mary Neighbour, for editing and book production. Thanks, Susan Winstead, for research assistance. Thanks to Lamar Marshall for collaborating on the maps. Thank you, Sherry Jarrett, for your friendship, encouragement and prayers. Thanks, Linda Brown, of the Old Buncombe County Genealogy Society, as well as Matt Bumgarner, for help with southern railroad history. I'm grateful for the men and women who work to preserve history so that all of us may benefit from the stories of those who lived before us; stories that allow us to see the imperfections of our own humanity.

Author's Note

THIS BOOK HAS ITS BEGINNINGS in genealogy research. When I climbed up into and shook my family tree, I knocked loose stories that compelled me to tell them. Over thirty years ago, my grandfather told me a shocking story. In 1885, my 2nd great-grandfather was murdered by his brother, who then escaped jail with two notorious outlaws. Nothing further could be learned about the murder or the jailbreak. Fast forward three decades to the digital age and online historical newspapers. And I began digging again.

Reading about the jailbreak, I learned that my 2nd great-grand-uncle was awaiting trial at the time he escaped. A local newspaper reporter interviewed one of the prisoners in another cell who'd watched the whole getaway. His name was Jack Lambert, and he'd also been convicted of murder and was awaiting execution by hanging.

Being married to a Lambert, I was curious. I asked my husband, "Are you by chance related to Jack Lambert?" To my surprise, he said, "Yes. He was my 2nd great-grand-uncle." Happy to relate what I'd learned, I said, "Your uncle, in jail for murder, watched my uncle, also in jail for murder, break out. What do you make of that?"

I'd also learned that at the time of the escape, Jack Lambert had been married to my 2nd great-grand-aunt for the previous eight months. This meant he and my uncle were brothers-in-law. Discovering that my husband's nineteenth century family had been so intimately intertwined with mine invited me to look deeper. And that I did, unearthing long-buried stories of true crime in nineteenth-century western North Carolina.

The research of Madison County's Nancy Franklin came about many years prior to this book being an idea. Seventeen years ago, my friend and fellow historian Dan Slagle shared his research with me, and since then, Nancy has lived in my imagination.

Exploring what her outer and inner worlds must have been like, I wrote essays about her, and some of that prose made its way into this book.

The process of researching, writing, and publishing *A Demand of Blood* taught me much about correlating the attributes of the past with the realities of the present in order to reach a deeper understanding of ourselves and the world around us. In discovering our past—whether it's our collective experience or individually—we come to a knowledge of our humanity in ways nothing else can provide.

In all but one story in this book alcohol—either the consumption of it or the dealing in it—figures prominently in the act of murder. As a culture today, we might joke about the proverbial drunk Irishman or small-town drunk, but in reality, many lives were deeply marred by alcohol. Moonshine, guns, and hot tempers stole the lives of many young men. The North Carolina mountain region was every bit as fraught with danger as any town in the American Wild West, and in some cases, perhaps more so. As I searched for compelling stories from the history of the Smoky Mountains, I found a common thread that runs through all of them: resentments allowed to grow out of control, in the end, control everything.

—Nadia Dean

CHAPTER ONE

Emotional Insanity

THE SOCIAL EVOLUTION OF THE people of North Carolina had been slow in coming in the decades previous to 1851. The pattern of life, especially in the mountain region, had changed little. Strong influences of individualism, demonstrated by "unbridled freedom of speech," as one historian put it, often led to "physical combat or the duel to settle disputes." In the mid nineteenth century, some North Carolinians exhibited a lack of patience in the "orderly process of legal and social control and cooperation."

Nowhere are these truths more evident than in the story of Samuel Fleming—almost a caricature of the self-made American man. Born in 1810 in Maryland, Fleming became a big, braggadocious "rugged mountain man," and was likely self-educated. Others considered him a powerful speaker. Primarily a buyer and seller of horses, Fleming's business ventures ranged from livestock and planting to selling liquor. Caustic and sarcastic, he sought to emulate President Andrew Jackson in both politics and demeanor, and he entered government as a twenty-two-year-old Democratic member of the North Carolina House of Commons.

He campaigned in a freewheeling, populist way, gesticulating wildly from on top of a dry goods box in front of his store and promising supporters a "treat" of whiskey—an unscrupulous but effective method of getting votes.

In 1850 and 1851, one of the main issues in North Carolina politics and in the House of Commons was "free suffrage"—a movement to eliminate the requirement for a man to own fifty acres of land in order to vote. (When achieved in 1857, its passage gave an estimated 125,000 North Carolinians a right to vote.) Fleming supported fulfilling free suffrage through a constitutional convention, believing it would bring other benefits to the state's western counties. When he failed to do this through a bill in the legislature, he launched a grassroots campaign and even attempted to form a new political party.

In 1835, Fleming had married Hannah Greenlee, the daughter of a colonel. Five children came from their union. Shortly before she died, Hannah came into a large inheritance. The Greenlees' money left Fleming "one of the biggest landowners and slaveholders" in two counties. A proud bully, he angered quickly—a trait that gave rise to increased conflicts with his adversary, William Waightstill Avery, a fellow attorney and statesman.

Avery was known as "Waightstill" to his friends but as W. W. Avery to history. His life presented a photographic negative of Fleming's. Avery was born in 1816 into North Carolinian aristocracy. His grandfather Waightstill Avery had been an Indian commissioner at the Cherokee treaty of 1777, practiced law and became North Carolina's first attorney general. W. W. Avery's father, Isaac Thomas Avery, lived as a wealthy landowner and livestock breeder. His mother, a woman of "strong Christian convictions," also came from a prominent North Carolinian family. Avery's relatives included lawyers, doctors, and "many titled officeholders" in the area. In 1846, he married Mary Corrina Morehead, the daughter of a former governor, which further cemented his social class.

As a child, he had severe illnesses that likely stunted his growth and may have damaged his heart. He was taught to read and write at home, and later studied Latin, Greek, and mathematics at a private grammar school in preparation for college. Although at times he helped his father in his business, bargaining for supplies or taking droves of livestock to market, he graduated as valedictorian of his class at the University of North Carolina at Chapel Hill and studied law under a respected jurist. He grew into a slight, delicate man with large, somber eyes and a square, clean-shaven jaw.

He received his first license to practice law in the county courts of the state on April 9, 1839. This may have been the first time his life crossed paths with that of Samuel Fleming, who received—on the same day, from the same court—a license to sell liquor in his store. It would not be the last.

Avery built a large and successful law practice. At twenty-six, two years after an unsuccessful run for the legislature, Avery was elected to the House of Commons. He could be shrewd and caustic in the courtroom and aggressive in the legislature, but his peers generally regarded him as gentlemanly and affable.

Avery and Fleming both served as Democrats from the western part of the state in the North Carolina House of Commons. While Fleming—a Jacksonian Democrat—fought his grassroots battle for a constitutional convention, Avery—like John C. Calhoun, a believer in states' rights—favored legislative action. He wanted the less populated but wealthier eastern counties to continue to dominate the state. During one of their bitter debates, Avery accused Fleming of being an unscrupulous demagogue. Fleming called Avery a traitor to the western counties.

Their political differences soon overlapped in a brewing court battle wherein Fleming and his deceased wife's relatives were feuding over her father's estate. Avery had been retained to represent the Greenlees, and he secured an injunction barring Fleming from collecting a claim. Fleming was particularly incensed because he had "received a judgment against one of the Greenlees." Nevertheless, Avery successfully argued that Fleming "used fraud to acquire the notes on which the claim rested." Fleming told a friend he blamed Avery, not the Greenlees, for the fraud allegation, and that Avery had previously worked against him before. Fleming more than once tried to provoke Avery into challenging him to a duel, although he had not succeeded. Now Fleming said he would "be damned if he did not cowhide him."

Making his clients' case in court in Marion, North Carolina, on October 21, 1851, Avery again accused Fleming of fraud—this time alleging his entire career, in both politics and business, was a sham. The *North-Carolina Star* would later report his words were "not more severe than most other lawyers would have used under similar circumstances."

Fleming left court and purchased a cowhide whip. Outside the courthouse he waited with the lash hidden under his coat and a rock in his hand.

After court adjourned, Avery left the courthouse with some other lawyers and Judge William Horn Battle. The judge went one way and Avery and his client went another. When they encountered Fleming, the client gracefully bowed out and continued on his way.

Fleming dared Avery to repeat his remarks from the courtroom. The press would later report Avery "remarked that what he had said was in his official capacity, and that he had nothing to say to him, or was not accountable to him out of the courthouse for such acts."

"Will you fight?" Fleming demanded.

Avery said he wanted no fuss and walked away.

Fleming pulled out the hidden whip and lashed Avery several times. The *North-Carolina Star* later wrote it included "from 4 to 10 licks in rapid succession"—a brutal beating.

A November 19, 1851 account in the *Raleigh Register* reported that "Avery immediately turned and knocked him down with his fist, behind unarmed," although reports conflict, and it's far more likely that the larger and stronger Fleming got the best of Avery.

Fleming beat Avery's face and head with the rock, "felling him and rendering him entirely insensible."

A crowd, including Judge Battle, gathered quickly and separated the two men. Avery bled profusely from his forehead, and his face was badly bruised. Fleming cursed Avery, saying he would fight him "with anything from the point of a knife to a cannon's mouth."

Before Avery "could properly avenge the indignity offered to his person," the *Tri-Weekly Commercial* reported, "the parties were separated, and he was taken to his room, and all weapons of offense denied him."

Avery's cousin, Dr. John W. Erwin, tended to his wounds. Avery's close friend and fellow lawyer, E. P. Jones, was also with him. Avery asked what he should do about Fleming. He insisted they get him "a pistol, or other weapon, saying he did not know what he might do before he left." Both men withheld their counsel. They knew Avery's honor had been insulted and his reputation "as a man, a citizen, and a lawyer was at stake . . . for the public would regard any attempt to seek redress through the courts as a shirking of his moral

A cowhide is a whip used to drive cattle—not by striking them with it, which would cause injury, but by startling them with its cracking sound. They also had long been used as a tool of power and punishment against slaves, and slave owners had fewer qualms about whipping the human beings they owned than their cows.

Since cowhiding was seen as a tool of authority over slaves, Southern White men felt it carried extra dishonor when applied against a White man. One newspaper at the time wrote, "A man might bear the fist of another, or his cane; or any other weapon without dishonor except a cowhide, for to no other does such a stigma attach itself as to that. . . . According to the unwritten law, any man who cold-bloodedly cowhided another forfeited his right to live."

duty." According to the *North-Carolina Star*, Erwin eventually decided to procure a pistol and gave it to Avery.

Avery left his hotel after nightfall to return home. During the twenty-plus-mile ride, he decided to kill Fleming as soon as possible. Later he said that he had no intention of giving his assailant a chance to defend himself—deeming Fleming "too far beneath the dignity of a gentleman to entitle him to be treated as one."

For the next three weeks, Fleming boasted about whipping Avery. He said he had "cowhided one lawyer and would treat the whole profession so, if they spoke disrespectfully of him." Of Avery specifically, he said he was a coward who "would not even resent a cowhiding."

In the meantime, Avery went about his usual business but fell into depression. Judge Battle thought Avery would be driven hopelessly insane if his despondency went on another month. Yet when the court reopened for its fall term on November 10 in Morganton, Avery appeared to represent his clients, despite seeming distracted and unable to conduct serious business. He likely heard that Fleming was around.

The next day, November 11, Fleming appeared in town with his fourteen-year-old son, John. He sent John ahead to Charleston with some horses, telling him he'd catch up to him on the road within a day. Fleming checked into the Mountain Hotel, where he left his saddlebags and pistol. He made a point of being seen around town and in the courthouse. He told others he wasn't afraid, and "always went where his business called." Hoping his taunt would make its way to Avery, Fleming told an acquaintance, "Give my regards to your lady. I understand she said to you, were you to come to her after a cowhiding without resenting it, she would be tempted to give you another." That afternoon, Fleming went to the courthouse to appear on a matter he was involved in.

Avery had arrived first. He was engrossed in conversation with two drunken clients and hadn't yet taken off his cloak. Judge Battle sat on the bench.

Fleming walked up to the clerk's table, and as he bent down to talk to the clerk, he put himself in close proximity to Avery. This gave rise to the first time Avery saw Fleming since the flogging.

Avery, clearly irritated by Fleming, may have felt that Fleming's deliberate adjacency was the last straw. Suddenly, Avery stood up, pulled a pistol from under his cloak, stepped forward, and shot Fleming at point-blank range.

Fleming straightened, held his hand to his chest, and pulled out his watch—perhaps an attempt to draw a weapon— then fell over. Avery threw his pistol at him, breaking it.

Avery likely shot Fleming with a Derringer .50-caliber pistol.

Burgess S. Gaither, a solicitor and a relative of Avery's, rushed Avery out of the courtroom.

"Judge Battle automatically swung his gavel, and with the familiar sound came a sickening realization that he had been a reluctant witness to the tragic drama," reported the *North-Carolina Star*. So had the rest of the courtroom, the bailiff, and the clerk.

Fleming died without a word. The bullet passed below his ribs, through his heart, and exited through his chest, only to get caught on his vest. Avery had orphaned Fleming's five children.

Avery left the courtroom and headed toward the jail and surrendered himself to the sheriff. The *North-Carolina Star* would later report on the extraordinary murder "in a public courthouse under the eyes of the judge upon the bench, in his official capacity, in the presence of the solicitor of the district, the sheriff of the county, and several other official dignitaries," writing, "well may the sense of a whole community be shocked, well may its mind tremble and quake, when such an act is committed in such a place, in such a way, by men who stand high in the community, men who are the legal representatives and expounders of law and order."

The paper would go on to write that Fleming had been "passionate, ambitious, of quick temperament, daring and inconsiderate, and in consequence of it has lost his life."

For the next several days, a cold rain drizzled. Fleming's two oldest children, John and Mary, were brought to town to view Fleming's body; they buried him in the Presbyterian churchyard in Morganton. The following week his body was moved to be reburied beside his wife.

Avery was arraigned before Judge Battle, who set the trial for murder three days later, on Friday, November 14, in the same courtroom where the crime had occurred.

The day before the trial, a relative of Avery's, W. W. Lenoir, weighed in on Avery's situation. Lenoir, like Avery, came from a family with Revolutionary roots and aristocratic bearing. He was a descendant of Revolutionary General William Lenoir, a large landowner. Lenoir wrote that Avery had been like a character out of Aeschylus, facing a "dilemma either alternative of which is dreadful." Avery either had to kill Fleming and face the consequences, or be cast out from his family and society for allowing anyone to dishonor him so severely. As Lenoir saw it, Avery had been driven insane by Fleming's cowhiding, and would not have been able to return to sanity without shedding Fleming's blood— not a murder, but "an act of righteous retribution."

A jury was empaneled and witnesses summoned. Some men who had seen the killing sat on the jury, and Judge Battle, who had observed both the fight and the murder, sat on the bench.

The packed courtroom gave Avery a standing ovation when he was brought in. He sat with his father and brothers as the trial began. The *North-Carolinian* reported that Avery "was cheerful during the progress of the trial. . . . Indeed, he felt a relief from the stigma which has been put upon him that buoyed him up and made him feel all the pride of vindicated honor and avenged insult." Witnesses testified to a belief that Avery was not "in his right mind."

The prosecutor spoke for forty-five minutes, "his arms flailing the air like the sails of a windmill caught in a storm." He argued for the principle of impartial justice for all "and of maintaining the dignity and supremacy of the law."

But Avery, the scion of a patrician family of attorneys, was represented by the best. That day, two of Avery's defense lawyers spoke, one for forty-five minutes and the other for an hour.

The next day, the gray weather finally cleared, and one of the most highly esteemed lawyers in the state, John Bynum, spoke in Avery's defense. "A careful student of human nature, he skillfully appealed to every prejudice that could in any way aid his client's cause," and argued the charge against Avery should be reduced from murder to manslaughter. Fleming, he asserted, had provoked Avery to kill him by appearing unarmed and so close to him in the courtroom. "No doubt God forgives Mr. Avery," Bynum said. "And whom God pardons, men dare not punish."

In his instructions to the jury, Judge Battle said it was his job, not theirs, to determine the law. Avery had been correctly charged with murder, not manslaughter. But if the witnesses' testimony convinced the jury that Avery's mind was so deranged he hadn't known he'd committed a crime, they should find him not guilty.

The jury took only ten minutes to declare Avery "not guilty by reason of emotional insanity."

The *Asheville Messenger* reported that Judge Battle believed "that the jury would have found him and every member of the bar guilty before they would have convicted Avery."

The judge later wrote that the room was silent. Almost everyone shook Avery's hand, in tears. "Battle's voice adjourning the court until 2:00 that afternoon was the first sound to rise above a whisper."

One newspaper reported a crowd of a "thousand people responded with tears of rejoicing." The *North-Carolinian* called it "undisguised joy."

There had been fewer than five full days from Fleming's death to Avery's acquittal.

The *North-Carolina Star* wrote that it believed the jury's verdict came from "the true belief that this unfortunate man's reason was dethroned, and that he was the creature of distracted, harrowed, outraged, ungovernable passions and feelings, when the fatal deed was committed."

Another paper wrote of Avery, "As a man of the world, situated as he was, outraged and insulted as he had been, and with precisely such a state of public opinion upon such subjects as exist in the community in which he lives, no other course was open or possible for him, and instead of blame, he deserves sympathy."

The *North-Carolinian* later bragged, "As we anticipated, we have the pleasure of announcing Mr. Avery's acquittal. . . . There probably never was a case tried in this country the decision of which caused more universal satisfaction; and we may say, gratification."

Within a few days, Judge William Horn Battle wrote to his wife, "This case illustrates the verity of the statement. . . . [T]hat truth is often stranger than fiction." Battle, who had been on the Superior Court bench for over a decade, thought the jury's verdict showed that the unwritten code of honor that dictated Avery's actions and long guided Southern elites had spread as unwritten law among White Southern men regardless of class or status. The jury ignored his instructions and acquitted Avery according to this code of honor, not the law of the land.

For years afterward, Avery suffered insomnia and depression; he often seemed preoccupied. But his social and political standing didn't suffer: he was reelected to the House of Commons and later to the state Senate, where he served as speaker from 1856 to 1857.

He became a secessionist and argued for North Carolina to leave the Union after the election of Abraham Lincoln as president in 1860. On May 20, 1861, North Carolina was the final state to secede from the Union, and Avery successfully ran for the provincial Congress; he served until the permanent government took over.

Avery lost his reelection bid. When his term ended, he went home to Morganton and raised a regiment to fight in the war. His four brothers were already in active service; they and Avery's eighty-year-old father argued that Avery was too old to fight and had a duty to stay home. Avery did, and gave large sums of money to the Confederacy's support of soldiers' families. Within a year, two of his brothers were killed in battle.

In June 1864, a band of Union sympathizers, Cherokees, and Confederate deserters led by Col. George Kirk invaded the state. Kirk captured conscripted Confederate soldiers, sabotaged a railroad, and looted the countryside. Compelled by a sense of duty to his own honor and to North Carolina's, Avery commanded a group of several hundred older men and boys in a hastily-organized Home Guard in pursuit, hoping to free the conscripts. They attacked Kirk's forces in a skirmish in the mountains about twenty miles from Morganton. Avery was mortally wounded and carried home to Morganton, where he died on July 3.

His father buried him in the Presbyterian cemetery—the same cemetery where Fleming had initially been interred, their lives and deaths forever linked.

The newspapers, the jury, and the public all seemed to have diminished Fleming's very existence. As for Avery, he had committed murder with a gun and had his own life ended with one; he'd killed for, and been killed by, the "emotional insanity" of honor.

CHAPTER TWO

Bloody Madison

SHELTON LAUREL, A PLACID REALM of earth in Madison County, is a valley with deep, hardwood forests, thickets of rhododendron, and picturesque coves that define its boundary. The Laurel River streaming through Madison supplies creeks and streams with fresh water and an abundance of fish. In Laurel country's higher elevations with cascading waterfalls and blooming mountain laurel in spring, the early inhabitants must have felt grateful to have been granted land in such a magnificent spectacle of God's creation.

Shelton Laurel was named for some of its earliest English settlers including Roderick, James, and David Shelton. Other families that put down roots included Franklin, Gosnell, Gunter, and Norton. These determined men and women and their descendants founded an enclave of settlements in the Smoky Mountains called Big Laurel, Little Laurel, and Shelton Laurel.

Nancy Shelton Norton Franklin, born in January 1825 in Shelton Laurel, was a striking brunette with steely eyes and a strong disposition. Like others in her early nineteenth-century mountain community, she never learned to read or write. The mountains into which she was born and where she would raise her own had always been home. What lay beyond the high ridges of her realm held no fascination for Nancy. It was enough to be a woman, in her day, tasked with managing the exquisite suffering of sheer survival; there were no allowances for thoughts of folly about other worlds.

Nancy grew up surrounded by trees with roots as deep in the earth as hers were in the people of Shelton Laurel. Nancy's grandfather had been a soldier in the American War of Independence, and of that she held a special pride afforded only those who could rightly claim it. Shelton blood, she was taught, was strong enough to withstand whatever horrors life might inflict upon her. Being of Shelton stock, she felt the bond between the blood of her people and the land they survived upon. The Sheltons had long been a preeminent family in Laurel Valley, and with that history, Nancy experienced a solid sense of belonging that aided her in troubles times—the cloud of love and connection that the old ones spoke of surrounded her daily life. On every crest, on every vista, in every direction

The inset is the only known photograph of Nancy Shelton Norton Franklin. The original, likely not much larger than a postage stamp, is not dated, but in those days a woman had her picture made only on special occasions. Perhaps her wedding day, and her second husband, George, was later cut out of the picture? (It appears cropped on the right.)

Artist Bryan Koontz sketched this to see more clearly the details of her face and clothing.

she gazed, Nancy's province of the Smoky Mountains engulfed and enhanced her very existence.

Nancy Shelton, granddaughter of Roderick Shelton, had married Drury Norton in about 1840. They lived as their ancestors had—by farming and raising children, having four sons and two daughters. The Norton's farm was in the high hills between the tiny hamlets of Gunter town and Franklin town. The boys worked the cornfields, tended the hogs, tanned hides, and hunted wild game, while the girls learned to milk cows and take care of the chickens. The family owned two horses, a work steer, and a large number of sheep, cattle, hogs, and poultry. The Nortons were better off than some of their neighbors and lived in a so-called "mansion house," meaning a milled wood-framed home rather than a log cabin.

Despite the pastoral nature of Shelton Laurel, lives could be cut short by deep political divisions, unfettered hatreds, and ubiquitous alcohol. Madison County eventually came to be called "Bloody Madison," not only for the Civil War event but also for the high rate of killings and familial violence—a scourge soon to overtake Nancy's life with a stunning and unexpected change.

The Murder of Drury Norton

One morning in May 1854, Drury Norton drank a lot of whiskey before going to work. His father-in-law, Roderick, and brother-in-law Lewis were with him, helping to plow up a fallow field. By day's end, Drury had sobered up, and when he and Lewis got back to the house, they found Nancy's other brother, James Shelton, and his friend, Tilman Landers, there. The men argued. It got heated, and Drury ordered the men to leave. Tilman spat chewing-tobacco juice in Drury's eyes and threw liquor in his face. Drury "was about to tell James Shelton he could stay," when suddenly James threw Drury out of his own house.

The fight was on. Drury picked up a maul and James drew an axe. James swung the axe, and Drury missed being hit by jumping into the house through the window. He next headed to his stable while loudly threatening to swear out a warrant. James threw stones at him. Drury quickly saddled up and rode off while James continued hurling rocks and cursing.

A half mile down the road, Drury arrived at his neighbor's, Mr. Gunter. He asked Gunter to lend him his gun, but Gunter refused. Drury pleaded with Gunter to go home with him, but the neighbor stayed out of it.

Fifteen minutes later, Drury stabled his horse. Thinking it too dangerous to return to the house the usual way, he snuck through the orchard. But as he did, he stepped on a stick that made a noise. Just then, someone hit him on the head. Moments later, Nancy and her father found Drury bleeding and prostrate in the orchard.

The next day Drury lay in bed and spoke to Nancy about their boys: Bayliss, James, George, and Josiah, saying he didn't think he'd be able to help them in "making a crop" that year. Later, an unnamed man visited Drury as he hung precariously between life and the afterlife. The man described the wound in Drury's forehead as "very severe," and said his skull had been fractured. Drury was weakening, but still able to speak. He told of the fight with James and Tilman. That night, Drury lingered for hours in delirium. Three days later, on May 17, 1854, Drury Norton died.

Meanwhile, James and Tilman had fled Shelton Laurel. On May 25, the *Asheville News* headline read: "STOP THE MURDERERS!" James Shelton and Tilman Landers had reportedly "waylaid the road" and killed Drury Norton. Calls went out throughout the region to capture the two men, saying the killers were "unsafe men for any community."

Weeks later, while James and Tilman were still on the lam, the NC governor issued a $350 reward for their arrest and delivery to the sheriff of Madison County. The notice described James Shelton as thirty-five years old, five-foot-ten and 160 pounds. He had sandy-colored hair, wore whiskers, and had a "rather fair" complexion, scarred by gunpowder burn. Tilman Landers, twenty-five, had red hair and a ruddy complexion, and was about the same height as Shelton. Tilman had a painful boil on one hand near the first joint of the middle finger that made it hard to use his hand, and when spoken to he tended to have "a downcast look."

James and Tilman were hiding in East Tennessee when a relentless posse hunted them down and brought them back to

Marshall. At trial, the jury found James Shelton guilty of murder and Tilman Landers guilty of manslaughter. When the jury foreman pronounced their verdict, "the prisoners manifested very little emotion."

James Shelton appealed. At issue: what portions of Drury Norton's dying words should the jury have been able to hear, and should James have been charged with murder or manslaughter?

In any trial, testimony is usually only admissible if it can pass two tests of truth: both an oath and a cross-examination. "A sense of impending death is as strong a guaranty of truth as the solemnity of an oath," said the court, so the declarations of a dying person pass the first test, but not the second, since there's "no opportunity for cross-examination." Dying declarations can be valuable, because "knowledge of the facts attending the killing is confined to the party killed and the perpetrator of the crime," but the circumstances for making them admissible evidence are limited to homicides, not murder. Allowing for any broader use of them would mean dying declarations become admissible "not merely to prove the act of killing, but to make every homicide murder by proof of some old grudge."

If the fight had been one continuous act, from the house to the stable to the orchard, "the killing was but manslaughter" and the dying declarations would be inadmissible. But if it ended at the stable and there had been a cooling off period before violence again broke out in the orchard, killing Drury would be an act of premeditated murder.

The trouble with Drury's account, "being a full narration of the whole fight," indicated that the fight had been a single, continuous act. In this case, James should have been charged with manslaughter. The high court concluded that, considering all the events as one act, the dying declarations had been "properly admitted as evidence." The lower court erred and "the judge should have instructed the jury" in light of the crime being one act, that "the killing was manslaughter." If the killing had been two separate acts, the dying declarations relating solely to the second act should have been admitted, however, the court erred by admitting the declarations that related to the first fight at the house before Drury left for Gunter's. The lower court judge should have "withdrawn from the jury all the declarations" except for the part which related to what "took place in the orchard when the fatal blow was struck."

The court concluded that Drury's death resulted from an armed provocation on both sides and that James had been "impelled, by blind fury, to kill his adversary." Miraculously, James won his appeal, and the judgement was reversed. James Shelton lived to be eighty.

Widowhood

At the age of twenty-six, Nancy became a widow with six children, by the hand of her brother James. Drury died intestate, "in possession of considerable personal estate," but included insurmountable debt. In July 1854, Nancy petitioned the court for a writ of dower (the court's decree for the care of a widow), which would give her a year's provision to support herself and her children. To pay down some of Drury's financial obligations, Nancy sold fifty acres, but she was able to keep her "mansion house" and remain on their farm on Big Laurel Creek. She also sold a few farm animals:

One horse sold to **David Farnsworth** $50.50
Sold **Roderick Shelton** one yearling $4.30
One work steer sold to **William Norton** $21.80
Four head of sheep and one pair of gears sold
    to **Wiley Gosnell** $9.00
Five head of sheep sold to **Hezekiah Franklin** for $7.50
Three head of cattle and three head of hogs sold to
    Nancy Norton for $32.50
Four head of sheep sold to **Nancy Norton** for six dollars
    and 31 1/4 cents
Five head of hogs sold to **Baxter Shelton** for $3.70

Nancy managed to keep some hogs, cows, sheep, and poultry. She also kept two hundred bushels of corn, the kitchen furniture, her farming tools, a pair of gears, and five dollars to buy coffee. She struggled to adjust to life as a widow with six little ones, but she drew strength to do what had to be done to keep body and soul together.

In May 1857, Nancy married George Washington Franklin, but it would be a tumultuous relationship. "I won't say that I lived with him all the time uninterruptedly, as he would sometimes go off and stay a long time," Nancy later recalled. "He was a drinking man." She said he didn't work, but "just lived on me and done little toward his own support before the war." During the first year of their marriage, Franklin made a living out of the farm, but after that, Nancy said, "I don't think he did any more than to support himself."

Nancy and her four boys were staunch Unionists. Her sons had joined the Union Army and were serving under the infamous Col. George Kirk of East Tennessee.

Kirk's all-volunteer North Carolina Mounted Infantry units spread fear and terror in western North Carolina. Aiming to undermine the Confederate cause, Kirk's guerrilla tactics sparked fear and hatred throughout the region by burning homes, bridges, and barns, earning them the moniker, "a notorious band of scoundrels and thieves." Cherokee Indians joined Kirk's ranks, serving as

Colonel George Washington Kirk (with his wife, Mariah) was a former Confederate soldier from East Tennessee who deserted and eventually became a colonel in the Union Army. Major General Schofield ordered then-Major Kirk to raise 200 men to undermine Confederate General Longstreet's strength by destroying support resources.

scouts. North Carolinians who refused to join the Confederate Army and had evaded the Home Guard, had joined his ranks. In 1864, his men attacked a conscription camp in Burke County and destroyed much property in the area.

Slavery existed in every county of North Carolina when the Civil War began, but in the high hills of Shelton Laurel, Nancy had no slaves, nor had she need for a war that would help another man own them—and spilling the blood of poor White farmers didn't figure into Nancy's view of the world. The way she figured it, every man and woman should have leave to exercise his or her view of things.

The state of North Carolina, initially reluctant to secede, did finally succumb to breaking from the Union. And the Conscription Act of 1862 led many in Shelton Laurel to feel imposed upon. As war came to Shelton Laurel, Nancy's sense of foreboding grew worse by the day. Times were desperate, and Nancy needed more than the bare subsistence that her farm provided. She hungered to be free from the tyranny of those whose views on the war stood sharply distant from her own.

Across Nancy's mountainous world, there were Confederates aplenty who daily were expectant and hopeful to run roughshod over any Lincolnite they encountered. There could be little doubt in her mind as to the nature of the coming tide. Nancy was vexed, haunted by worries about her sons and in what direction the state of things might turn. It was not the general uncertainty of life in Shelton Laurel that had as of late grown worse, but more like the eternal feeling of a thing—that life itself might be too fragile to hold with too firm a grasp. She'd sensed the foreboding cloud moving overhead like a large, dark hand that threatened to reach down and choke the life out of her world. Trouble from beyond the encompassing sphere of her mountains menaced sometimes, and her mind would glide into a fearful and unknown world where whispers and taunts gave hint to a groundswell of misfortunes that would soon rise up and entangle her body, soul, and spirit.

War in Shelton Laurel

Shelton Laurel men and women saw themselves in a continuum of the human saga of struggle to give their progeny the secure right to be free. They felt it was God's divine will that they live on the land their ancestors had won, and that their time had come to enter their own exploits in the historical record for their children to remember.

The Civil War came and split apart families as well as the community of Shelton Laurel. Being a Unionist in Shelton Laurel was a tenuous way to live. In January 1863, Confederates and Unionists clashed in a mass murder that shocked the nation.

Shelton Laurel Massacre

In the nineteenth century, salt meant survival. In Madison County in January 1863, Confederates were hoarding it and depriving Unionists of their share. In a desperate effort for survival and revenge, Unionists raided Marshall. They shot the salt guard and made off with salt, food, and supplies, then raided homes including Colonel Allen's. Ironically, Allen and the 64th Regiment were in East Tennessee guarding salt. In response to the raid, Lieutenant Colonel James A. Keith's unit from the 64th swooped into Shelton Laurel. Keith's men tortured women, including the elderly, by whipping and hanging them from a tree. Troops burned houses and slaughtered livestock. The Confederates rounded up suspected Unionists, and after a forced march, herded the thirteen men and boys into the woods. Ordered to kneel, they were then each shot in the head. All were buried in a mass grave. The women of Shelton Laurel removed the bodies and buried them elsewhere. Outrage spread throughout North Carolina and beyond. Madison County officially earned the moniker of "Bloody Madison." The shocking Shelton Laurel Massacre exemplified the razor-sharp divide in the community. Nancy Franklin, who lost six of her kinsmen, was likely a witness to the massacre or its horrifying aftermath.

In addition to Union guerrillas, other roving bands of marauders, outliers, and deserters roamed the countryside, terrorizing women and children throughout the mountains by stealing food, horses, and whatever else of value they could carry off.

Meanwhile, in Strawberry Plains, Tennessee, following a large cavalry raid, Confederates captured Nancy's fourteen-year-old son Josiah. Because of his youth, he was paroled. As Nancy put it, "They told him to go home, and he came home in citizen's clothes."

Nancy described Bayliss, eighteen, and James, sixteen, as "nearly grown up." Her middle son George and his brothers were all serving under Colonel George W. Kirk. In 1864, Nancy and her daughter Delany Jane went to Knoxville, cooking, sewing, and caring for the Union wounded. She later went to Kirk's camp at Bulls Gap, Tennessee. When she told the Colonel she was going home, Kirk gave Bayliss a furlough to go with her. The next day, James and George received verbal leave to return to Shelton Laurel as long as they'd report back in five days.

George would later say, "I think there was no written leave. Kirk had a habit of letting us come home on mere verbal permission." James and George came home on detached duty, meaning they were to forage for food. "The men in this command came and went as they pleased," a report read years later. "The colonel allowed it." The report dubbed it "a time and place where strict discipline was unknown."

Bayliss, James, and Josiah had been home for three days. Fearing an ambush by the rebels, they'd spent nights sleeping outside near the house. On their fourth day home, the boys were preparing to return to the army when their greatest fear came upon them.

On the morning of September 27, 1864, Nancy was not at home and George was away. In the early morning light, while Bayliss, James, and Josiah were eating breakfast, Confederates began surrounding the house. The boys saw the soldiers and ran outside. Bayliss and Josiah were immediately shot. James had run "some distance from the house" before being gunned down. The Confederates, soldiers from the 14th North Carolina Battalion, then set fire to Nancy's home.

Nancy was in earshot of the gunfire and came quickly. "I heard the shooting, and I saw them after they were dead," she later testified. "I never can forget the scene."

Years later in 1883, Nancy's surviving son, George, detailed the killings in a deposition. He said a squad of 140 rebels had come to the farm and killed his brothers. "I suppose it was not more than two hours after the shooting that I came over and saw them dead—all three."

An investigator later wrote, "There can be no further evidence obtained as to the shooting as it is not at all probable there were many spectators around about that time."

Nancy was forty-two when she came upon her murdered sons. A freed African slave helped Nancy bury Bayliss, James, and Josiah together in one grave with no coffins.

A Valuable Union Spy

The killings became fuel for Nancy's hatred for Confederates. She quickly utilized that energy to become a spy, later being lauded for her effectiveness by a Washington, DC, examiner. Her accomplishments as a Union spy have been lost to history, but part of her exploits did include directing Unionist bushwhackers.

From her vantage point on a hill hidden in the trees, she pointed out to her snipers every Confederate coming through her valley. "If one half of the stories told about her are true, she must have been a real heroine," Commissioner of Pensions M. E. Weeks would later write. Weeks dubbed Nancy "one of the most remarkable women of the war."

Speaking of the economic situation he observed while in Shelton Laurel, he said, "The land in these mountains has no value scarcely . . . [but] the land makes good crops and the people live well. There's no want in this country." Weeks noted that none of the county's men were hard workers, "and it's not a good place to hunt for angels." Weeks called Nancy "a thoroughly immoral woman," referring perhaps to Nancy's reputation for violence, or that she was living with a younger man. Weeks nevertheless lauded her patriotism, saying, "There can be no question raised as to her loyalty to the Union during all the war. After her three sons were murdered, she became desperate and was one of the most efficient spies in the whole Union Army."

Even though her husband George Franklin returned home after the war, Nancy testified, "I never recognized him as my husband." A year after the war's start, George Franklin had enlisted in the Confederate Army. "He done so against my will," Nancy later recalled. "I told him if he enlisted in the rebel army, I would never live with him another day, but he did enlist." Before long, George deserted and joined the Union army, but Nancy said, "I never lived with him after he joined the rebels."

George had been shot by Confederates, which left him disabled. He began drinking heavily and eventually began drawing a Civil War pension. There remains, however, some indication that from time to time, he'd stay at her home. But during that time, he had apparently taken up with other women.

When she learned of this, Nancy was furious. She boldly accosted her husband's paramour and commenced attacking her physically. In 1866, Nancy was charged with assault and battery against Mary Wilson. In another outburst, in 1868, Nancy, "in a fit of jealousy," stabbed a woman named Susan, inflicting a wound so severe that "for a while the life of the injured woman was thought to be in danger." Nancy's fits of rage did not stop there. In 1870, "she nearly killed a woman with whom she thought her husband was too intimate." Asked why she and Franklin had divorced, Nancy said, "He drank and got into some difficulties and I did not want to become responsible for his debts. I own all the property." (Earlier, in 1868, Madison County granted Nancy the power to hold her property independent of her husband. George had deserted Nancy, whose half-dozen children had made up her world where the struggle to feed hungry mouths grew progressively worse by her lay-about husband who loved the bottom of a bottle more than the family of seven he'd married into.)

Eventually, Nancy left Shelton Laurel and moved to Greene County, Tennessee. In July 1876, a notice appeared in the

Tennessee newspaper *Union and American*, notifying Nancy Franklin "to plead, answer, or demur to the petition filed against her for divorce" by her husband, George Franklin.

A Civil War Pension

The federal government passed a pension law on July 14, 1862, allowing Union veterans and their dependents to apply for a pension based on death or disability. In 1875, Nancy filed for a pension from the US government to make up for the loss of her sons' income, on which she claimed she'd been dependent. At the time of her application, the fifty-year-old Nancy was living with 28-year-old John W. Ballman.

In her request, she stated that her two eldest sons, Bayliss and James, would at times hire themselves out to work for other farmers. Nancy got part of their wages. "The fact is all my sons assisted me before the war, but I think that James assisted me more than the others," Nancy testified. "He was at home more."

Nancy faced obstacles to getting a pension. Her claim was investigated and initially denied because her sons "were not in the line of duty when killed"—and worse, they were suspected of desertion. "The soldiers' captain, lieutenant, and sergeant know nothing about it. It is absolutely impossible for one to get the facts," investigator Howard Miller wrote. Colonel Kirk's lenient leave policy worked against Nancy's case. However, "these boys, all parties agree, were good soldiers, and the record of the mother precludes the idea that they were deserters."

Even if there had been no cloud of uncertainty over their service record, obtaining a pension as a deceased soldier's parent would still have been difficult. Extensive proof that the parent had been dependent on their son's army pay had to be provided. Sworn affidavits from two credible and uninvolved witnesses were required. For women claiming their sons' pensions, there was an extra hurdle: "If the mother has a living husband, the fact is regarded as prima fascia evidence that she was not, in any degree, dependent upon her son for support. . . . It must be clearly proved by witnesses having personal knowledge that her husband has refused or neglected to provide for her support . . . or else, that having deserted her, he is beyond the reach of legal compulsion to contribute to her maintenance."

Son George and his sister Delaney Jane, as well as Nancy's brother John, supported her claim. John testified that his nephew James had helped support Nancy and had "always considered it his duty to aid and assist her." James had a "careful regard for her comfort and welfare" and "constantly and regularly" contributed to Nancy's support for three years from September 1861 until his death on September 27, 1864.

John further described Nancy's husband, George Franklin, as "a man of very bad habits," who had deserted her. John testified that George was "generally drunk" and for many years had not given Nancy any assistance. George Franklin had abandoned Nancy and had gone to Tennessee with another woman.

Another witness said James had passed by his mother's house frequently with bacon, cornmeal, flour, and sometimes coffee and tea and "spoke about his stepfather doing so bad and drinking himself to death."

In a report to the North Carolina Commissioner of Pensions, M. E. Weeks debunked the idea that Nancy was dependent, saying, "I don't think such dependence appears." He noted that Nancy still lived on the hundred-acre farm she'd inherited from Drury Norton "uninterruptedly from his death until now" and was "better off than a majority of her neighbors." Although Confederates had burned down her house in 1864, by 1875, she obviously would have had another home.

Asked to estimate his mother's worth at the time of his brothers' killing, George said, "Probably $500," which in today's buying power would be roughly $15,000. George testified that Nancy's husband, George Franklin, "never has been stout," a nineteenth-century expression meaning healthy or strong. George said Nancy's dependence on his brother James for support had been "her only chance."

M. E. Weeks's report went on to say, "There is not one particle of evidence to show that she was ever dependent on said son, who was only 18 years old when he was killed." Of George Franklin, he wrote, "I can find no evidence that he was different from any of the rest of the men in this country. None work hard."

M. E. Weeks concluded that Nancy was a "hard case," and that she had been made "a great sufferer by the war." He recommended she be granted a pension. Finally, eleven years after applying for a pension, in 1886, by an act of Congress, Nancy's name was added to the pension roll, overturning the previous denial of her case. A report accompanying the law read, "There is no question as to the woman's loyalty, poverty, and patriotism. She gave everything she had, and now has the poor house staring her in the face."

Nancy lived in Tennessee with her son George and his wife, Nancy. On January 5, 1903, Nancy died in Greene County, Tennessee at age seventy-eight. She was buried in Mount Olive Cemetery.

Over the years, several accounts about Nancy's story have been published, but rarely with much truth and often with misinformation not based on public documents. What clearly emerges in the pages of her affidavits is a portrait of a woman of her time. To have endured a husband's murder, at the hands of one's own brother, no less, would have measured the strength of any woman; but to have found her sons murdered seems more than a person should be called upon to bear. If anyone could have survived that kind of hellish trauma, it was Nancy—an extraordinary woman who belonged to the enclave known as Shelton Laurel.

CHAPTER THREE

The Tragedy of Montraville Ray

MONTRAVILLE RAY had a problem. At age twenty-seven, he'd wholeheartedly joined the Confederate Army. "Mont," as his friends called him, had enlisted in the 16th Regiment North Carolina on May 1, 1861. Not long afterward, however, he realized he'd committed to something he could no longer countenance. Mont, along with others in his unit (known as the Black Mountain Boys), went AWOL.

Born in 1833, Montraville grew up in the shadow of his father, Amos, who was sheriff, justice of the peace, and seller of "Spirituous Liquors" in one of several taverns he owned. Amos Ray came to own most of the land embraced in the Caney River basin, roughly twenty thousand acres. After going AWOL,

Flag of the 16th Regiment NC. Montraville's regiment served at Ox Hill, Harper's Ferry, Sharpsburg, Shepherdstown, Fredericksburg, Chancellorsville, Frazier's Farm, Cedar Run, Manassas, Seven Pines, Mechanicsville, and Cold Harbor.

Mont Ray was described as 5' 8", 160 pounds, with a dark complexion, "countenance downcast," dark eyes, low forehead, and dark-brown hair. He spoke "slowly, but precisely, with a fine and somewhat whining voice."

Montraville made his way home to Yancey County in the Toe River Valley. Of all the mountainous counties in North Carolina, none features a more isolated and rugged terrain than Yancey. In the annals of its early history, the county residents earned a reputation for being harsh and violent, in keeping with the likeness of its landscape.

Soon after his disappearance from the Confederate Army, on August 21, 1862, the *Asheville News* published a reward notice for the arrest of Corporal Montraville Ray and his brothers, Privates Samuel Paul and James Lafayette Ray. Thirty dollars would be paid if they were delivered to any Confederate officer, or fifteen dollars if taken to the county jail. Ironically, the Confederacy had money to pay rewards for turning in deserters, whom the army would shoot at the head of the troops, and yet they'd failed to adequately provide for the men who stayed. Rectifying conditions might have lessened the number of desertions in the first place. Many became fugitives because they were sick of eating green beef and wormy hardtack while reading letters from home about women suffering under the burden of farm labor and constant threats from marauders, outliers, deserters, and the dreaded Home Guard. Some stories tell of Confederates defecting to the Union Army because federal troops had coffee.

After the Confederate Congress passed the Conscription Act on March 3, 1863, men who refused to join the Confederate Army were hunted down. Since Mont and his comrades were mountaineers "acquainted with the unfrequented recesses of the Black Mountains," few were ever captured. Mont Ray "foiled the efforts of hundreds of Indians to effect a recapture," meaning Cherokee scouts had been used to hunt the renegades. Ray at various times was chased through Burnsville, "his fleeing form always dodging minnies [minie´ balls] and losing itself behind the sheltering woods."

This 1862 illustration depicts sharply divided Confederates and Unionists.

On April 16, 1862, the Confederate Congress passed a national conscription act to fortify its dwindling numbers. The illustration shows a Confederate pulling a reluctant recruit's neck, saying, "Come along you rascal! And fight for our King Cotton." The man protests, "Let me go, I tell you I'm a Union man, and don't believe in your southern Confederacy." Another soldier yells, "Blast your Union! Them as won't go in for the war must be made to do it. Go ahead, or we'll hang you on the next tree."

Montraville Raids Burnsville

Many North Carolinians were unwilling to be drafted into the Confederate Army, and "swarms of men liable to conscription" had joined Union units. Montraville and three of his brothers joined the Union Army—a bold, brave thing for a young man to do in Confederate Appalachia. Scores more ran away from the Confederate ranks. Eventually, these men realized they could challenge the Home Guard. By March 1863, after Confederates had passed the Conscription Act, Mont had already begun rallying like-minded men.

At age thirty, Mont Ray assembled a gang of anti-Confederates and planned a raid on Burnsville. His intent was to disrupt Confederate conscription efforts and capture the cache of weapons and supplies stored there. On the night of Sunday, April 10, 1864, Ray set his plan into motion. When he and his seventy-five men rode into town, they took the Home Guard by surprise; none offered any resistance. The raiders attacked Captain Lyons, the Confederate enrolling officer, who, though slightly wounded, made his escape. They snatched five hundred pounds of bacon from the Home Guard commissary and broke into the powder magazine, seizing one hundred guns, plus ammunition. They looted Milt Penland's general store and then took him captive. Penland was the town's largest slaveholder, a sore spot for Unionists like Montraville. The violent mob yanked Penland from his home and threatened to hang him unless he paid their price and promised to move from the county. Penland struck a bargain. In exchange for his freedom, he agreed to give them eight head of cattle, one hundred pounds of bacon, and fifty bushels of wheat. He also consented to leave the county.

By April 1864, several hundred Union sympathizers were occupying Burnsville. Some frightened citizens sympathetic to the Confederacy fled to Fayetteville, and others to McDowell County. Ray's men occupied Burnsville for about a week, until they were dislodged by Colonel J. B. Palmer and a detachment of the Home Guard dispatched by General John W. McElroy. On April 28, 1864, the *Daily Confederate* reported that Col. Palmer had engaged Unionists in Burnsville, capturing fifteen, and killing eight or ten. Mont Ray, the leader of the band, had "skedaddled." In retaliation for Mont Ray's violent incursion, angry citizens set fire to three town buildings owned by his father, Amos.

Countrywide famine gave rise to violence in Burnsville. In an incident reminiscent of food riots elsewhere in the Confederacy, fifty women marched into Burnsville and seized "sixty bushels of army wheat." (See Appendix 1.)

By the time the Civil War ended, conditions in the western mountains of NC were dire for most people; not only from the deprivations of war but also because of widening political divides. Many continued to identify as Confederates or Unionists, inflaming tensions that often led to conflict.

After the emancipation of slaves, racial violence burgeoned in western North Carolina, giving rise to the Ku Klux Klan. Members were Whites who refused to accept the idea that Black men, who were once property, had become citizens with the right to vote. The prospect of Blacks being elected to govern over Whites was fundamentally intolerable to them.

The Klan used gangster-like tactics of burning down churches, barns, and homes, as well as severely beating men and women—Black and White—to drive home their message.

Montraville and Andrew Jackson Brown

In late September 1870, Mont Ray was in Burnsville to pay his taxes. Fresh on the heels of Colonel George Kirk's campaign earlier that year, the fact that Mont had

Mont Ray's Provost Marshal Card (top) and ID card (bottom). On July 18, 1865, Mont Ray took the oath to become a Union Provost Marshal. The oath included a promise to "abide by and faithfully support all laws and proclamations which have been made during the existing rebellion with reference to the emancipation of slaves." As a Provost Marshal, he did solemnly swear to "preserve the peace, prevent crime, and arrest criminals," and to obey all military laws.

1870 photo of Colonel Kirk.

The Kirk-Holden War, as it came to be called, was a militia campaign to quell KKK violence in North Carolina. Shocked by the murder of Senator Stephens, on July 8, 1870, Governor Holden declared Caswell and Alamance Counties to be in a state of insurrection. Holden suspended the writ of *habeas corpus* and imposed martial law. To help restore order, Holden summoned the aid of former Union Army Colonel George Kirk.

During the Civil War in Tennessee, Kirk had led the North Carolina Mounted Infantry troops, which launched terrifying, destructive raids into Confederate western North Carolina. Montraville Ray and his brother Samuel Paul Ray joined Kirk in Holden's campaign.

On July 29, 1870, the *New York Herald*'s reporter in Burnsville observed that twenty-eight men were locked up "in close confinement" in the Burnsville Court House. The prisoners were allowed no visitors and feared being tried and convicted "by a court of Kirk's ignorant, illiterate and partisan officers." The *Herald* called Kirk's men "half-starved jay-hawkers," who were accused of nightly plundering "chicken-coops, hog-pens and storehouses." On the public square, the militiamen had "completely gutted" a store and others were closed up. Recruits of Kirk's command were drilling in the streets in squads, and the *Herald* reporter wrote "a more slovenly and dirty set could scarcely be collected." After Holden's military campaign that did abate KKK violence, the governor paid a price for ordering it by being impeached and removed from office.

also raided Burnsville during the war fostered bitter feelings among former Confederates.

That afternoon, Andrew Jackson Brown, a notorious and assertive Confederate, was in his store near the eastern foot of Burnsville Hill when Mont and Sam Ray passed by. Brown came out into the road and assailed the brothers as "Kirk's damned pups." Brown had apparently been drinking.

Sam Ray and Brown exchanged words, and an argument over politics grew violent. Brown's friends came to his aid by dragging him into his store and locking him inside. Sam left for the post office. Suddenly, Brown broke out of a window, and started down the road after the brothers. Brown again picked a fight with Sam, who struck Brown on the head with his pistol. Mont came up and jumped in the fight, stabbing Brown several times. Brown died instantly, and Mont made his escape.

Montraville Ray lived in Egypt township, Yancey County. Below, a drawing of a Cane River farm.

At the 1870 fall term of the Yancey County Superior Court, the grand jury endorsed the issued indictment. The jurors stated that Montraville Ray and Samuel P. Ray, "Not having the fear of God before their eyes but being moved and seduced by the instigation of the Devil . . . with force and arms" did willfully, and "of their malice aforethought," assault Andrew Jackson Brown. Montraville Ray used a knife "of the value of sixpence," and Samuel P. Ray, with his gun, pistol whipped Brown "in and upon the head, the breast, the left side, and the belly," causing "several mortal wounds and bruises of the breast . . . 3 inches and . . . 6 inches deep."

The jurors further presented that Hiram Wheeler—knowing that Montraville Ray and Samuel P. Ray had killed Brown—had "against the peace and dignity of the state," harbored and maintained the fugitive Rays.

Sam Ray and Hiram Wheeler offered an affidavit for removal of their case. They swore that they could not safely be tried in Yancey County. A. J. Brown had "influential relations and a large number of influential friends," who had used their clout "to prejudice the public mind" against them. The homicide had been "much discussed" and many "distorted and untrue versions of the facts" had been circulated, they argued, concluding that they could not get "a fair and impartial trial."

The court ruled that the trials of Sam Ray and Hiram Wheeler should be moved to Madison County. Sam Ray and Wheeler were to be brought to the bar of Madison court in the custody of Yancey County Sheriff W. E. Piercy. Afterward, Sam was remanded to the jail in Marshall, and Hiram remained in the custody of Sheriff Piercy.

Meanwhile, Mont Ray was still on the lam. On February 15, 1871, North Carolina governor Caldwell offered $200 for the capture of Montraville Ray. Ray stood "charged by indictment" in Yancey County for the murder of A. J. Brown, and was "at large and so conceals himself that the ordinary process of law cannot be served upon him." The governor pleaded with citizens to "enjoin all officers of the peace, as well as all good citizens to aid in securing the ends of justice in this case."

In the 1871 fall term of Yancey County Superior Court, the case of *State v. Montraville Ray* was presented. It appeared "to the satisfaction of the court" that Mont had failed to appear, so the court ordered the issuance of an *alias capias* (a felony bench warrant when a suspect fails to appear in court). Yancey County Sheriff Piercy was ordered to arrest Montraville Ray on a charge of murder and "him safely keep" until the case could be heard in the next term of court.

No primary documents survived to give further details of where Mont would spend the next eleven years of his life, but according to historian John Preston Arthur, Mont Ray went to Buck's tanning yard, "west of Carver's gap under the Roan mountain." There, he earned a living making and mending shoes. He stayed in hiding until "many of the most important witnesses against him had gotten beyond the jurisdiction of the court—by death or removal." Mont was never more than forty miles away, while no one "ever suspected that he was a fugitive from justice." Arthur observed that, at that time, "So sequestered were many of these mountain coves . . . that persons living within only short distances of each other" were like an ocean away.

While Mont Ray continued to stay in hiding, his case remained on the docket for several years. Finally, eleven years after the homicide, Mont Ray was brought to trial. No records survived to inform how he was apprehended.

In 1882, medical expert Dr. J. A. Hague began to testify at the Yancey County Superior Court. On the day of the murder of A. J. Brown, he'd been sitting on a wagon in front of Samuel Flemming's store. Sam Ray came into town riding a gray horse. Suddenly, A. J. Brown burst out of the store, hollering, "Aren't you one of Kirk's pups?"

Sam retorted, "I'm neither pup nor dog." Brown grabbed Sam's arm and tried to pull him off his horse. Brown didn't succeed in dislodging Sam, but Sam dismounted on the other side. Hague and others took hold of Brown, while others restrained Sam. Sam drew his navy pistol, but someone snatched it. Meanwhile, Brown's friends carried him to his store and locked him inside.

About that time, Hague saw Montraville Ray coming from Milt Penland's store. Hague approached him and pleaded for him to take Sam away from town. Brown was very drunk and "bordering on delirium." Hague thought if Sam went home until Brown sobered up that Brown would make "satisfactory apologies" for his assault on Sam. But Montraville said he wouldn't be run out of Burnsville. Hague reasoned with him, and he eventually agreed to take Sam away, and the two Ray brothers started down Marion Road.

Hague recalled that shortly thereafter, he could hear Brown cursing. Hague ran as quickly as he could and found the badly wounded Brown in the gully, in front of Joshua Williams's gate. Brown muttered, "Doctor, they have killed me." Hague and others carried Brown into Joshua Williams's yard. Brown had seven or eight wounds on his body and limbs, including bruises on his head.

Next, W. B. Banks testified that on the day Brown was killed, he heard a noise and looked out the courthouse window and saw men tussling. When Banks went outside, he saw Sam Ray on his horse, while several men were carrying Brown to his store to lock him inside.

Banks then said that a short time after Sam and Mont were out of sight, Brown climbed out a window and went down the street. Brown was loudly swearing that the Ray brothers were horse thieves and he intended to kill them both. As Brown got closer to the Rays, Sam drew a navy pistol and waved it. Brown kept advancing, so Sam got off his horse. He struck Brown with his pistol and Brown fell. Then Brown got up, and he and Montraville began to fight. Banks said he'd heard of Brown's previous threats and said he regarded Brown "as a boisterous man when drinking."

Next, Montraville Ray's defense began with Henry Wheeler called to the stand. He testified that while he was on his way to the Baptist Association meeting, he ran into Mont. Henry knew of Brown's threats to kill Mont, and warned him: if Mont went to the church meeting, his life would be in danger.

Joshua Williams testified that Mont showed up at his apple orchard and told the men about the tussle between Sam and Brown. Williams heard loud talking and went out and saw Brown and Sam in a fight, while other men were yelling, "Separate them!" Williams said that Brown threw a "pretty good size" rock at the Rays, which passed just over Joshua's head and within a few feet of Sam. Williams saw Mont grab Brown, put his arm around Brown's neck, and begin stabbing him. Joshua testified that he "heard the blood flowing" from Brown's body as he fell.

Garrett D. Ray, a distant relation of Montraville, testified that the killing took place about eleven a.m. Garrett had been at the harness shop and heard Sam and Brown arguing. He went outside and saw men dragging Brown to his store to lock him up. Moments later, as Garrett was walking down the street, he heard a noise and saw a window blind fall as Brown climbed out of a window. Brown asked Garrett where "Kirk's pups" had gone, and Garrett sent him in the wrong direction. Brown took off but came back and said, "They're not going the way you pointed. You knew they didn't go that way."

Garrett testified that Brown, about twenty-five years old, looked "to be a man of good strength," who could be "terribly mean and violent, when drinking." Garrett said he'd never heard of Mont being in a ruckus.

Marcus Renfro testified that he'd been in town that same day. He didn't see the fight, but he did see Brown near his store, yelling, "G-d, d-m them, they shan't stay in this town. Kirkite horse thieves!" James Gibbs, W. H. McClellan, and W. C. Parsons all testified that "up to the killing of Brown," Mont Ray's character was good; but they described Brown as a violent, "bad, overbearing" man.

The Testimony of Montraville Ray

At the time of his trial, Mont was forty-nine years old. He testified that on the day of the killing, he'd come to town to see the sheriff and to pay his taxes. He first saw his brother, Sam, while he was at Penland's store; Sam was on his horse in front of Brown's store. Mont called out to Sam and wanted to see him. Sam answered, and when Mont asked where he was headed, in reply he pointed toward a shop.

Just then, Mont saw Brown grab Sam and try to pull him off his horse. "He come down on his feet with some staggering, as if almost thrown by quick pulling." Mont immediately started toward Sam. Mont saw men take hold of Brown and stopped "about midway between Sam and Brown." When Brown saw Mont, he turned toward him and said, "There is that dammed Mont Ray; I want to get hold of him." Mont said, "I don't know what for."

Mont stood between Brown and Sam, insisting Sam put away his pistol. Mont told Sam to avoid the fight and to go take care of his business. Then Brown's friends took him to his store and locked him in, with Brown yelling, cursing, and raging. Sam got on his horse, headed to Jerry Boone's blacksmith shop, and Mont followed him.

Mont got down to the lower side of the town square, opposite Jules Abernathy's drug store, and then remembered there was someone else he needed to see. Sam said he had to go to the post office and Mont said he'd meet him there. Minutes later, however, Mont "heard some excitement and a female voice," yelling, "Run! Joshua! They will kill Sam Ray!" Mont quickly went up the road and saw Sam and Brown on the ground.

By the time Mont passed Joshua Williams's gate, the men let go of Sam, who began punching Brown. Banks came running, saying, "Part the men!" As he stooped to catch Sam, Mont caught Banks by the collar by mistake. Banks caught Mont by the wrists and dragged him down the hill five or six steps, then turned him loose.

Mont then looked up, opened his pocket knife with the buckhorn handles and four blades, and walked toward the place where Brown and Sam were on the ground fighting.

Someone said, "I'll part them," and came forward. Sam got up and the men ushered him across the street. Brown stood up and gathered some rocks, and threw one at Mont. He kept coming toward Mont, rock in hand. Mont managed to throw his left arm around Brown's body, and struck him with his knife. Mont testified that he stabbed Brown several times, while Brown yelled, "He is cutting me all to pieces!" Mont then turned away from him. Brown staggered and fell in a ditch.

Mont's lawyer asked him several questions. "Why did you strike the deceased?"

"I did not touch him after he fell. I did not know whether I had cut him, but I believed it and was assured of it pretty well when he exclaimed (that) he was killed. I did not make an effort to strike after he was."

The lawyer asked, "When the deceased advanced upon you did you believe he was intending to kill you or do you some great bodily harm?"

Mont replied, "The rock size was sufficient to fill his hand. I thought it weighed three to five or six pounds. I had heard of threats against me said to have been made by Brown."

The existing court notes don't include a verdict, and no verdict exists in any surviving newspaper. However, according to historian John Preston Arthur, Montraville Ray was acquitted.

Montraville Ray died November 20, 1913, at the age of eighty. He was buried in the Hanging Dog Baptist Cemetery in Murphy, Cherokee County, North Carolina. At the time of his death, he was alone, without any family members nearby, as stated on his death certificate. The person who found him deceased, perhaps a landlord, noted him as a "wanderer," a euphemism for being a vagrant. Perhaps his was the saddest ending of a life; although Mont Ray had been one of nine siblings with eleven children and countless grandchildren, none were with him when he passed from this earthly realm into eternity. What remains of his history in the collective memory reveals a man whose wild youth and passionate political strains came to fully characterize the mountain region in the nineteenth century, making Montraville Ray a man of his time.

CHAPTER FOUR

The Weston Family Massacre

IN 1871, POVERTY LINGERED IN the coves and valleys of western North Carolina. Earlier hopes of prosperity, kindled by railroad construction before the start of the war, had dissipated. Economic desperation became widespread. Industry had been stymied by the war and its aftermath, and some areas in the South were submerged under the hands of ubiquitous Union troops.

In post-Civil War Rutherford County, the proud mountain people continued their production of alcohol as they had for generations. Whiskey was not illegal to make, but it was unlawful to do it without giving Uncle Sam the lion's share of the profits. Those who made liquor and didn't pay the tax had to be clever and skilled to run a still undetected. These men were called "blockaders," and they hid themselves and their stills from agents of the Bureau of Internal Revenue. Blockade distillers did not pay tax on the whiskey they produced, in part, because the tax rate was exorbitant, given all the labor and resources invested in running a still.

Some families found a way to profit from moonshine other than just producing the brew. The Adair family of Rutherford County indulged in the enterprise of brewing, bottling, and selling whiskey. Henderson Adair and his four sons—Columbus, Govan, Craton, and Avery—were not only blockaders, but they operated a side hustle stealing liquor from a neighboring blockader. The family became extreme, radical Republicans, and for that they were despised by some of the mountain people. In return, the Adairs disdained people whom they called *secesh*, Confederates who'd started the war.

In their mid-twenties, Henderson Adair's two oldest sons, Columbus and Govan, had earned a reputation for being violent and dangerous. On Election Day, they'd wield their clubs and harass men waiting to vote, specifically targeting Democratic voters. To avoid potential violence, some men left without casting their ballot. The Adair boys were notoriously heavy drinkers who enjoyed fighting as well as stealing and selling whiskey while evading the revenuers. Into their crafty schemes, they conscripted a man named Martin Baynard.

One evening, freedman Silas Weston heard a rattling noise outside his cabin. He opened the door to see Govan Adair, Martin Baynard, and Columbus Adair with a wagon hauling a keg of brandy. Silas, who had purchased his liberty before 1863, had married Polly Steadman, a White woman. Their three children were David (five), Theodosia (six), and baby Mary. Polly's son William, whom they called Lee (ten), was from a previous marriage.

The Adair boys and Silas had enjoyed congenial relations. Aside from being neighbors, together they attended Republican rallies. Assuming that their friendly neighbor Silas would comply, Govan offered him a gallon of brandy if he would help them bury the barrel of brandy they'd just stolen from "two young Morgans." But Silas refused.

The Morgans and the Adair boys were also reputed to have been "good friends and lived near together." Another newspaper stated that the stolen brandy had been swiped from a smoke-house. The Morgan brothers, one of whom was the town constable, suspected Baynard and went to his home and found him drunk. They dragged him out and threatened him, so he confessed: he and Govan had stolen the brandy, and he told them where they could recover the keg.

Warrants were issued, and Silas Weston was summoned as a witness. Govan and Columbus went to Silas and "ordered him not to swear against them." Govan threatened Silas: if he testified, they would kill him. Silas apparently did not believe them. Silas said "he had no desire to injure them" but that if put on the witness stand, he'd tell what he knew. Silas could not have imagined what would come of his resolve to testify.

The Adair boys went home and told their father about their predicament. Already arrested for stealing the brandy and facing an upcoming trial in neighboring McDowell County, the Adairs feared Silas's testimony would send them to jail.

An hour after sunset one evening in late April 1871, Silas and Polly were just finishing supper. Their three older children were already tucked in bed. Still sitting at the table, Silas was feeding his fifteen-month-old baby, Mary. In an instant, Silas and Polly's domestic bliss would soon be shattered.

Out in the yard, their dog began barking wildly. Polly scurried to a corner of the cabin and peered out through a space in the chinking. Through the gap, Craton Adair fired a pistol, and the gunpowder burned her eye.

Polly reeled back into the room, screaming, "I am killed! God have mercy on me!" Just then, Govan and Columbus Adair and Martin Baynard smashed down the door of the cabin and burst in, guns blazing. Govan shot Silas, who jumped up from the table and tried to retreat to the other end of the house, but Govan shot him again. Govan and Martin next grabbed Silas and cut his throat.

Columbus walked over to the children's beds and pumped bullets into David and Theodosia. He then shot and killed Lee, who gurgled, "They have killed me!" through his own spurting blood before he, too, succumbed to death.

Polly rushed to the corner of the cabin to squirm underneath the bed, but Govan and Martin grabbed her and dragged her out. Govan aimed to shoot her, but his pistol misfired. Martin stabbed her repeatedly, cutting her seven times and slashing her throat. As she finally sank down, they kicked her body into a pile of nearby broom straw. Columbus hoisted up baby Mary in his arms and slashed her throat.

This 1872 drawing, called "Visit of the Ku-Klux," depicts KKK violence. Since the Klan was known for making midnight raids, the Adair boys committed their horrific murders in a way that mimicked the KKK, and they would later accuse the Klan for their crime, hoping to get away with murder.

The Weston family lay in quiet heaps on the floor. The three assassins set fire to the bedding and clothing. Feeling certain that the burning cabin would conceal their vicious crime, they ran off into the night.

The Adair boys were in for a big surprise.

Polly, her eye horribly injured, her body mutilated and bleeding, lay semi-conscious in her blazing home. As the flames crept into her hair, she began to stir. With a determined effort to stand, she staggered toward the door. She heard a sound at the other end of the room. Miraculously, her baby Mary was still alive. Polly snatched her up.

Polly dragged Theodosia—not knowing whether she was dead or alive—across the burning floor, while crawling and clutching baby Mary. Her arms and shoulders were slashed and bleeding, and Polly's strength was rapidly draining away. On reaching the threshold of the door, Polly could no longer hold Theodosia. Leaving her at the door of the blazing cabin, and with Mary in tow, Polly staggered half a mile to her nearest neighbors, the Williams family.

Mrs. Williams opened the door and was stunned. Polly's face was black with soot and gunpowder burns, her hair wild and charred. Blood streamed from her copious wounds as she clutched her bleeding baby. Immediately, Mrs. Williams sent for the doctor. Polly begged her to run and fetch Mrs. Morgan, the Westons' landlord, who lived nearby, saying, "I want to tell Mrs. Morgan all about it, and who did it, before I die, as I expect and believe I will die." She urged Mrs. Williams to hurry.

Magistrate Squire Hanes came to Polly's bedside and took her statement. Certain her death was imminent, Polly gave him the names of the three men and what they'd done, explaining that the Adairs had not worn disguises or covered their faces. Hanes listened to her recount her ordeal, and felt he had enough probable cause to make the arrests.

The following morning, Polly and Mary were still alive, with the doctor at their bedside. In the morning light, the Weston cabin lay in ashes, containing the burned bodies of Silas, Lee, David, and Theodosia.

Squire Hanes, accompanied by a posse of armed men, arrived at the Adair home to arrest Govan and Columbus. Henderson Adair demanded to know who had accused his sons of such a heinous crime. Hanes showed him Polly's statement, and a shocked Henderson exclaimed, "Is she not dead?!"

Hanes asked the whereabouts of Martin Baynard and where he'd been the previous night. Govan insisted he had no idea, and claimed to have had no part in the murders. Magistrate Hanes figured they were lying, and arrested Govan and Columbus, who swore they'd burn the neighborhood and anyone who led to their arrest. Baynard was found, and all three were taken into custody and jailed. Rutherford County residents, who'd "long been in terror of the young desperadoes," likely breathed a sigh of relief at hearing that the Adair boys and Martin were locked in the cage of the county jail.

Randolph Shotwell, the notorious Ku Klux Klansman, had also been arrested and put in the Rutherford County jail. Placed in an iron cage along with Baynard and the Adair boys, he wrote of his experience spending a month in the miserable jail. Govan tried to ingratiate himself with Shotwell by offering him his "large, wadded bed-comforter, as thick as a mattress." He refused Govan's offer, even though "the temptation was great," Shotwell wrote.

Randolph Abbott Shotwell migrated from Virginia to North Carolina after the Civil War. As an editor of Democratic newspapers in Rutherfordton and Asheville, he denounced Republicans. Shotwell was arrested for the lynching of James Justice and for destroying the *Rutherford Star* newspaper office. In his defense, he claimed to have led the KKK in an effort to modify the Klan's violent acts, but the prosecution proved that Shotwell "guided a desperate body of men to the residence of James M. Justice for the purpose of beating and killing him." Shotwell was convicted of conspiracy due to his efforts to "coordinate the activities of the Ku Klux Klan" in Rutherford and Polk counties, and was sentenced to six years, serving time in three federal penitentiaries. He was offered a pardon if he would testify against fellow Democrats, but he refused. In 1872, Ulysses S. Grant gave him an unconditional pardon. After his release, Shotwell bought the *Farmer and Mechanic* newspaper in Raleigh and stayed in the newspaper business for the remainder of his life.

"For there was no one to bring me any bedding." What bedding the other prisoners had, was "swarming in lice," and the flies and fleas "require the constant slapping of handkerchiefs, and hats, to secure a moment's relief." Shotwell also complained of the enormous jailhouse rats that scurried around the cells.

Shotwell described the cell as a cage "about 10 feet long and 7 feet wide," and that the seven inmates "occupied every inch of the floor." He wrote that if he'd tried to lie down, he "must lie lengthwise at the feet of the whole party, subject to the kicks of the long-legged, and the odor of fourteen last year's socks." So, he sat up for three nights in a row. With no ventilation, the air in the Rutherford County jail was "almost suffocating." The squalid conditions were made slightly less noxious after one of the prisoners procured a piece of wood "to shut in the odor of the slop bucket," which the jailer emptied only once a day.

In the cage, Shotwell despised his "shamefully enforced association with the Adair boys." One day, Govan whispered some things to Shotwell. Govan's father had been conniving ways to bust out his boys. Henderson Adair had noticed that there were only three guards downstairs, and he suggested that ten well-armed men could creep up in the rear of the jail and then rush and overpower the guards who were known to set aside their guns and keys. Govan bragged that he and his brother "kin take this jail any dark night, if we was foot loose, and had our poppers."

Govan went on to say: "Now, me an' the boys has been a thinking in case we got things fixed for you, you would see fair play done us you know, and so, I'll just tell you, we've been a talkin' to our daddy, an' he's right ready. An' he says if you'll give the name of one, or two plucky boys in South Carolina, he'll take the best team on our place, and a light three seat wagon, and go like lightnin',' and bring 'em; and the old man says he'll lead 'em."

Apparently, Henderson had been studying the situation for the previous three weeks, and wanted to tap Shotwell's miscreant contacts in South Carolina. Govan said his father "kin make the trip to South Carolina in one night, an' come back the next night, lay in the woods over thar on the town hill, where they kin see this here winder," but Shotwell declined being involved in any scheme of the Adair boys.

As for Baynard, Shotwell described him as a "small, yellow-faced, shock-headed, mountain boomer . . . [who was] . . . ugly to look upon, ignorant in the last degree, and with no intelligence save the trickery of a wild fox." The Adairs were evidently afraid of Baynard turning state's evidence, especially since he'd confessed to the Morgans. As an inducement to insure against that, Henderson promised to give Baynard after the trial a forty-six-acre farm with livestock and wagons. Shotwell was certain that if Baynard had been put in a cell by himself, and "shown the certainty of his conviction and execution" he would quickly confess the details of the massacre.

Govan climbed up on a rear window of the cage, and pulled out a foot-long piece of iron from the top of the window frame. He next went to the fireplace to demonstrate what he'd learned from a brick mason who'd worked on the jail and who knew of its construction defects. He lifted a flagstone, which revealed several bricks that could be easily removed. Govan suggested taking out dry bricks, cutting a hole in the floor, and lowering themselves into the room below, which had no bars on the windows. Govan's father had told him that Sheriff Walker slept in that room, and that "his bed will furnish more blankets for lowering us from the second story windows." Shotwell said Govan "judged from my weary and suffering aspect that I would take any means to regain my liberty," but they were wrong. Govan begged Shotwell not to say anything about their plans, which ultimately never materialized.

The men in the cage spent evenings singing, "old sacred songs, hymns, and camp-meeting choruses." Shotwell wrote that, "The Negroes really sing well, as most Negroes do, and their rondo of 'The Old Ship of Zion,' roared out by four voices, has a strange, pathetic sound under the circumstances."

The Adair boys and Baynard had committed horrific murders that sparked public outrage. Authorities expressed concerns about the safety of the prisoners if they were tried in Rutherford County, so the trial was moved to Henderson County, where they were held until the fall term of court.

November came and the trial began. The prosecution sought to present the case involving all four murders, while the defense insisted on dealing solely with testimony involving the murder of Polly's oldest son, Lee. The court overruled the request and heard all available testimony.

In the meantime, Polly Weston had miraculously recovered from her injuries and appeared in court. As the main witness for the prosecution, her compelling testimony was a stunning account of that night of horror just seven months earlier.

The three killers each took the stand. All three claimed to have been elsewhere that night. They said Polly had mistakenly identified them, and coolly suggested that the killings and arson had been the work of the Ku Klux Klan.

While the trial was underway, there was an unexpected interruption. Two men were abruptly brought into the courtroom before the judge. They'd been fighting in the street, and one was bleeding. Polly, who'd already given her testimony, saw the badly bloodied men and fainted. She was brought back to consciousness, but became so distraught that she had to leave the courtroom. Apparently, her ordeal on that night of terror had triggered a post-traumatic stress response.

On Saturday, November 11, the case was finally given to the jury. A verdict was returned the following Wednesday, November 15: All three men were found guilty of murder. Judge James L. Henry pronounced their dreaded sentence: they were to hang from the neck until dead.

Martin and the Adairs immediately appealed the case. Their attorneys argued before Judge Henry that the verdict should be set aside. They requested a new trial to allow for new witnesses. Judge Henry refused to set aside the verdict, telling the Adair boys, "Your counsel have done all in their power for you. Your case has been ably defended . . . [but] the stubborn facts which have paved the way to the gibbet have been insurmountable, and they have at last to give you over to the penalty of the law you have so fatally incurred."

The judge went on to say, "You slew four human beings and burned down the house above them that your handiwork might not be suspected, and left the mother and babe whom, too, you thought dead, wounded and maimed for life. You have taken that which you have not the power to return—the life of a fellow man—over which you had no control, for God himself, the Maker, has reserved the right to destroy that which His Almighty arm alone can create.

"For this, you must die!"

Judge Henry continued, "Your life is no longer yours; it has been forfeited by your baseness and misconduct, and must now be offered on the altar of retributive justice, an oblation for those poor, helpless ones whom you, and your fiendish malignity, hurried unbidden into the presence of their Maker."

> *How it could've entered the heart to conceive the horrible design and execute its dreadful purposes, staggers belief, and makes us tremble for the depravity of a soul so irretrievably low, and so besottedly debased.*
>
> JUDGE HENRY

Due to the severity of their crimes, the judge said the guilty Adair boys should not expect executive clemency from the governor. He repeated the sentence of the first court, that on June 14, 1872, they would die by public hanging. With last-minute motions, the execution was postponed until July 12, from which there would be no final appeal.

Meanwhile, a trial was pending against Henderson Adair, suspected of participating in the Weston family murders. That case required Martin Baynard's testimony, so Baynard was not scheduled to hang on the same day as the Adair brothers. He was to give his testimony first and later be hanged on October 18, 1872.

On July 11, the day before their execution, a reporter from the *New York Herald* visited the condemned Adair boys. During their final interview, Govan and Columbus were sitting in their cells—as was their father Henderson and their two younger brothers, Craton and Avery, who had also been arrested as accessories to the murders.

The older Adair brothers asked the reporter if he thought that Martin Baynard's testimony, which had led to the arrest of their father and brothers, would lead to their conviction. Govan swore that Henderson, Craton, and Avery were innocent. The reporter asked how he could be so sure. Govan slyly replied that he had led the killings and that they hadn't been there.

Govan claimed he massacred the Weston family on behalf of the Ku Klux Klan, but clearly, this was not a Klan killing. Most Klansmen in Rutherford County belonged to the Democrat party, and the Adairs were Republicans. Contradicting Polly's testimony, Govan said they'd been disguised the night of the killings, which must have been an admission of guilt. In light of these improbable comments, the reporter asked how it was, then, that Polly Weston had named the three men and said that they'd not been disguised. Govan answered, "The Lord only knows."

On Friday, July 12, 1872, a large crowd of 5,000 gathered at the jail to see the Adair brothers hanged. In those days, public hangings were social events, often attracting hundreds and sometimes thousands of people. Many would bring a picnic basket and considered it a treat if the prisoner made a speech before the noose. On that morning, the Adair brothers gave the crowd extra entertainment value: each made a speech.

Columbus spoke first, claiming innocence, and saying that Martin Baynard had wrongly incriminated his father and brothers. Columbus said he could have proven his innocence if only he'd been given a new trial. He said the governor had refused to pardon him, "because I will not confess." He turned and thanked the sheriff, his deputies, and the jailer for their kindness through the months of his incarceration. He asked that their bodies be taken to Rutherford County for burial, and he bid farewell to the crowd. He asked to be shown his coffin, and after contemplating it for a moment without expression, sat down.

Govan stood next and addressed the crowd. He said he'd made an affidavit that would soon be published. He, too, claimed he wasn't guilty, saying that the murders of Silas Weston and his children were "a most atrocious crime, but I did not commit it."

Like his brother, he said the governor had refused to pardon him because he was a brave man. He also blamed Baynard for lying, but concluded, "I will show you that there is one man in western North Carolina who is not afraid to die." The convicted psychopath made these absurd comments after he'd told the *Herald* reporter that he did the killings, and that he'd done so on behalf of the KKK.

The minister then stood to speak from the scaffold and prayed for the condemned. Columbus knelt, but even after he asked his brother to kneel with him, Govan remained seated. After the prayers, the sheriff made them stand. He affixed the nooses around their necks and bound their arms and feet. The sheriff asked if they were ready. Columbus answered, "Yes," and the sheriff released the trap door. Their bodies fell through. Death was nearly instant.

Baynard eventually gave testimony in the Henderson Adair case, and his execution was slated for October 18. On that fateful evening before he was to be hanged, his wife came for one last visit. Weeping into a handkerchief, Sallie Baynard made an appeal to Sheriff Terrell Taylor, on duty that night at the jail. She begged Taylor to let her spend the night with Martin. She promised Taylor that she'd leave at six o'clock the next morning. He agreed, and locked the husband and wife in the cell for their final night together.

At six o'clock the next morning, Taylor unlocked the cell door. Sallie, wearing a large bonnet and weeping into a handkerchief pressed to her face, quickly brushed past Taylor and scooted out the door. Taylor watched as she left, and then re-locked the cell door.

Two hours later, Taylor returned to Baynard's cell. Taylor opened the cell door and stepped in with Baynard's breakfast. Suddenly, Taylor dropped the tray of food when he discovered that the poor soul huddled against the cell wall wasn't Baynard. It was Sallie, wearing her husband's clothes.

Two hours earlier, Baynard had scuttled past Taylor, dressed in Sallie's clothes. By this time, Baynard was long gone. Despite an intense manhunt, he was never found. Rumor had it that he went to Texas, and was later joined by Sallie and their three children. He never returned to North Carolina.

And there ends the story of the ferocious Adair murders—horrific killings that the murderers had tried to pass off as a Klan act. Had Polly not survived to identify and testify against them, no one would have ever learned the truth. Because of Polly's unusual strength and fortitude, her descendants live on today. The Adair boys, however, left no posterity other than their evil, which will be remembered for generations.

CHAPTER FIVE

The Whipping of Aaron Biggerstaff

THE CIVIL WAR HAS OFTEN BEEN CALLED the war that pitted brother against brother. What came after the war, however, bred a whole new level of chaos. The Biggerstaff feud, as it would come to be known, is one such story.

Half-brothers Aaron V. and Samuel P. Biggerstaff had deep roots in Rutherford County, being descendants of British loyalist Aaron Biggerstaff, who died in the Revolutionary War at the battle of King's Mountain.

Aaron was twelve years older than Samuel. At the start of the Civil War, Aaron vociferously opposed secession from the Union, while Samuel joined the Confederate Army. Aaron was reputed to have been a member of a secret society called the Red Strings, aka Heroes of America, which aimed to end the war. By early 1865, Aaron had been helping Union soldiers steal horses from Confederate sympathizers, including from his brother Samuel. Aaron had also aided Union prisoners in their escape from the Confederate prison in Columbia, South Carolina. Local histories

The Ku Klux Klan

The beginnings of the KKK emerged after the defeat of the Confederacy. Many southern Whites who'd supported the CSA felt disenfranchised, and believed they were being "put upon" to accept the Enforcement Acts. In 1868, members of the Ku Klux Klan began undermining the new state governments formed under the federal mandates of Reconstruction. The KKK attracted a wide base of support, with members holding political, judicial, and publishing positions. In several North Carolina counties, the Klan's attempts to assert their philosophy of White supremacy generated lawlessness and violence.

suggest that he additionally piloted a detachment of Union cavalry through the Carolina backcountry. Viewed by some as a traitor, Aaron was most intensely resented by his half-brother Samuel.

After the war, Aaron became an active Republican, and Samuel a Democrat. During Reconstruction (1865 – 1877), the Republican Party attracted Black voters and some White southerners who begrudgingly and marginally accepted the provisions of Reconstruction as a consequence of losing the war. In contrast, many members of the Democratic Party—then called "Conservative"—were avowed White supremacists.

Aaron supported racial and political equality, but Samuel would not or could not accept those terms. He became active in raids with the Ku Klux Klan (KKK).

The oath of the so-called "Invisible Empire" was dedicated to opposing the principles of the Republican party and "forever maintaining and contending that intelligent white men shall govern this country." The KKK attracted many to its nefarious order. One contemporary said of the secret society: "It cannot be longer disguised or denied that the ku klux is a bloody reality, and that it is a murderous, scourging, burning, desolating organization, in the political interests of the conservative party." The Klan did not limit their violent assaults to Blacks; Whites who promoted the rights of the newly-freed also became targets. As the Ku Klux Klan rose in power both politically and culturally, the brothers

This 1874 engraving, published in *Harper's Weekly*, depicts a member of the "White League," a paramilitary domestic terrorist group, shaking hands with the Ku Klux Klan standing over an African-American couple with a dead baby, and a man in the background hanging from a tree.

The Enforcement Acts.

The adoption of the Thirteenth, Fourteenth, and Fifteenth Amendments to the Constitution extended civil and legal protections to former slaves. The new laws prohibited states from disenfranchising Black male voters "on account of race, color, or previous condition of servitude." The Ku Klux Klan sought to deny Black men their new voting rights. The KKK terrorized Blacks with horrifying beatings and house burnings aimed at intimidating them from exercising their right to vote, running for public office, or serving on juries. In hopes of ending the violence, in 1870 and 1871 Congress passed a series of Enforcement Acts. These empowered the President to use military force to protect Black people. During Reconstruction, Union troops remained stationed in southern states, in part, to ensure those states adopted constitutions guaranteeing the rights of men of color to vote. Ensuring that right, however, brought unimaginable suffering for those who took a stand for their deeply-held beliefs.

continued to be at odds. In the wake of increasing KKK violence, their toxic relationship came under great scrutiny, though some contemporary accounts, eager to deflect responsibility away from the Klan, claimed the brothers' mutual hostility stemmed from a family squabble.

By February 1870, the KKK in Rutherford County had begun to suspect that James McGaha—a Unionist and a Republican—had become an informant on their illicit whiskey trade. The KKK had a habit of exacting severe revenge on suspected informants. A snowy February night became the backdrop for a rush of fear and terror.

First, a demonized, violent horde donned in white robes and pointed hoods stormed the McGaha home. They were angry to learn that James was out hunting but nevertheless traumatized his wife, Malinda. The Klansmen ransacked the house and shoved, pushed, and intimidated Malinda. Some news reports indicate she had been "outraged," a nineteenth-century euphemism for rape; other accounts don't report the men as going that far.

James was furious when he returned to find his home raided and his wife terrorized. Immediately he formed a posse that included fifty-nine-year-old Aaron Biggerstaff, a "bold, determined, and fearless Republican." The group trotted through the night, following horse tracks left in the snow—which led right to Samuel Biggerstaff's home, in a remote area in Rutherford's Golden Valley section, near the Cleveland County border.

That bitter-cold night, the brothers' feud came to a head. James McGaha, Aaron Biggerstaff, and the rest of their posse were on Samuel's doorstep. They fired their pistols at the house. Aaron discharged shots into Samuel's bedroom, intending to kill him in his sleep. Later, bullets and slugs were found buried in Samuel's bedpost. Samuel survived the shooting by having providentially fallen asleep by the fireplace.

McGaha's quest for vengeance didn't end with Samuel Biggerstaff. The next morning, Malinda told James more details about the Klan's raid on their home. Even with their faces disguised, she'd recognized one of the men as Decatur DePriest. Straightaway, James saddled up and rode hard to DePriest's home. Out in front of the house, he summoned DePriest to the door. In a fury of scalding, Scots-Irish anger, James shot DePriest dead.

James McGaha took his family and disappeared from Rutherford County. Aaron Biggerstaff was left to face the consequences of that night of familial fury and rage. Samuel Biggerstaff, enraged over the attack on his home, swore out warrants for Aaron's arrest. Aaron was convicted, but Judge George Logan—an ardent Republican and a friend of Aaron's—merely fined him $25 and released him. KKK members of the Democratic Party resented what they felt was an abuse of power by a Republican elite. Logan, who'd been elected in 1868, had once published a statement about Aaron, saying, "His character for honesty, morality, and fair dealing is unimpeachable." To the Klan, Logan became a symbol of what was wrong with the judicial seats in Rutherford County, of the influence of the Republicans, and of Internal Revenue Collector John Mott; in their minds the country was going to pot.

The Terror of the Nightrider

On Saturday, April 8, 1871, the sixty-year-old Aaron experienced a shocking catastrophe. Around midnight, he was in bed sleeping when dozens of Klansmen descended on his farm. Disguised in flowing robes and pointed hoods, the "midnight assassins" stormed into Aaron's farmhouse. Violently seizing a nearly-naked Aaron from his bed, they dragged him outside. Wielding "limbs of ash, hickory, and white oak," they began "unmercifully" whipping him. For more than an hour, they lashed Aaron two hundred strikes using "hoop-poles and sticks and withes." They beat him to within an inch of his life, "until he could neither sit, stand, nor lie."

The horde announced that they were whipping him for being "a damned radical," and for testifying against them in the James McGaha case. They made Aaron swear that he would "never again vote the Republican ticket," and told him that they'd kill him for sure if he ever swore out a warrant against them another time.

Aaron wasn't the only one who suffered that night. His daughter, Mary Ann, was beaten, and his sixty-three-year-old wife, Margaret, was also abused. But Aaron got the worst of it. A Klansman broke a bottle of turpentine over Aaron's head and then whipped him again. When the gang left, Aaron was left so severely injured that for weeks he was confined to his bed.

With great resolve, Aaron swore out warrants for members of the mob of terror, including his brother Samuel. On May 24, 1871, US Marshal Joseph G. Hester and "a squad of US soldiers" from Camp Pettigrew were sent to arrest thirty-one of the disguised men who had attacked Aaron.

Judge Logan, who had previously ruled over Aaron's punishment, faced the responsibility of deciding the Klansmen's sentencing. Those arrested were for two days jailed in Rutherfordton and released only "upon giving heavy bonds." They appeared before Logan in mid-April, ready to be tried. But Logan postponed hearing their case and "bound them over to appear in June." Logan charged them to post bonds of $500 each. When June came around, Logan said he was still not prepared to hear their cases. Again, he required them to post bonds of $500 each, and said he'd hear their cases in July. Even though a federal court sat at Marion, just twenty-five miles from Rutherfordton, they were herded onto a train and taken 250 miles away to Raleigh, where the trial was held. These farmers had been arrested at harvest time, creating a great hardship for them and their families, which was clearly Judge Logan's intent.

Meanwhile, Aaron had been summoned to testify against his attackers. Undaunted by the severe beating he'd endured earlier,

Aaron set out with his family, horses, and wagon, determined to testify before the US Commissioner in Shelby, some twenty-five miles away.

Just ten miles from Shelby, they stopped to get some sleep near Grassy Branch in Cleveland County. Suddenly, Aaron and his family were overtaken by a mob. From out of nowhere, a KKK horde surrounded them. Not in full Klan attire, and only partially disguised, Aaron recognized Samuel.

Aaron had been asleep in the wagon, since he was still much too injured to easily climb out. The miscreants yanked Aaron from the wagon, put a rope around his neck, and dragged him into the woods, announcing they were going to kill him this time. They beat Aaron while his family looked on helplessly as he screamed in agony.

Govan Biggerstaff—Aaron's nephew—took off running, escaping gunfire. As the crazed mob encircled them, Margaret, Mary Ann, and Mary Ann's husband remained to face the Klan. The terrorists began dragging each of the women into the woods but were miraculously stopped when suddenly their mules and horses got spooked and took off running. Before the Klansmen left to find their mounts, they threatened Aaron and his family: don't testify in Shelby tomorrow, they demanded. The family turned around and went home. Aaron was again summoned to testify, but he refused. The risk to his life was too great.

Meanwhile, Judge Logan sought military aid from Governor Tod Caldwell. Civil order, he explained, had broken down in Rutherford and Cleveland counties, and he feared for his life if he tried to convene regular court sessions. People needed protection. Since the state militia was primarily composed of Klansmen, North Carolina asked President Grant for troops; roughly two weeks later, federal soldiers were dispatched to Rutherford County.

Next, the Klan targeted James M. Justice, a Republican member of the North Carolina legislature and publisher of the *Rutherford Star* newspaper.

On Sunday night, June 11, heavy rain came pounding down on rooftops in Rutherfordton, drenching anyone walking the streets. Undaunted by the extreme weather, a band of Klansmen descended on the town. Dressed in red gowns and horned hoods, they stampeded into Justice's home. Chief among them was the head of the KKK in Rutherford County, Randolph Shotwell. Busting down the front door with an ax, the rapacious mob had come for blood. They stormed into his bedroom and grabbed Justice by the throat. Snatching him out of bed, one of the brutes bellowed, "Oh, you damned radical, we have you at last." Dragging him into the entryway of his home, "a gang of them completely surrounded him." Justice began yelling to alert his neighbors. For that, Klansmen struck him with a pistol. He "fell down and became insensible," but he still felt their kicks and blows on his sides.

The Klansmen next pulled Justice into the street while beating him. When Justice hollered for help, the Klansmen again pistol-whipped him. "It was raining very hard, and I had on only a shirt and no other garments," Justice recalled. "The rain revived me and I soon came to my senses and heard many voices that seemed familiar to me. It was dark, cloudy and lightning . . . [The Klansmen] commenced firing guns and pistols along the street, and shouts, screams, and expressions of exultation were raised and exceeded anything I ever heard."

The Klansmen interrogated Justice: they wanted to know "where that damned Logan was." Justice said he didn't know. The Klansmen dragged him toward the courthouse, while asking him what his business was; Justice said he was "engaged in the practice of law." They asked what kind of cases, and he replied he took on a variety. "You made a distinguished speech the other day," a Klansman said. He recalled Justice had, in his remarks, proposed to hang the leaders of the Klan. "Now what if *you* should be hung," the Klansman asked, "a leader of the radical party?"

Upon reaching the courthouse, the gang became angry at not finding Judge Logan there, so they pulled Justice into the woods.

"I was carried away to some men with horses," Justice would later testify. The Klansmen continued their harangue, saying he should be "ashamed of being of that party that put Negroes to rule and govern." They said White men would not stand for it and announced they would drag him into the woods to kill him. Justice, faint and bleeding, asked to sit down, but they refused, while one of them said that standing "would do him good to take the Negro-equality blood out of him."

The initial plan for the raid on Justice was to whip him, and then turn him over to a South Carolina KKK den. There, they had intended to "carry Justice to the river, tie a sack of sand to him, and lose him." The Klan spared Justice that terrible fate on the condition he swear to retire from public life and reveal the whereabouts of Aaron Biggerstaff and Judge Logan. Finally, they let Justice go after he promised to "surrender his principles." That same night, others of the crazed mob went to Justice's *Rutherford Star* office, and by morning, the office and press were destroyed.

Congressional Inquiry

Klan violence became so rampant throughout the South that the US Congress formed a "Select Committee to Inquire into the Condition of Affairs in the Late Insurrectionary States." The congressional inquiry in 1871 outlined the goal for North Carolina as: "To ascertain whether the laws of your State are efficiently executed, and whether property and life are safe there."

J. B. Carpenter, clerk of the Superior Court in Rutherford County, had reported that within a thirty-day period, "not less than fifty persons have been whipped and scourged by masked and disguised men, generally known as Ku Klux." Aside from Biggerstaff and his family, the Taylor family had been beaten, as well as "a crippled man seventy-five or eighty years of age." Carpenter, who'd been threatened to be "skinned alive" by the Klan, noted the KKK targeted both Blacks and Whites, and that Mrs. Jackson, a cousin of Senator George M. Whiteside, had been "whipped and tarred and feathered." Mart Pearson's home had been burned, and "a colored church was burned the night of the whipping of Mose Hammilton." The whipping of Aaron Biggerstaff and the Biggerstaff feud became focal points of the congressional committee.

KKK leader Plato Durham, summoned to testify, responded by positing the argument that the issue between Aaron and Samuel was simply personal animosity, not politics.

When asked to give an account of the Biggerstaff feud "from beginning to end," Durham shared what Aaron's attorney had told him: That at "about the close of the war," Aaron piloted federal cavalry troops to neighboring farms to hunt for horses, including at his brother's plantation. There'd been a bitter hostility ever since, with "one thing leading to another." Durham expressed what he believed was an unfair judicial situation in Rutherford County. "I think that if Mr. Aaron Biggerstaff had been punished by the courts for his assault upon Samuel Biggerstaff, with deliberate purpose to kill, there would have been nothing of this assault upon him."

When asked to explain his comments, Durham launched into a diatribe about the incompetency of Judge Logan. That opinion was shared by most members of the bar in his circuit, he claimed, except for some lawyers who had begun their practice under the "twenty-dollar rule." (In North Carolina, if any man paid $20 and could prove himself to be of "good moral character," he could be licensed to practice law.) A meeting of the bar in Charlotte was called because members "were so fully convinced

Plato Durham was a Confederate soldier in the 12th NC regiment from Cleveland County. He became an attorney, and was elected to the State House as a Democrat. At the 1868 Constitutional Convention, he strongly resisted Reconstruction. He believed that although newly freed Blacks had gained liberty, government should remain strictly in the hands of White men. Durham, a leader of the Ku Klux Klan, appointed Randolph Shotwell to lead the Rutherford County clan. Durham was defense attorney for several Klansmen named for whipping Biggerstaff. Although indicted, he was never brought to trial.

of the incompetency of Judge Logan," they unanimously signed a petition to the legislature to remove Logan. When asked, "In what respect [does] his incompetence manifest itself?" Durham replied there'd been "many cases" in which Logan had been over-ruled by the State Supreme Court. In one case, a trial for murder, Logan had charged the jury "that upon an indictment for murder a verdict of manslaughter could not be found," although this was not true. Durham went on to say that ever since the war, Logan had been "a very bitter partisan." He argued not only was Logan incompetent, he "carried his partisan prejudices upon the bench." In many cases, men of color who'd been convicted of "larceny and other crimes," in Logan's court were allowed to go free after paying court costs. Others "of his own party," who were "strong partisans," were given "very light fines for very serious offenses." Durham further assailed Judge Logan's competence by pointing out Logan's treatment of those arrested for beating Biggerstaff.

Durham claimed that since the passage of the Congressional Acts, members of the Union Leagues that supported the newly freed, had told Blacks to believe White men were their enemies, and their only friends were Northern men. Blacks further regard-ed as true, he said, that Whites wanted to "restore slavery at the earliest possible moment." Black people were "ignorant and superstitious," and had been taught to believe the US Army had set them free and the US government "was their only protector."

The committee report that followed the testimony of Durham and others concluded the Biggerstaff feud had led to "much dis-order" in Rutherford County. Despite the Klan's brutal assault of James Justice and Aaron Biggerstaff, the committee called the feuding Biggerstaff brothers "obscure criminals," and acknowl-edged "the cases of outrages proved before the committee" could be traced to "personal or local feuds," regardless of political party.

Surprisingly, the uncivil feud between the Biggerstaff broth-ers ended civilly. One newspaper reported that at the end of the trial, judgment was not executed on Samuel Biggerstaff "at the instance" of his brother Aaron, "on account of reconciliation, they being half-brothers."

Although the Biggerstaff feud came to an amiable resolution, the KKK remained a force of terror. The 1870 Kirk-Holden campaign had suppressed Klan activities in Alamance and Caswell counties, but the KKK had nevertheless remained active in Rutherford County, as demonstrated in the 1871 beating of Biggerstaff. Scores of other county residents suffered terrifying beatings and barn and church burnings.

The force and policies of Reconstruction cracked down on the Klan in North Carolina, and in targeting the KKK, the Enforcement Act of 1871 gave federal officials the power to assemble a posse in order to execute arrest warrants for Klansmen.

While many wealthy and influential supporters of White supremacy disapproved of the tactics of the Ku Klux Klan, they nevertheless applied their sympathies to the Klan's political and social agenda. Night whippings and church burnings eventually diminished, as White supremacists adopted other forms of public expression to promote their religious and political ideologies.

Chapter Six

The Hanging of Jack Lambert

O N A BITTERLY COLD DECEMBER night in 1884, a group of young men gathered in a Jackson County stable, singing, joking, and drinking heavily. Their host, Bragg Jones, was a blockade distiller—an illegal moonshiner—who sold them contraband whiskey and brandy.

Richard "Dick" W. Wilson joined the gathering, held a few miles outside of the town of Webster. Wilson was a revenue officer, tasked with collecting taxes on liquor. Living up to revenue officers' general reputation of being heavy drinkers, he participated in Jones's party instead of enforcing the law.

The men all came from a tight handful of mineral-rich counties at the western-most tip of North Carolina, close to the border with Georgia and Tennessee, and knew each other well. But a stranger to most of them drank with the group that night too: Andrew Jackson "Jack" Lambert, a mica miner twice their age.

Lambert, an Eastern Band Cherokee, had grown up in nearby Cherokee County. He had joined the Confederate Army as a private in the first North Carolina cavalry as a young man, and "engaged in some of the most hotly contested fights of the war, but Lambert passed through them all unscathed," wrote the *Asheville Weekly Citizen*. He was at Appomattox when Lee surrendered to Grant.

The author's 2nd great-grand-aunt and Jack Lambert's widow, Louisa Jane "Jennie" Reece Lambert.

After returning home, his grip on a stable life seemed to loosen. In 1867, "another Indian" on the Cherokee reservation broke Lambert's jaw with a club. In the 1880 Federal Census, he appears three times, living in three different places with three distinct sets of people—a historical oddity, but also an indication of instability at home or work. He became a miner and a painter, traveling around Tennessee and North Carolina for employment. He married and had children, but later divorced. His second marriage, to Louisa Jane Reece, nicknamed Jennie, took place in 1884.

The *Asheville Weekly Citizen* reported that during a mining trip to Macon County, North Carolina, in the fall of 1884, Lambert quarreled with others and was fired. Following a drunken spree, Lambert accused Dick Wilson of being the informer who cost him his job.

Did anyone else drinking in Jones's stable on the night of December 17 know of Lambert's recent past? Did any of the men have a sense of foreboding of what was about to happen?

An hour later on that intensely cold night, Lambert appeared at the home of Wilson's sister-in-law, drunk and vomiting. He asked to warm himself at her fire. She acquiesced and gave him some wine. As he sat at the stove, drunk and likely unaware of who she was, Lambert "declared that he had killed a man named Wilson up the road."

Around midnight, deputies showed up at Mrs. Wilson's house, arrested Lambert, and took him to jail in the nearby town of Webster.

Wilson "lingered" until two o'clock the following morning and died of his wound.

The next morning, Lambert told a friend he had done the shooting but was too drunk to remember why. Later on, Lambert claimed to his family, "I didn't kill Dick Wilson, but my gun did."

The people of Jackson County, where the murder took place, were so inflamed by the killing of Dick Wilson that Lambert didn't think he could get a fair trial in that county. He asked that the case be moved, and it was relocated to Swain. Judge John A. Gilmer presided over the trial, which the *Citizen* later reported "consumed two and half days and was regarded as the most extraordinary one that had ever taken place in the county."

Bragg Jones testified in court that ten or twelve people met that night, drinking liquor near a public road. Wilson had been with the group at Jones's house and left around dark. Jones accompanied him to fetch Wilson's mule. Once outside the fence in front of the house, Jones said, the two found Lambert in a wagon bed about seven feet away from the gate.

"Who are you?" Lambert asked.

"It is us," Wilson said.

Lambert swore. "Wait until I get my pistol, and I'll show you who 'us' is."

He fired his gun. According to the court record, Jones "swore positively that it was the prisoner who did the shooting; that he recognized him by his voice, and the blaze of the pistol shot."

Wilson fell to the ground. Jones waited a moment to see if Lambert would shoot again, then went to hide in the stable. As soon as he reached it, he heard another shot. He went back and found Wilson still on the ground. He carried Wilson back into the house.

Wilson's sister-in-law later testified to Lambert's confession at her house.

Lambert, represented by four lawyers, then took the stand in his own defense. Clearly, Wilson's death had been caused by a deadly weapon, yet Lambert bore the burden to show mitigating factors. He told the court he hadn't been present when the shooting occurred—instead, he claimed, he had been a mile and a half away from the scene of the murder at eight o'clock.

Lambert testified Bragg Jones offered to sell Lambert some illegal whiskey if he kept it secret from the revenue officers. Since Wilson was a revenue officer, Lambert argued, that gave Jones a motive to kill him. He claimed he and Wilson hadn't met before and were introduced for the first time that evening "and took a drink together, and parted apparently in a friendly manner."

The jury deliberated for thirty-six hours and found Lambert guilty. "The verdict was generally regarded as a righteous one and gave universal satisfaction," the *Asheville Weekly Citizen* wrote.

Lambert moved for a new trial on a technicality—that one of the jury members was underage. But because Lambert hadn't objected to the juror until after the verdict, a new trial was denied.

Judge Gilmer sentenced Lambert to death by hanging.

Lambert appealed the verdict to the North Carolina Supreme Court. On July 4, The *Wilmington Morning Star* reported that "Jack Lambert, who was to have been hanged to-day at Webster, has taken an appeal, and will be given another trial."

Pending his appeal, the judge ordered Lambert held in the jail in Asheville, deeming as unsafe the jail in Charleston (now called Bryson City), where the high court was located. At that time, the conditions of most of the jails in western North Carolina were often deemed "unsafe" to hold Lambert. Doctors and charities made inspections of the county jails and the consistent complaints were overcrowding, vermin, and jailhouses vulnerable to escape.

The Buncombe County jail in Asheville, however, had been referred to as the "Bastille," as it boasted a sophisticated lever and lock system on their steel and iron cages. Lambert was transferred to the Asheville jail and put in the same cell as prisoners Ed Ray and Waightstill Anderson. At some point, Lambert got into an argument with the two men. The uproar grew violent, so the jailer moved Lambert to another cell. Shortly thereafter, Ray, Anderson, and the others in the cell escaped. Had Lambert not argued with Anderson, he may have escaped with the rest of them.

After several weeks, Judge J. Ashe of the Supreme Court of North Carolina denied Lambert's appeal, ruling, "We have carefully reviewed the record in this case, and find no error." Ashe poked holes in Lambert's defense by saying, "There was no evidence proposed to be offered to connect Bragg Jones with the homicide, except that he was a distiller of illicit liquor, and the deceased was a revenue officer."

In mid-June, Judge Shipp re-sentenced Lambert: on Friday, the 9th of July, Lambert was to hang by the neck until dead. "Friends of the unfortunate man will make an effort to induce the governor to commute the death sentence to imprisonment for life," the *Asheville Advance* reported, "but it is generally believed that such an effort will be in vain."

Until the day before his execution, Lambert remained jailed in Asheville. Sheriffs took him by train across three counties to Charleston, Swain's county seat.

A view of Bryson City.

Lambert's execution would be the town's first, and the train ride was a spectacle that would rival any outlandish reality show of today. According to a long account in the *Asheville Weekly Citizen*, written later by a reporter who accompanied Lambert and the sheriffs, crowds gathered at every station. Lambert recognized a lot of people and called out to them, in his "attempts at wit." He chatted "gleefully"—almost "painfully so." Along the way, Lambert spoke extensively with the reporter from the *Citizen*.

"I want you to publish as my dying statement what I am going to tell you today," Lambert said. "But I don't want you to put it out until the day after my well [sic], if they kill me."

The reporter promised to respect his wishes, and Lambert gave him a copy of a manuscript he'd written. He read it aloud to several people on the train, calling it the true, last, and only statement he would make on Wilson's death. Lambert's version of the story follows.

In December 1884, he left his family to go to Macon County to prospect for mica. On the road, he met a man he had worked with before, Leon "Corn" Webb, and a stranger named Bragg Jones. Webb and Lambert talked over old times, and Webb invited Lambert to Jones's house. They would have brandy there and spend the night, and then Webb would lead him to a mica prospect.

Intoxicating Drink

Most of the stories in this book involve a murder committed while under the influence of intoxicating drink. Alcohol has existed in nearly every culture for thousands of years. European immigrants to the American colonies brought with them the skill to make alcohol and that skill was taught to each generation. In the colonial period, it was normal for people of all classes to drink heavily. Fermented and distilled drinks were, in some places, the only beverage alternative to drinking contaminated water.

In nineteenth-century North Carolina, alcohol was everywhere. Liquor was sold in every country store and was a part of social life at gatherings such as gander pullings, county fairs, and barn raisings. Doctors at times wrote prescriptions of whiskey for prisoners in the Buncombe County jail. During Reconstruction (1865-1877) in the mountains, addiction to alcohol became widespread. Men returning home from the Civil War, who were too maimed to perform farm labor, often became alcoholics. The federal government enacted a new tax to pay for the Civil War and Reconstruction; every family-run still was suddenly required to pay an exorbitant rate. This led to violence and bloodshed as moonshiners had shoot-outs with US Deputy Marshals that persisted for decades. Citizens concerned about the deleterious effects of alcohol organized the Temperance Movement, aimed to limit or outlaw alcohol. In 1908, North Carolina made state-wide Prohibition the law—twelve years prior to nationwide Prohibition.

At the Jones house, Lambert bought a quart of brandy from Bragg. Lambert tried to use a $20 bill to pay for it (about $500 in today's economy), but Jones couldn't make change for it. Lambert put the large bill back in his vest pocket and paid in smaller bills. Webb also bought brandy from Jones.

A number of men arrived in a wagon and joined them in the stable to drink, including Bragg Allison, who ran a retail store in the nearby town of Webster. Lambert considered Allison a friend and believed he was "on intimate terms" with him. Bragg Jones's brother Willie was there as well. "We all commenced drinking freely," Lambert wrote.

Soon, Dick Wilson arrived. Allison introduced Lambert to him.

Lambert asked Wilson to take a drink, but he refused.

"Dick, take a drink with him, he is all right," Allison said. Lambert wrote in his manuscript that he "pressed him to drink, and we all drink [sic] together."

"Do you remember seeing me before?" Lambert asked.

Wilson said he did, saying that he had met him not far from Quallatown, on the Cherokee Indian Reservation.

"There has been a damned lie told on me," Lambert said.

Wilson said he didn't know about that.

"Do you remember seeing a young man with me?" Lambert asked.

"I do," Wilson said.

Lambert said the young man had gone up to the mica mine, where he'd been living. He told the owner, Captain Gregory, that he left Lambert in Webster on Saturday, drunk.

Wilson said that was a lie, to his knowledge, and would tell Captain Gregory so. Lambert and Wilson "began joking rather in a vulgar way."

Everyone took another drink. Lambert said that Wilson left on his mule, but this contradicts his other testimony. Yet, Lambert insisted that while Wilson was riding away, "I made a remark that made him laugh and all heard him till he got to the turn of the road. He was laughing as far up the road as we could hear him."

Bragg Allison asked Lambert to sing for him. Lambert sang a few words of "The Old Ship of Zion," a hymn that starts, "I was standing on the banks of the river, looking out over life's troubled sea." But Lambert wrote that after "a few words, I broke down and told them I was too drunk to keep it up." He sat down on a log, leaned against the fence, and fell asleep.

He woke up to the cold, nearly dark night. He found Jones's father preparing to make a fire to heat water.

"I'm a stranger to you, and drunk," Lambert told Jones, "but I'll pay you in the morning if you let me stay all night."

Jones said he would take care of him and sent him into the house. Lambert sat by the fire with Mrs. Jones and Mrs. Webb, but soon felt sick and went outside to vomit.

He sat down in the wagon bed just outside the fence, fell over, and stayed there.

Lambert wrote that after a while he heard footsteps and voices draw near.

"He is asleep," a man said.

"Yes, he is asleep," said another.

They began feeling in his pockets. Lambert shifted.

"We will take his money and pistol and keep them for him until he gets sober," one of the men said. "Then we will give it back to him." They took the $20 bill from his vest and his pistol from his overcoat pocket and walked off. Lambert listened to the men talk about how to divvy up their stolen goods.

"Suppose he wakes up and makes a fuss?" one asked.

"Let him do so," another said. "We can soon settle him. I don't like him nohow."

Lambert raised himself to take a look, and he recognized them. "Bragg Jones had the twenty dollar bill in his hand," Lambert wrote. "Will Jones had the pistol. Will Jones was to keep the pistol and have five dollars, Corn Webb and Bragg Jones was to divide the remainder."

Later on, Will Jones came out to the wood pile near the wagon bed. Lambert asked who had his money and his pistol.

Jones said he didn't know.

"You boys taken my money and pistol to keep for me until I get sober, then you will give it to me, won't you?" Lambert asked.

"Damn you and your money," Jones said. "I know nothing about it."

"We will see in the morning," Lambert said.

Jones said if Lambert accused them of taking any money, they would kill him.

Lambert laughed. He said he didn't suppose they were very dangerous.

"There is some here don't like you," Jones said, "and if you are here tonight, you will be killed."

Lambert asked about his friend Bragg Allison. Jones said he had gone home, and went back into the house.

Lambert climbed out of the wagon and headed for Webster, "where I expected to find Mr. Bragg Allison and get him to go back with me and try to get my money back, thinking that they would give it back as soon as they got sober for we was all drunk."

He made it a mile and a half or two miles before he remembered Allison had planned to stay at his father's house that night.

Allison's father lived a short distance from Jones. Lambert turned back. He would have to pass Jones's house to reach Allison's. It was now after dark.

"Who is that?" Jones called out as Lambert passed.

Lambert was about to answer when another voice—Dick Wilson's—said, "It is me."

Jones called out again. "Damn you, did I not tell you if you was here tonight, you would be killed?"

A shot rang out.

Wilson fell against the fence. "Boys, catch my mule and I will go home," he said.

Another shot.

Willie Jones ran out and said, "I have shot that mining man or Mr. Wilson, go and see which."

"Keep your mouth shut," someone said.

The men gathered around Wilson. "Who is this?" one asked.

"It is me," Wilson said again.

They asked if he'd been shot. "I do not know," Wilson said.

"Are you sick?" they asked.

"Yes," Wilson said.

"Drunk?"

"Yes," Wilson said.

Corn Webb asked if Lambert had shot him. Wilson couldn't say.

"Lambert shot you," Webb pressed. "Where did he go?"

Wilson said the man who did the shooting had gone into the house.

"Mr. Wilson, Lambert shot you," Webb said. "We seen him do it."

"What did he shoot me for?" Wilson asked. "We never had anything against each other in our lives."

Webb said he didn't know, but it was Lambert that had shot him. Webb went to Lambert, standing some distance away in the road.

"Corn, you know I did not shoot Wilson," Lambert said.

"Well, who did it?"

"You know who shot him," Lambert said.

"Do you?" Webb asked.

Lambert said yes.

"Who?" Webb asked.

"Willie Jones," Lambert said.

The rest of the men came down the road.

"Boys," one man said, "the least said about this matter the better it will be for all parties." But Corn Webb told the men that Lambert had named Willie Jones as the shooter.

Jones drew a pistol—Lambert's pistol—and told Lambert he would shoot him if he accused him of shooting Wilson.

"You did shoot him," Lambert said.

The others told Jones to be quiet and to put the pistol away. They would all be arrested, and if they all kept their mouths shut, they would all get out of it.

A group of the men traveled with Lambert when he left, claiming it was to "show me where to turn off to go home," but clearly to secure his silence. They made him stay quiet as they rode past Bragg Allison's house, then beat and kicked him. They asked where his pistol was, and Lambert told them they knew who had it.

They forced him to drink more brandy. "I pretended to drink when one of them struck a match and looked at the bottle and said I had not drunk a drop. They then jerked me down again. Two of them held my hands and one of them held my head while the other one poured about a half pint of brandy into my mouth, swearing if I did not drink it he would shoot my brains out." They kicked him again.

"There is your pistol," Will Jones said, giving it back to him. "I knew you had it." The men told Lambert to go away, "and if I ever told who shot Wilson, they would kill me if they had to follow me to the end of the earth."

Lambert woke in the road sometime later, calling out for Jennie, his wife. He was frightened, armed, full of brandy, and insensible.

He went to Mrs. Wilson's house. "Being crazy from drunkenness, and fear, in trying to tell Mrs. Wilson what had occurred down at Mr. Jones's, I perhaps told her in a way that she mistook me for Wilson's murderer," Lambert wrote. "I did not have my right mind for several days at all times. Everything seems like a dream from the time I was left in the road."

Lambert was arrested that night by several of the men who had been drinking at the gathering, including Bragg Allison.

At the jail the next morning, when a friend asked Lambert if he had done it, he wrote that he "was afraid they would shoot me if I said no and I said yes, I did, but I was too drunk to know any better."

Lambert spent four months in the Asheville jail awaiting trial. In the meantime, his lawyers arranged to have his trial moved from Jackson County to Swain County.

A lawyer named Davidson met with Lambert while he was in jail. Lambert answered his questions about the case and told him Willie Jones had shot Wilson. Davidson agreed to defend Lambert, but never did. Instead, he appeared against Lambert on behalf of the state in the trial—a highly unethical move for a lawyer to have made.

Bragg Allison and Sheriff Rich asked Lambert why he'd shot Wilson.

"I did not shoot Wilson," Lambert said. "You will see on trial that I did not shoot him."

The next morning, Corn Webb appeared and threatened Lambert with death. Lambert said he would tell Bragg Allison about this, but Webb threatened him again—this time, he said he would tell the authorities that he had heard Lambert's brothers and father planning to break him out of jail.

"Then they will have you taken out and killed," Webb said, "for they have said that if they had any idea that your people would break you out, they would never get the chance for they would take you out and kill you. They said if you get away, they will kill every one of the breed they can find"—a threat and a racial slur combined.

During the trial, Webb returned to the jail every day to threaten Lambert into silence. "He told me if I swore who shot Wilson, I would not live to see the sun rise again," Lambert wrote. Webb told him the group of men who had been present the night of the shooting were afraid Lambert would "tell on" Willie Jones "and besides that, they are afraid you will kill all of them." Webb said his brother would gather a crowd, take Lambert out of the jail and kill him, "for he did not care any more for killing a man than he did a dog."

Webb, returning again to threaten Lambert, told him, "it was better for one man to hang than for one man to hang and four men to go to the penitentiary." He warned Lambert that "they have already brought kerosene oil to throw on the jail and set a fire if you open your mouth to tell anything against them."

Lambert believed him, and furthermore knew every member of the Jones family would swear against him in court. He decided he would rather risk being sentenced to hang than being burned up in jail.

Lambert's manuscript concluded, "I kept getting my hand in the lion's mouth deeper and deeper, and when it was too late, I tried to get out. God knows all things and he knows I am innocent. I did not kill Wilson."

The day came that was to be Lambert's last. They erected a scaffold in a field on the east side of the Tuckasegee River "near the beautiful slope of the Unaka range of mountains." Lambert would now be standing on the banks of the river, looking out over life's troubled sea, just as he'd sung that fateful night of drinking. Just across the river, Charleston's streets were crowded and the atmosphere was festive. More than 1,500 people gathered to watch the town's first, and last, hanging. Lambert's father, wife, four brothers, and an uncle came to visit him. Lambert asked the sheriff to deliver his clothing to his wife, and his body to his brothers. At one o'clock, Lambert was presented with his coffin and said he was perfectly satisfied with it.

The *Asheville Weekly Citizen* reported that the night before, Lambert had stayed up writing "until late." Lambert gave his brothers a handwritten note that read, "Brothers, I ask of you to see that my wife & children is taken care of. If you all leave this country, take them with you. Jennie says she will go."

At 1:15, Jennie left. The crowd watched her go, and "the sobs of the heartbroken woman brought tears to all the bystanders." Lambert's father left too. His brothers and uncle stayed, standing quietly under the scaffold.

Robert Lee Madison, a schoolteacher and newcomer to town, recorded the events of the day, and noted "a nervous posse of heavily armed men stationed nearby." When he inquired about them, "he was told that persistent rumors indicated that friends of Jack Lambert intended to attempt to save his life."

At 2:15, Lambert was led to the gallows by Buncombe County's Sheriff Rich, Sheriff Welch of Swain, and a reverend. Three doctors were present. Lambert went to the scaffold "with unusual coolness" and spoke to the audience for about six minutes.

Lambert gave a version of the story he'd told to the reporter the day before, and concluded by telling the young men in the crowd, "Refrain from drinking whiskey and keeping bad company. I give you this warning from a dying man."

One of the guards called out, "Did you kill Wilson?"

"I did not," Lambert said.

The *Asheville Weekly Citizen* reported that Lambert kept calm during the entire execution. The sheriff bound his arms and legs and adjusted his black cap. At the last moment, Lambert called Sheriff Rich to come close, and whispered to him. Lambert asked him "never to reveal his statement to a living soul" and bade him goodbye.

The *Citizen* observed, "The prisoner stepped forward and placed his head in the noose, and, upon a motion from the officers the spring was touched, the drop fell, and Andrew Jackson Lambert's soul entered upon the great unknown."

As he fell, a woman screamed. The crowd "uttered a low moan." A young teacher from Ohio fainted.

But the shorter-than-usual rope hadn't broken Lambert's neck. The authorities kept his body hanging for over fifteen minutes, "suspended between heaven and earth." The crowd watched silently as Lambert strangled, the only sound his "desperate struggle to breathe. . . . Lambert's shoulders rose and fell in hitches."

One of the doctors wanted to cut him down quickly, but the other two objected. After fifteen minutes, "the physician listened for the beatings of the heart and felt for the pulsations and finding none, declared to the other two attending physicians that Lambert was dead."

Sheriff Welch cut the noose into pieces and tossed them as souvenirs to the crowd. Local superstition held that they could ward off evil and cure sickness, and people scrambled to catch them. Meanwhile, Lambert's brothers took possession of his body and "made such haste to leave town that remarks were made of their eagerness to get away."

The 1898 hanging of James Fleming Parker in Prescott, Arizona.

The Gallows

Punishment by death pre-dates the Bible and appears in the code of Babylonian King Hammurabi. The death penalty in North Carolina is a carryover of English Common Law. In 1868, the new state constitution set limits to the types of cases punishable by death. It was not until 1893 that murder was divided into first and second degrees. In the nineteenth century, the state called for the death penalty for "murder, rape, statutory rape, slave-stealing, highway robbery, burglary, arson, castration, buggery, sodomy, bestiality, dueling where death occurs, hiding a slave with intent to free him, taking a free Negro out of state to sell him, bigamy, inciting slaves to rebel, circulating seditious literature among slaves, accessory to murder, or mayhem."

Public hangings became a social event. In nineteenth-century North Carolina, hundreds, sometimes thousands of people traveled long distances, picnic baskets in tow, to attend a hanging. After the hanging, crowds would vie for souvenirs, such as pieces of the victim's clothing or bits from the rope that hanged him.

The *News and Observer* would report that one of Lambert's last requests to the sheriff was to use as short a rope as possible. The *New York Times* later wrote that "the fall was only 12 inches. . . . That the prisoner preferred a slow death by strangulation was thought to be novel and strange."

Public executions were a social event including tickets for admission.

They loaded his coffin into a wagon and drove it up the Tuckasegee River then up a stream called Deep Creek. Once they reached a secluded place, they took him out of the coffin and "in a moment the cool waters of the creek were applied by loving hands to the body." For over an hour, they "coaxed the still heart to throb again, and watched the leaden eyes for some sign of latent animation." Lambert's brothers tried "every act that loving hands could do and active minds suggest" to bring him back to consciousness.

Madison, who decades later wrote a series of articles called "Experiences of a Pedagogue in the Carolina Mountains," recorded a rumor. Lambert's family had arranged in advance to meet a doctor on the Cherokee Indian Reservation, and that the doctor had attempted to revive Lambert's heart with a "galvanic battery."

The *New York Times* reported that the family had outfitted the chosen spot on Deep Creek in advance with "a fire and pots full of boiling water, two pairs of heavy woolen blankets, an electric battery, brandy, aromatic spirits of ammonia, and other materials prepared for the effort to cheat the law."

A legend arose in Jackson and Swain counties that Lambert survived and was seen alive in Jackson the Sunday after his execution. "It is astonishing what credence is given to this rumor," the *News and Observer* wrote.

A few days later, the *New York Times* covered the rumors swirling around Lambert's supposed revival, reporting on demands for Lambert's grave in the Old Cherokee Boarding School Campus Cemetery in Cherokee to be exhumed and his body put on display. Lambert's brothers refused and guarded the grave to keep it from being disturbed. "This refusal to satisfy morbid curiosity has only added confidence to the belief that Lambert is alive," the *Times* wrote.

Many years later, Lambert's family supposedly gave a twenty-page letter to Dick Wilson's descendants. Lambert had stayed up late writing it to his family on July 8, the night before his execution. The letter mirrored the account Lambert gave to the

Asheville Weekly Citizen, elaborating on some details. Contrary to Lambert's court testimony, it confirmed that he had been at the scene of the crime when Wilson was killed, and not a mile and a half away. But he remained adamant that Willie Jones, not him, had committed the murder.

The letter concluded, "Knowing that I shall soon stand before God, there to answer for my sins in full, I believe it nothing but a duty I owe myself, my friends, and the friends of R. M. Wilson, and more to God, to tell to the people who did kill Wilson. . . . I am as clear of killing Wilson as a babe. . . . One of God's commands is that thou shalt not lie. God forbid I should."

According to Lambert family lore, when Willie Jones was on his deathbed, he confessed to the killing of Dick Wilson. Bolstering this claim, Madison recorded that an unnamed man on his death-bed in the town of Dillsboro, in Jackson County, "admitted that he had killed Dick Wilson and that he had stolen Jack Lambert's pistol to do it."

A common ploy used by families was to whitewash an executed relative's reputation. Lambert's family claims that in addition to this deathbed confession, at one point they were in possession of a letter in which Jones confessed to the crime.

Who can know the truth about that dark, drunken winter night in the mountains, more than 130 years later? The most likely sce-nario is that Lambert shot Wilson, but was too drunk to remember doing it. Lambert's letter and his account to the *Asheville Weekly Citizen* are compelling, but they at times conflict. Despite drink-ing enough to render him insensible, as he had put it, Lambert recorded details, dialogue, and a coherent chronology. His story seems contrived.

To modern eyes, Lambert seems like a man who should have been set up for success. He was literate, had some access to mon-ey, and inspired deep support among family and friends. Was rac-ism a factor? What was the real story between him, Dick Wilson, Willie Jones, and Bragg Allison? Even the authorities seemed to agree something was amiss—it is a matter of record that Lambert's trial was moved to improve his chances of an impartial jury, and that safety precautions were taken when he was jailed.

Lambert's elaborate stories, his family's faith they would revive him, his determination to control his legacy in the press and among his descendants, and the legend that he survived his execution all combine into an alluring mystery surrounding a resourceful scoundrel who left us certain only of this good advice: "Refrain from drinking whiskey and keeping bad company."

CHAPTER SEVEN

"Buncombe's Boasted Bastille Busted"

J ULY OF 1885 WAS A sultry month for six men who were finding the thick, hot air more humid than usual. For them, the stakes were much higher than just surviving the heat in a miserable jail cell. All were condemned, and their crimes invariably involved alcohol, sudden passion, and guns. Nearly all had been convicted of murder. As they languished in the most secure jail in western North Carolina, they awaited their dreadful fate of hard labor in the penitentiary and the death walk to the gallows. So secure was the Buncombe County jail in Asheville reputed to be, that it was hailed by a newspaper man as the "Bastille."

Twenty-six-year-old Waightstill Avery Anderson sat among the prisoners. Accompanying him was his forty-one-year-old cousin, Edward W. Ray, who'd been convicted of two counts of manslaughter. Anderson and Ray, also brothers-in-law, had each married a daughter of Jacob Weaver Bowman, a prominent judge.

The historical record offers no details about precisely how Anderson and Ray communicated with friends on the outside;

nevertheless, as they wasted away in the Buncombe County jail, contemplating the noose and the pen, those friends were earnestly hatching a plan. But first . . . .

Fratricide

Among the six in the Asheville jail was another man guilty of murder, Charles York. At the time of his arrest, he'd been living with his brother, John York, of Cooper's Station. John, twenty-nine and married with children, had invited his younger, unmarried brother Charles to live with him and his wife, Eveline. John also allowed Charles to work with him in his lumber business.

> There is a little boy inside the man who is my brother. . . . Oh, how I hated that little boy. And how I love him too.
>
> ANNA QUINDLEN

John and Charles had been made fatherless during the Civil War. Their father, William York of the 60th Regiment of NC troops, died of pneumonia at Chattanooga when John was seven and Charles five. Over 650,000 men died in the Civil War. The widespread loss of fathers greatly impacted the generations that followed. The trauma of the war and then growing up with no access to education in impoverished post-Civil-War southern Appalachia became contributing factors in the widespread addictions to alcohol. Sadly, the two brothers were apparently alcoholics.

On a Thursday afternoon in May 1885, John and Charles were returning home from Asheville. They'd delivered a load of lumber and were on their way back to the Swannanoa Valley. Driving a wagon with a team of oxen, they commenced doing two things: drinking liquor and bickering. At one point, the two got off the wagon and began to lead the ox team while they walked. An acquaintance who walked with them to within five miles of their home, said the two brothers argued the entire time.

As soon as they arrived outside their home, John's wife, Eveline, heard a strange sound, "like cattle running." She heard her husband yelling. She swung open the door and ran to John, who was on the ground, stabbed, bleeding, and "in the agonies of death." Her screaming caught the attention of neighbors, who carried her husband inside the house, but John was dead before they got him through the door. Their six-year-old son, William, witnessed his father's murder, and for the rest of his life the trauma haunted him.

Authorities arrested Charles for murder. In trying to explain away the stabbing, he said that his brother had been whittling with a knife as they walked along, and that he'd tripped and fallen on the open knife, which pierced his heart. The coroner's examination revealed otherwise. John had been stabbed in the heart multiple times—his coat displayed seven gashes. In a blind, drunken rage, Charles had made Eveline a widow and her children fatherless.

No records survived to reveal what they fought about. Was it an old resentment? Jealousy that John was married and Charles was not? Whatever the case, it was made worse by the quantities of alcohol consumed that day. According to local witnesses, both were "addicted" to liquor.

Dr. Watson, county coroner, empaneled a jury. After a week, there was sufficient evidence to continue detaining Charles pending a grand jury. On May 23, 1885, Charles was committed to the Buncombe County jail. While awaiting the outcome of the next grand jury session, Charles was put in the same holding cell with Anderson and Ray.

Waightstill Avery Anderson

Waightstill Anderson, or "Wates," as his friends called him, was born in June 1859 and grew up in the turbulent eras of the Civil War and Reconstruction.

The author's 2nd great-grandmother Eveline "Vicey" Reece York, taken eleven years after John's death, on the day of her marriage to Doc Gibson in 1896. Vicey would have been considered what we today call a "cougar," since she was thirty-seven, and Doc was twenty-five.

He spent his childhood in Yancey and Madison counties, places of excessive violence during and after the war. One contemporary observer described Anderson as "intelligent and genteel," while another remarked that he had "Fair complexion, light hair, blue eyes." Anderson was "slender built," about five feet, nine inches tall, and weighed about 135 pounds.

As he was growing up, Anderson fell under the influence of his older cousin Ed Ray. Described as five feet, nine inches tall and 190 pounds, with blue eyes and auburn hair, Ed Ray was "a large, fine looking man . . . of Herculean make." Ray lived in Madison County and was the son of a preacher, but he earned an unsavory reputation as a US Deputy Marshal who assisted agents of the Bureau of Internal Revenue. He had a violent history and was reputed to have killed seven men. Newspapers described him as "very active and quick spoken," a "reckless violator of the law," and reported that he'd been charged with assault "with intent to commit a rape." In his defense at a hearing, Ray said that he'd done everything "in the line of duty" as a Federal Revenue officer.

Under Ed Ray's tutelage in the Wild-West atmosphere that characterized the mountain region, Anderson became a skilled gunman. Quickly, he developed a penchant for shooting when he got mad. He also earned a notorious reputation for carrying concealed weapons as well as cornering unsuspecting folks with his six-shooter.

Anderson carried a Smith & Wesson single-action revolver.

Anderson, the son of a Confederate veteran and Baptist minister, was married with two small children. They lived nine miles from the town of Bakersville, near the road that led to the Flat Rock mine, a place that would ultimately change his life in unthinkable ways.

On July 21, 1880, Anderson and Ray got into a fight with another Mitchell County man. Marshall "Marsh" Keener attacked Anderson "contrary to the law and peace and dignity of the state." Anderson, "with force and arms violently assaulted" Keener by throwing a brick at him, hitting him on the head, and "inflicting a bad wound." Anderson then pulled his pistol on Keener. In the fray, Ray picked up a chair and hit Keener with it, and the court charged Ray, saying he "beat and seriously injured" Keener. Anderson and Ray were each handed an indictment of assault and battery with a deadly weapon.

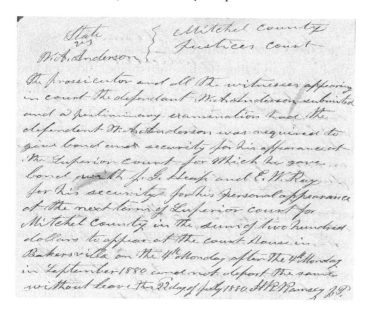

Warrant for Anderson for Assault and Battery, issued July 22, 1880, and executed the same day. Anderson was ordered to appear at the next term of Superior Court in Bakersville.

In October 1882, Anderson, who for some time had been noted for "making attacks on peaceable men with weapons unawares and at disadvantage," again did just that. One afternoon, while walking down the street, Anderson hailed Thomas C. Greene, a wealthy Mitchell County Republican. Anderson demanded to know if Greene had written an article published in *Mountain Voice*. Greene said no. Not believing him, Anderson stepped back, drew his pistol, and called Greene insulting names. Anderson was holding his ground when John G. Heap, hearing the commotion from a nearby store, ran to the scene. Heap begged Anderson to put away his pistol and behave. At that moment, Clerk of Court

The Mountain Voice, was a weekly Republican newspaper.

David Alexander Bowman (Anderson's in-law) showed up and began calling Heap a liar. Heap retorted, and Anderson and Bowman punched Heap in the face. Exactly how that clash of manhood was resolved, the historical record does not say, but the episode characterizes the thread of violence that would run through Anderson's life.

Murder at the Flat Rock Mine

The mining boom in the mountains brought an increase of violence. In the 1870s, mica was in high demand, and the mountains were yielding up tons of the shiny mineral. Men claiming mineral rights, as well as the leasing and subleasing of these rights, gave rise to fierce rivalries. A friend of Mark Twain, writer Charles Warner, wrote in 1885 that "scores of visionary men" had been disappointed. Lawsuits about "titles and claims" multiplied, and disputes ending in murder had become frequent.

The Flat Rock mine was located "between Spruce Pine and Bakersville." John Blalock had a previous mineral rights claim to the mine, but he had forfeited it, because he'd failed to complete the claim, and his two-year grace period had lapsed. Based on Blalock's incomplete entry, Ed Ray decided to assert ownership, and in this regard, Ray intended to become a *claim-jumper.*

Ray brought Anderson in on the deal by promising him a stake in the mine, of which Ray falsely claimed "peaceable possession." His plan was to work the mine until it became exhausted. If any

State
vs
W. A. Anderson

} Mitchel County
Justices Court
Recognizance

Be it remembered that on the 22d day
of July 1880 before the undersigned
a Justice of the Peace for said County
personally appeared came J. G. Heap and
E. W. Ray and severally acknowledge
themselves indebted to the State of North
Carolina in the Sum of two hundred
dollars lawful Money of the United
States

The conditions of this Recognizance is
such that if the said W. A. Anderson
shall appear at the next term term of
Superior Court to be held in and
for the County of Mitchel at the
Court house in Bakersville on the 4th
Monday after the 4th Monday in September
1880 and shall not depart the same
without leave then this recognizance
to be void otherwise in full force
Taken subscribed and acknowledged
before me H. R. Ramsey, JP
this 22 day of July 1880

W. A. Heap (Seal)
Jno. G. Heap (Seal)
E. W. Ray (Seal)

Ed W. Ray and John G. Heap signed
a $200 bond for Anderson. Keener
was fined one dollar and released. No
further records were found to indicate
the results of these serious charges,
but Anderson's rage would again flare
on a fateful evening at the Flat Rock
mica mine.

Gaugers & Storekeepers

In July 1882, at age twenty-four, Waightstill Avery Anderson swore an oath. When he became a gauger for the Department of Treasury, Bureau of Internal Revenue, he promised to act with "carefulness and accuracy." Revenue gaugers were appointed to truthfully determine the volume of alcoholic spirits being produced in breweries and distilleries. Anderson's work required the ability to make quick, accurate math calculations, specifically using decimals. Gaugers inspected, weighed, and marked the alcohol. Anderson was one of eight revenue officers in Mitchell County with annual salaries between $1,200 and $1,500, considered a good income for the period. Anderson and his family were more affluent than others who earned a living by farm labor or mining.

Anderson held a commission initially to work during fruit brandy season. Three months later, however, he was sworn in as a deputy collector and storekeeper, which meant he was authorized to carry a gun and was made a US Deputy Marshal. Anderson was also in charge of the keys to distillery houses.

All gaugers and storekeepers for the Bureau were required to post a $5,000 bond, which acted as surety against cheating. Civic leaders, who favored Anderson's appointment due to his respected family and his fervor for Republican politics, agreed to be his bondsmen. One of them was John G. Heap, publisher of *Mountain Voice*, a weekly newspaper in Bakersville. But only two months after his appointment as a deputy collector, Anderson shocked one of his bondsmen by accosting him on the streets of Bakersville.

Stamps were issued to show a distiller had paid the revenue tax.

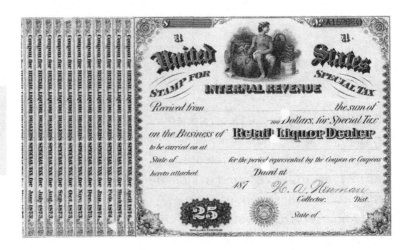

legal dispute did arise, he'd have extracted the profits from the mine before a legal claim could be adjudicated. But according to newspaper accounts, three other men—Ceborn "Cebe" Miller, Milton Buchanan, and a man named Bailey—were also working the mine and claimed rightful ownership.

One evening, Ray built fires at the tunnel's opening and fanned the smoke inside, hoping to drive out Miller and Buchanan or suffocate them. When that didn't work, he tried to starve out the men by blocking the entryway, but the miners slipped out another tunnel to replenish their food supply.

One day or so later, Anderson went to Ed Ray's home, where he stayed the night with Ed and his wife, Malissa. While the men were talking about going to the mine the next day, Malissa said, "I would not go, Ed, if I were you." He'd been gone a lot, and she wanted him home. But apparently, her pleading went unheeded. On February 17, 1884, Anderson and Ray rode horseback, trotting down Mountain Road toward the Flat Rock mine. Ray was carrying Anderson's .22 Flaubert handgun. As a gauger and deputy collector, Anderson carried his six-shot pistol in his hip holster. Anderson and Ray arrived at the mine about sunset and sent their horses off to feed.

Earlier that day, Miller and Buchanan had hired additional men to work with them to sink a shaft to a tunnel below. Among the workers at the mine was Ed Horton. Folks said Horton was usually a peaceable man, but when he got drunk, he became dangerous. For two years, he'd had an ongoing murderous grudge against Anderson. Months prior to Anderson arriving at the mine, Horton had waylaid the road, hoping to ambush and kill Anderson, who by some miracle survived but came "within three minutes of being killed." Horton felt justified in his desire to kill Anderson, and hoped he'd soon get the chance.

At the mine, Anderson went to the opening of the upper shaft while Ray went to the lower shaft. There, Ray saw Miller, Horton, and other men with tools. Ray began voicing claims of ownership and said forcefully to

The Flaubert was also called a saloon or parlor gun. Developed in 1845 by French inventor Louis-Nicolas Flaubert, it was the first to integrate a rimfire metallic cartridge.

Miller, "You can't put any more tools in the mine 'til this matter is settled." At the mouth of the lower pit, Miller and Ray squatted down and began talking. Miller told Ray that Bailey would come the next day to show deeds. Ray seemed to think that the dispute would be resolved in his favor. Miller called Horton over, and Horton squatted down on Ray's right side.

Bill Burleson came by with shovels and took them down into the pit, but Ray protested. He pulled out his gun and repeated his demand: "You can't put any more tools in here!" Just then, Miller struck Ray so forcefully that they both fell down the shaft, landing on Milt Buchanan and brothers Stephen and Bill Burleson at the bottom of the mine.

Hearing the fighting, Anderson climbed down to the lower shaft. Suddenly, Horton was just a few steps away on Anderson's right. He picked up a rock and threw it, but Anderson ducked. Horton jumped on Anderson, shoved him down, struck him on the head, and straddled him with his knees. Anderson went for his pistol. Horton grabbed Anderson's Smith and Wesson six-shooter and tried to wrench it from his grip. Horton yanked Anderson's hand over rocks on the ground, leaving Anderson's hand and wrist torn and bloody. Anderson attempted to shake him off, but Horton caught Anderson's left forefinger in his mouth. He bit down hard through the first joint to the bone. Anderson managed to get on top of Horton and hit him on the head with his pistol. He had raised his pistol to strike him again when Horton yelled, "Don't hurt me. Let me up, and I'll leave!" Anderson accepted this, got off Horton and started walking toward the upper pit. Anderson's hat had fallen off, and when he bent over to pick it up, Horton came toward him with a large rock. Anderson cocked his pistol, and Horton yelled, "Don't! I will leave, I will leave. I'll leave."

Anderson again told him to leave him alone or he'd shoot him. Horton said, "I will. I will." Anderson stepped off the path to his right, up the slope, and Horton walked on by. As he got just past Anderson, Horton leaned down, grabbed a large rock, and threw it at Anderson, hitting him hard on the right shoulder, knocking him backward. Horton kept coming toward him. Anderson aimed his gun at Horton, who cried out, "Don't. You'll kill me!" as Anderson fired his fourth shot. Horton fell to the ground mortally wounded. He was twenty-five years old.

Meanwhile, Ray was struggling to free himself from the grip of four men who intended to finish him off. He begged for his life. They let go of him on the condition that he abandon his supposed claim. He conceded, and began climbing the ladder. A few steps up, however, he reached down and grabbed a pistol from his boot and started firing. He shot Miller in the face, killing him instantly. The second bullet killed Stephen Burleson, and the third hit his brother Bill Burleson in the shoulder. Ray raced up from the pit, leaving three men "lying weltering in their blood."

Ray and Anderson took off on foot, heading into the mountains. Meanwhile, the bodies of Horton, Burleson, and Miller were carried to a former slave outbuilding of the old Penland homeplace. When people heard about the killings, they grew infuriated, raising $4,300 in reward money for information leading to their capture: $800 from the state, and $3,500 from private donors.

For the next three weeks, Anderson and Ray hid in the mountains that they knew so well. Desperate to have them found, Governor Jarvis ordered a company of the Third Regiment of troops to pursue them. In addition, a posse of two hundred men went searching for Anderson and Ray. Even though they'd fled without horses or provisions, they nevertheless had family members who helped them survive in the February cold of the Smoky Mountains. One afternoon, the search party found "a gun, six blankets, two overcoats, a pair of overshoes, a satchel of biscuits, and a ham." This discovery on Pumpkin Patch Mountain, about four miles west of Bakersville, excited the posse, who soon expected to capture the two outlaws. But despite their fervor, the posse never found them, and eventually abandoned their search.

Three weeks after the shootings, and believing that they'd be acquitted at trial, Anderson and Ray gave themselves up. They thought folks would vindicate their plea of self-defense. Their father-in-law, Judge Jacob Bowman, received their surrender and handed them over to Judge Graves, who was then holding court at Marshall in Madison County. Anderson and Ray were immediately spirited away to the Buncombe County jail in Asheville. Six weeks later, on Saturday, April 19, Anderson and Ray were escorted to Burnsville to be arraigned in Mitchell County Superior Court. An "immense crowd" packed the court, so Judge Shipp ordered his courtroom cleared, with the help of "27 extra deputies, who hustled out all but about fifty of the citizens." After the arraignment, Anderson and Ray were returned to the Buncombe County jail.

The murder case became such a sensation that the Buncombe County sheriff developed concerns over the safety of the prisoners. He feared an angry mob would storm the jail and drag the men out and lynch them, or that their friends would break them out. Hearing the sheriff's apprehensions, Judge Graves requested state troops, saying that based on his best information, Anderson and Ray in Asheville jail were "not safely kept." Authorities expressed fears of being overwhelmed by a gang of Anderson's and Ray's friends. Graves believed the two men were so influential that the threat of their friends breaking them out was very real. In light of these revelations, the judge ordered that Anderson and Ray be moved to the Henderson County jail.

A lengthy series of jail transfers unfolded. In an effort to enforce Judge Graves's order, Governor Jarvis authorized troops to be sent to protect the Buncombe County jail and to serve as a military escort for moving the prisoners to Hendersonville. A detail of fifteen men was stationed around the Asheville jail, and by 10:00 p.m. the guard had assembled and was on duty.

At six o'clock the next morning, a fourteen-man detail escorted Anderson and Ray to the Henderson County jail. Before starting out on their twenty-five-mile trek, they had a two-hour delay getting breakfast, but eventually "took up the line of march for Hendersonville." On account of heavy rains, and the road being muddy and flooded, they were "compelled to use horses." The entourage arrived at the Hendersonville jail at six in the evening, and the troops remained on guard until nine the next morning.

Due to Anderson's and Ray's privileged status, one newspaper reported, "With the array of counsel which they have retained and the amount of money that they can command . . . the prisoners can easily defeat justice in the Court House." The despised US Deputy Marshal and US Revenue agent were active Republicans and inspired their enemies to write an article in a Democratic newspaper suggesting that vigilante justice should supplant the judicial process, and that "unless they are hung by order of Judge Lynch they will never be hung at all."

Anderson and Ray were in the Hendersonville jail a few weeks when Judge Graves ordered that they be transferred to the Mitchell County jail in Bakersville. Sheriff Hickey of Mitchell County expressed concerns that it was "absolutely necessary to the protection of life, [and] the preservation of law and order" to have state troops guard Anderson and Ray while they were in Mitchell County jail. General Jones, commander of the state troops at Asheville, may have thought Hickey was being an alarmist. He wrote the sheriff, saying that he hoped people would let the law "take its course" without going to the extreme measure of deploying troops. Jones put Hickey under pressure to detail his "apprehensions of mob violence." He needed to explain why he thought that a "civil posse" would be unable "to preserve law and order" during their trial, or to keep the prisoners secure until then. However, if lives were at stake, and there was the need to preserve "law and order," troops would be sent.

Earlier, Governor Jarvis had heard the concerns of Mitchell County people who believed that a mob would try to lynch Anderson and Ray during their move for trial, but he was reticent to send troops, saying:

> I am a great worshiper of the civil law and a great
> believer in the majesty and power of its Judges. I
> have never heard of a man being lynched in this State
> while on his way to the Superior Court to be tried. Nor
> have I ever heard of such a thing being done while

the Court was in session, and I am loath to believe
that the people of Mitchell will attempt to do either.

Sheriff Hickey was then advised to summon a posse of "twelve resolute men . . . to protect life and preserve law and order."

The Mitchell County jail was in a poor state, as were other jails in the region. In 1885, writer Charles Dudley Warner visited the jail in Bakersville and described it as a two-story brick building with a room for the jailer. The lower room had a cage that was nine by ten feet square and eight feet high "made of logs bolted together and filled with spikes." The cage had a narrow door with a small opening through which prisoners received their food. In warm weather, the poor ventilation, overcrowding, and unsanitary conditions made for a miserable experience as Anderson and Ray awaited trial month after month.

Public sentiment over the shootings remained high. In Mitchell County, where the crimes occurred, authorities expressed concerns over being unable to deliver a fair trial, so the venue (aka *venire*) was moved to Lenoir, in Caldwell County. This change came about, in part, due to fears that the two prisoners had too much favor in Mitchell County on account of their Republican political connections. As a result, the trial was moved to the largely Democratic and more distant county of Caldwell.

On May 2, 1884, six heavily armed men, including ex-Sheriff Aden Wiseman of Mitchell County, escorted Waightstill Anderson and Ed Ray to Caldwell's county seat of Lenoir. The *Lenoir Topic*, a Democratic newspaper, denounced Anderson and Ray and suggested they "be taken out of jail and lynched." Regardless of threats instigated by the press, for the next eight months while awaiting trial, the two prisoners remained steeped in misery in the Caldwell County jail.

The Trials of Ray & Anderson

On December 4, Ed Ray's trial began in Caldwell County. Ray had hired "a fine array of legal talent." Testimony was heard from James Miller, brother of the man Ray had killed. Sherman Buchanan, one of the workers at the mine, was called to the stand. He told the court about Ray claiming to have a deed to the mine and "ordered them, with an oath, to vacate." He told of how Ed Ray and Hardy Sparks had tried to "smother them out" of the mine with smoke. Palmer Ellis was called to the stand and spoke about how Ray was at the mine ordering everyone around like he owned the place. He testified that J. C. Miller told Ray that if Ray had true ownership, he would bow out. After all the speeches, the judge gave the case to the jury. Within four hours, they returned a verdict of guilty of manslaughter. The judge congratulated Ray for "his escape from a conviction of murder." His sentence was twenty years of hard labor in the state penitentiary. After his sentencing, he was taken back to the Buncombe County jail.

On January 12, 1885, Anderson's trial began. One hundred and eight witnesses were reportedly summoned. His father, Rev. Jesse Woodson Anderson, was in attendance.

Ike Stewart, a fellow revenue agent and associate of Ray and Anderson, testified that he believed the two men had never been in actual possession of the mine. Stewart said that on the evening of the shootings, he left the mine about ten minutes after the two men arrived. He rode horseback to his house less than half a mile away. He put his horse in the stable and had just walked into his house, and was pulling off his spurs when he heard gunfire. Immediately, he ran outside and heard two more shots. Racing to the stable, he "caught a horse and rode over to the mine." Within two hundred yards of the mine, he saw Anderson and Ray, who were walking toward Bakersville. Based on Stewart's recollection, the series of events that took place after Anderson and Ray arrived at the mine couldn't have lasted more than twenty minutes.

Among the witnesses was John Butler, who had also been at the mine the night of the homicides. In his testimony, Butler told the court about the disputed ownership of the mine and about the fire Ray set to try and smoke out Miller.

Witness William Putnam testified that Anderson had told him, "If Baily shows title, I will have nothing more to do with it."

Some of the most interesting testimony involved Ed Horton's feud with Anderson, which began long before their altercation at the mine. According to witness I. N. Wilson, two years before the shooting, Wilson and Anderson were with a group of men target shooting in a meadow. They heard Ed Horton halloo from some distance away, and Anderson said, "If he comes in here cutting up as he did court week, he'll get his damned head busted. If nobody else does it, I will."

The men stopped their target practice about the time Horton walked up. Horton said that if they tried to run him over, he'd cut their throats. Anderson turned and said, "I'm a man." Horton retorted, "I'm a man." Anderson then hit him on the head with his gun barrel and knocked him down. He struck and kicked him again. Anderson beat Horton "severely," and was later indicted for assault and battery. Wilson testified that Anderson had said, "If I get into it [with Horton] again, I intend to kill." On cross-examination, Wilson told the court that at the time they'd been target shooting, Horton was drunk when he came into the meadow, threatening Anderson.

Mr. S. C. Gouge next testified to Anderson's character, saying he was truthful and honest, but that he had a reputation for being "a passionate, high-tempered man," known to "use weapons when he fights."

J. M. Buchanan testified that he'd known Ed Horton for several years. One day, Horton had told him, "Anderson ought to be in hell, and if he crosses my path I'll put him there." Buchanan had cautioned him not to make comments like that.

Charles Green testified that Horton had told him that one day he would "get" Anderson, and that he could take a good rifle gun and hit him from one hundred yards. Horton had remarked that the first chance he got, he intended to whip Anderson "and then kill the damned rascal." Eli Scoggins similarly testified that Horton had said of Anderson, "Damn him, I intend to kill him, and the sooner the better."

W. T. Garrison testified that he'd warned Horton about Anderson, saying, "Ed, you'd better let Anderson alone. You've had one fuss, and [one] of these days, he'll kill you." Horton had told Garrison about seeing Anderson in town, saying that the sight of Anderson made him so angry that "It seemed as if my heart would burst out." Horton grew more incensed as he was sure he'd spotted Anderson in a warehouse gauging liquor. Horton picked up two rocks and approached the door, aiming to kill him, but realized that it wasn't Anderson, and he left.

In court that day, Anderson testified at length. He said, "Ray told me that he had peaceable possession of the whole mine and that the parties regained possession of the lower pit." He told about being in fear for his life, and that he shot Horton in self-defense. He explained that when he arrived at the mine that Sunday, he was carrying a "Smith and Wesson six-shooting pistol, not a self-cocker." Anderson told the court, "I was a deputy collector and was authorized to carry a pistol."

Anderson did admit to having fights. The men he'd had brawls with included Stokes Penland, Marshall Keener, Wash Hyams, W. B. Councill, Tode Councill, John G. Heap, and Thomas C. Greene. In spite of his many affrays, the twenty-six-year-old had only twice been "indicted for violence."

Anderson relayed the showdown with Horton, saying he had gone down into the mine when he encountered

Court Week

In the nineteenth-century Carolina back-country, Circuit judges and lawyers rode horseback, often on bad roads through rain and snow as they moved from county to county holding court. Whenever court was in session, people flocked to the courthouse grounds.

"Court week" was a social affair at the impromptu open-air market with buying and selling of crops and dry goods, slaves, and horses. Some folks came "to be entertained by speeches, races, and games of chance." Still others showed up to hang around the whiskey wagons.

In 1853, Augustus S. Merrimon, a young Asheville attorney who later became a US Senator and Chief Justice of North Carolina's Supreme Court, kept a journal. In Buncombe County, he noted that the judge had "ordered the whisky wagons to be removed, and thus we have not been so much disturbed with drunkenness as yesterday." Merrimon complained bitterly about attendees at court week, saying, "Scores of women attend this court for the sole purpose of drinking and pandering to the lustful passions of dirty Men." Town inns and boardinghouses filled up during court week. A young Tennessee woman in 1828 bemoaned that court week had brought in so many boarders, that she had "a pack of men to work for." She lamented: "Some times I wish there was no men." Court week remained a tradition into the twentieth century.

Horton coming at him. Horton had heavy rocks in both hands and threw one at Anderson, injuring him, and Horton hurled more large rocks at him, which knocked him down. Anderson showed the court his scarred hand; Horton had bitten his left forefinger so hard that he'd lost a fingernail. Then he spoke of the final deed done in self-defense: "While I was firing, Horton was coming towards me with the rock raised. He was very near me when I fired the last shot. I didn't know that I had hit Horton until he fell at me. I shot to keep him from killing me." Having told his side of the story, Anderson was compelled to wait before hearing the court's decision of his fate.

The following day, the prosecution and defense attorneys summed up their cases for the jury. Six lawyers gave compelling speeches. On January 15, the state gave its final summation. By early afternoon, the judge charged the jury with their solemn duty. He told them that Anderson had been reasonable "to believe he was about to be killed or to receive bodily harm and found it necessary to kill to prevent such injury." The judge's sympathies stopped there, however, as he explained that the killing "was a necessity which he [Anderson] brought upon himself by his violent and unlawful conduct, and therefore he cannot shelter himself behind such necessity by a plea of self-defense." He likewise told them, "Because human life is sacred regarded by the law . . . life can never be lawfully taken unless when another is put in eminent [sic] peril and only when there is no reasonable means of protecting it but to take the life of the assailant." After a lengthy charge to the jurors, he sent them off to deliberate. Less than three hours later, the jury returned with a verdict.

The issues upon which Anderson's future hung were these facts: both Anderson and Horton had "indulged in threats" against the other, and Anderson had specifically said, "Leave here, Ed Horton, or I will kill you." Others testified that Anderson had said, "Damn you, I want to kill you anyhow." Unfortunately for Anderson, witnesses were unable to corroborate his account of Horton attacking him with rocks or biting his finger to the bone.

On the January morning that court was called to order, Anderson was ushered in, while outside there raged "a blinding snowstorm." Anderson's counsel requested a new trial, which was overruled, and when "sentence was prayed for by the solicitor, a motion and arrest of judgment was also made which was likewise overruled." After a grueling four-day trial, an anxious Anderson stood up to hear the verdict. One observer wrote of the atmosphere in the courtroom: "A solemn stillness prevailed, broken only by the closing of a blind by a deputy sheriff." Just then, the jury foreman stood to deliver the news: "We the jury find the defendant Waightstill Avery Anderson, guilty of murder." Anderson "dropped to his chair as though shot and, burying his face in his arms, gave vent to tears" as a murmur rippled through the courtroom.

The jury had heard about Anderson threatening Horton, and "this was the fatal fact against Anderson. . . . The fatal malice was indicated in his words." In the end, the jury judged the shooting as "willful and deliberate." In that heavy atmosphere, Judge Avery came to "one of the most trying duties that belong to a judge." Avery had an emotional conundrum. Certainly, judges were dismayed over having to pronounce the severest sentence of the law, but it was a bit more personal than that. Anderson belonged to a large net of kinship that linked him to Avery's family. Anderson had even been named after the judge's older brother, the notorious William Waightstill Avery.

You are trapped by the saying of your mouth and you are taken by the speech of your lips.

PROVERBS 6:2

Judge Avery's speech was filled with emotion. He commended the young man "to the mercy of a higher power," and pronounced the dreaded sentence of the law. Committing him to the only sentence for murder, on April 15, 1885, Anderson was to be escorted by the Sheriff of Caldwell County to the scaffold, to be "hanged until he is dead." Anderson filed an appeal, which automatically granted him a reprieve. While awaiting the outcome, Anderson was remanded to the Buncombe County jail in Asheville.

After the trial, folks in Caldwell County expressed "a very profound and heartfelt sympathy with the families of the condemned men," especially for Anderson's father and young wife. Nora Anderson's character was lauded in the press, saying she had "clung to her husband in the terrible ordeal through which he has gone, with the most heroic devotion," and that her sad situation had touched the "hearts of the humane people of Lenoir."

Concerns over an attempt to rescue Anderson and Ray induced Buncombe County Sheriff Rich to ask Governor Scales for a show of force. On May 2, 1885, the sheriff requested state troops to help him guard the Asheville jail. The Governor authorized six men to be assigned as extra security at the jail for six days.

By May 12, Anderson was still waiting for the outcome of his appeal. He and six of his fellow prisoners were growing weary of being cooped up in "Buncombe's Bastille," a two-story jailhouse. These seven inmates were in the second-story "cage," located at the rear of the jail and consisting of two iron cells. A locked door and passageway led to the cage. Access was secured by multiple doors, combination locks, bolts, and a lever that opened or shut the cell doors.

One night, the desperate men tried to break out. Their plan was to grab Sheriff Rich as he entered their cell and hold him until they got out. However, jailer Dan Henderson foiled their scheme. Henderson rushed in and a prisoner grabbed him, escalating the situation into a furious brawl. In the fray, Henderson discharged his pistol, and although no one was shot, the gunpowder scorched Anderson's scalp. Suddenly, Deputy Morgan, who was on the lower level, ran upstairs. He aimed his pistol at the prisoners and demanded silence. After that, everyone calmed down. Even if the prisoners had managed to overcome Rich and Henderson, the locked outer door would have stopped them from escaping.

A few days later, the North Carolina Supreme Court rendered its decision in Anderson's case. The court held that there had been sufficient evidence "to show a conspiracy" among Ray, Anderson, and Reuben Sparks "to take possession of the mine." The Supreme

Court framed its remarks, "In view of the very grave importance of our decision to the prisoner," and confirmed the lower court's "death sentence for murder." Anderson could expect no further redress from the courts. The news must have shaken him with great despair.

As the weeks passed, the prisoners seemed to have become more orderly, and were therefore permitted to socialize more than usual. During the day, their cell doors were unlocked, and they could enter a communal inner room, read newspapers, and talk with the other prisoners.

That inner room, usually cooler in summer than their cells, also served as a dining area, where they were permitted to take their meals as long as they remained quiet and compliant. Although the cell windows were barred, Anderson's and Ray's friends from time to time stood outside the jail and managed to communicate with them.

Around 8:30 on the night of July 13, Sheriff Rich began his usual rounds. He visited the secure upper level cage that housed Anderson, Ray, Sluder, York, Calloway, and Hensley, all charged with or convicted of murder. Deputy Sheriff Dan Henderson was with Sheriff Rich that night. When Henderson unlocked the cage door, Rich went in, and Henderson held his hand on the levers which opened the cell doors. As soon as he sprung the lever, however, York, Calloway, and Sluder jumped on Rich and stuck a pistol in his face. Through the cell's bars, Ed W. Ray pointed a pistol at Henderson's chest, warning him, "If you move, I will kill you." Terrified, Henderson asked him not to, and Ray answered, "I will not kill you if you don't move."

Anderson reached through the bars and "sprang back the bolts," which were erroneously not fastened, and the door to the cage opened. Within minutes, the escapees had opened the main door and confronted Henderson, demanding he surrender his gun. Ray seized Rich's "British bulldog." The prisoners bound and gagged Rich and tied him to a cell bed, locked in one cage. Henderson was bound, gagged, and locked in the other.

1870s Webley .44-caliber British Bulldog pistol. In 1881, President Garfield's assassin fired a British Bulldog.

Anderson grabbed the keys from Henderson and ran downstairs to the first floor, to the door leading to the jailer's room. Through the door's small window, Anderson handed the keys to Henderson's young son, and ordered him to unlock it. The boy, hearing a strange voice, thought there might be something wrong, so he took off and told his mother. She immediately ran to shut a door at the other end of the hall. As she was yanking it closed, Anderson said, "If you don't unlock this door, we will kill Dan." But she "slammed the solid iron door," and ran out to raise the alarm.

Meanwhile, Jack Lambert, a condemned murderer awaiting a death sentence, was still locked up within four feet of the escaping prisoners. He watched intently while "deeply interested to know if some provision would not be made" for his escape with the others. Lambert, "confined in the lower story of the cage, next to the side through which the prisoners would force their exit," watched Anderson run to the window after Mrs. Henderson refused to open the door for him. Anderson, hearing Mrs. Henderson raise the alarm, went to the east window and waved a lantern back and forth a few times, and then left it in the window. He grabbed a second lantern and went to the west facing window, where at least a dozen of his friends were standing on the outside. Lambert watched as someone on the outside passed Anderson an axe and two pistols through the window.

With the axe, Anderson made a vigorous attack on the brick wall, while one source claimed that men were on the outside hacking away at the same spot on the exterior wall. Anderson pounded away until the window sash fell out, and Ray grabbed the axe and continued busting a hole in the wall. Anderson, meanwhile, ran to the window on the other side of the room, waving a lantern back and forth as a signal to someone outside. Ray finished breaking through the wall, and Anderson again signaled with the lantern and threw it on the floor.

Ray crawled through but got stuck halfway, and Anderson shoved him out, pushing hard. Anderson passed through without difficulty. Then Lum Calloway, Charles York, and Philetus Sluder followed. Abe Hensley was last. Once outside, however, Hensley remembered that he'd forgotten his hat. He crawled back inside to get it, and as he did, he was captured. By that time, a Col. Williamson and two Asheville men named Will and Gus Reynolds had entered the jail and released Rich and Henderson.

Anderson's prominent family, including his father-in-law Judge Jacob Bowman, no doubt orchestrated the jailbreak for Anderson and Ray from what was then considered the most secure jail in western North Carolina. Five desperate escapees, presumed to be armed, were now on the lam. Governor Scales was notified of the jailbreak. The fire bell rang out the alarm. Asheville was "thrown into a state of excitement surpassing description." The townsfolk thought Sheriff Rich had been killed. Immediately, a crowd formed around the jail.

State militiamen under Charles Moseley's command sprang into action, as his Asheville Light Infantry troops dispersed in all directions. Fifteen hours later, Moseley returned from a futile search, while Sheriff Rich's posse continued their pursuit.

In his escape, Anderson had jumped from the prison wall, injuring his ankle, but he and Ed continued heading toward the French Broad River. At the banks of the French Broad, they hid in the weeds near Pearson's Bridge. A detachment of militiamen was stationed at the bridge, so the fugitives must have been terrified as they remained in hiding. One newspaper reported that "Fate intervened in their behalf . . . and the French Broad river . . . gave off a heavy fog that swept through the valley. The darkness was absolutely impenetrable, and to the men crouching near the river, it was a life-saver."

They swam and waded for fifteen miles down the river to hide their scent from the inevitable posse bloodhounds. They pushed themselves in a daunting trek through the woods until they reached the Big Ivy River. At dawn, they hid until nightfall and then made their way to an old slave cabin. "Aunt T.," a former

Anderson family slave, took them in. She nursed Anderson's wounded foot, and for nearly two months, hid and fed Anderson and Ray and "kept them posted on the intensity of the search being carried out for them." Soon, the two men figured it was best if they split up, and Ray disappeared.

Meanwhile, Anderson's wife Nora was about to give birth to their third child, conceived in the Caldwell County jail during one of the conjugal visits Anderson had been allowed. On August 29, 1885, Anderson held his newborn son, knowing that he'd never help raise him. He would also say goodbye to all that he'd known and loved; his mountain home, his wife, his children. After that, Anderson seems to have fallen off the face of the earth (or at least that's what he hoped folks would think.)

The escape of Anderson and Ray from the heavily guarded, ultra-secure jail became a sensation throughout western North Carolina. Sheriff Rich advertised a total of $800 in reward money. For information leading to the arrest of Waightstill Anderson as well as Edward W. Ray, he offered $400 each, but to no avail.

Anderson and Ray hid along the banks of the Big Ivy River.

As in other nineteenth-century jailbreak cases, suspicion fell on the sheriff and jailer. Rich and Henderson were arrested on charges of having been bribed to allow the prisoners to escape. This was not surprising; successful jailbreaks relied on the assistance of others. No one was more familiar with the Buncombe County jail and its security than Rich and Henderson, and no one would have been in a better position to help the criminals defeat it. Both men were put on trial and acquitted.

During their sixteen months of confinement, Anderson and Ray had been moved four times from one hell hole for the condemned to another. During those movements, "Threats were made to lynch and counter threats to rescue." Judges and sheriffs had requested state troops to guard the convicts in jail, as well as during their transfer to other county jails. And yet, in spite of all the extra security that was added after their initial attempt to escape, Anderson and Ray still managed to break free.

Waightstill Avery Anderson and Edward W. Ray disappeared from Buncombe County and were never again seen in western North Carolina. Although theirs was not the first nor last escape from the Buncombe County jail, their jailbreak likely inspired future escapes from what was then considered the most secure jail in the region. For more than a hundred years, locals have speculated about what might have happened to Anderson or Ray. After their disappearance, newspapers reported that Anderson

$800.00 REWARD.

Four hundred dollars reward will be paid for the arrest of Ed. W. Ray, who escaped from the Buncombe County Jail on the night of July 13th, 1885.

DESCTIPTION:—Height, 5 feet 9 or 10 inches; weight, 215 lbs, hair dark, slightly grey; complexion florid, eyes light blue, age about 43 years

Also Four hundred dollars reward will be paid for the arrest of Weightsell A. Anderson, who escaped from said jail at the same time.

DESCRIPTION:—Height about 5 feet 9 inches; weight about 135 lbs, slender built, hair dark brown, complexion light and rather pale, eyes bluish, age about 4 years.

The above reward will be paid by the governor of the State of North Carolina for the arrest of the above named individuals, and their delivery to me.

By order of the Governor of North Carolina.

J. R. RICH,
Sheriff of Buncombe Co. N. C.

jy 15—d 1waW1t

and Ray had fled to Honduras. Other stories surfaced claiming they were living in England. One newspaper reported that Ray had been killed in New Mexico "by cowboys with whom he got into trouble," and that of Anderson, "nothing has ever been heard."

When the historical record falls silent, some stories leave us with only speculation.

CHAPTER EIGHT

The Lynching of Bob Brackett

IN 1897, SUNDAYS IN BUNCOMBE COUNTY were customarily a day of worship for many. Kittie Henderson, the twenty-six-year-old daughter of John Henderson, was among them. Years earlier, she had been crippled by meningitis. Kittie lived with her family near the Coleman homestead, about a mile and a half from Weaverville. After attending Alexander Chapel one Sunday morning in August, the soon-to-be-married Kittie endured a shocking catastrophe.

Around 11:30 that day, Kittie was walking home alone from Sunday school when she reached the crossroads near her home. Suddenly, and seemingly out of nowhere, a man grabbed her by the throat and knocked her to the ground. He then dragged her into the woods, stopped and looked around, and then pulled her even farther away from the road. Screaming, Kittie begged him to let her go. The thug shoved a pistol in her face and said he'd kill her if he had to.

She struggled to resist her assailant's strength and cried out, "I'm only a poor crippled girl!" She prayed aloud for God to help her. Her assailant choked her until she was nearly unconscious and then sexually assaulted her. After he raped her, the man ran off. Terrified, injured, and panic-stricken, Kittie made her way to the nearby Coleman homestead. James S. Coleman notified authorities of the attack.

Before long, an angry mob of men went searching for "the brute." By that time, however, the unknown assailant had the advantage of a forty-minute head start.

Kittie eventually got back home. Dr. James Gill of Weaverville and Dr. D. E. Sevier of Asheville came to see her. She gave them a physical description of the Black man who'd assaulted her, saying he was heavily built and around twenty-three or twenty-four years old. She would recognize him if she saw him again, she was sure of it. The following day, she received additional medical treatment at the office of Dr. H. B. Weaver.

Meanwhile, the manhunt intensified. The posse included Charley Rymer, Goodson Ramsey, Will Smith, Mitchell Aiken, and Will Rymer. Forty-eight hours after the assault, the men were still searching. At four o'clock in the morning, they spotted someone walking along Whitemore Branch carrying a light. The men stopped the man and learned that he was a preacher named Sandy Ray, on his way to work. Ray told them that the night before, a young Black man had knocked on his door asking for shelter. The preacher had left his cabin with the young man still asleep.

Goodson Ramsey and his men hurried to Ray's cabin. When they got inside, they found the man in bed asleep. They woke him up and identified him as Bob Brackett, a twenty-three-year-old laborer from Caswell County. He said he'd come to work in Buncombe County about a year and a half earlier. Securely they tied Brackett with a rope and pulled him outside, barefoot. Deputy Joe Chambers led the men with their captive, as they marched down the road to a rendezvous point where the deputies from Asheville planned to take Brackett into custody.

Eager to hang Brackett on the spot, the outraged men attracted a crowd that grew in numbers and aggression. The deputies told the men to quell their violent ambitions, but they yelled, "Let's give him a hundred lashes on the bare back and then give him up to be taken to Asheville!" Deputies shot down that idea, but "Hats, guns, and hands were wildly waved," as the mob called for a vote to decide what to do next.

As they traveled, the group continued getting larger, while cooler heads tried to quell the spirit of violence. By the time they reached Weaverville, the mob had swelled to an estimated three hundred men and boys, with many toting shotguns. Before they would agree to hand over Brackett to the deputies, the posse took him to Kittie Henderson's home, for identification.

About that time, Deputy Reynolds rode up. He'd been sent by Sheriff Worley and Commissioner Brown with a message: If the men were certain they had the right man, a special term of court would be called at once. The swarm of enraged, heavily armed men crowded around the outside of Kittie's home, calling for immediate justice.

Dr. Gill, who was caring for Kittie, instructed Reynolds to tell the raucous crowd that they must stay away from the house while Brackett went inside to be identified. Kittie remained in a "highly nervous condition," and Dr. Gill was concerned that the throng of angry men would add more stress to his patient's fragile state. However, as soon as deputy Reynolds reprimanded the gathering, his words were forgotten, and the Henderson's backyard remained filled with men eager to see Kittie confront her attacker.

Several men from the posse ushered Brackett into the house. The rope on Brackett's wrists was removed so that he could take off the checkered shirt he was wearing and put on a plain one, like the rapist had worn at the scene of the crime.

Dr. Gill again gave orders that only a few men were allowed to stand nearby while Kittie was brought in to identify Brackett. Deputy McDonald repeated this instruction, but scores of men, armed with shotguns, stayed outside the house. Inside, Goodson

Ramsey and Charlie Rymer led Brackett into another room, holding the rope with which they'd led him from Preacher Ray's cabin. Dr. Gill ushered Kittie into the room and to a chair, while her mother remained close by.

Brackett backed toward the fireplace, with light from an opposite window full on his face. Kittie sat directly in front of him. As she gazed at him, she cried out, "Oh, what made you treat me so last Sunday, when I told you I was crippled and helpless! Why did you choke me as I prayed to God to defend me, and you threatened to kill me if I was not quiet? I would know you among a thousand, and do swear that you are the man!"

Dr. Gill said to Brackett, "Did you ever see this lady before?"

Brackett responded, "Never saw her before."

"Yes, you did!" Kittie cried. "I knew you the minute my eyes flashed on you!"

Reynolds told Brackett to put on his hat. When he did, Kittie said again that he was the man who had assaulted her.

Again, the deputy asked Brackett if he had been the man who'd attacked Kittie, and he replied, "Don't think I ever saw her; no, sir, never saw her."

By this time, the waiting crowd outside was told that Kittie had accused Brackett as her attacker. The men grew angrier and vocal, shouting that they wanted the rapist brought outside. Deputy McDonald, seeing their ugly mood, stood in front of Brackett as the two emerged from the house. McDonald told the crowd he had a warrant for Brackett's arrest and intended to take him to the jail at Asheville to await trial. "I will pledge myself," McDonald yelled, straining to be heard above the booming voices, "that the commissioners will call court next week for his trial!"

As Brackett stood with Reynolds and McDonald, one man yelled, "God knows he ought to be lynched!" The crowd took it up and began yelling, "Lynch him! Hang him! Bring him out; tear his head off!"

Kittie walked outside. She spoke to the men: "I prayed in my helplessness that God would spare my life and send friends to avenge me, and now they have come to help me!"

This inflamed the crowd even more. As they set out toward Asheville, Deputy Reynolds made sure Brackett was mounted on a horse directly behind his own horse. Reynolds attempted to quiet the rowdy mob, but the men were whipping into a red-hot frenzy, shouting, "Hang him! Hang him!"

"Men," Reynolds called, straining to be heard above the many louder voices, "if you hang him, *you are all known.* You'll all be tried for murder."

"That's all right," the crowd yelled back. "We'll take care of that!"

A voice of reason, Walter Vandiver of Weaverville, rose in his stirrups and spoke to the maddened men. He told them that a lynching would sully the fair name of their county. It would be a terrible crime, he said, and begged them to restrain themselves. A few other men who'd been trying to calm the crowd finally were heard, and eventually the mob reluctantly dispersed.

Brackett and the others started on horseback toward the jail at Asheville. As they rode, Brackett confessed to Commissioner Brown that he had, in fact, assaulted Kittie. He said he'd been in Asheville for a week and was returning to the Big Ivy settlement when he saw Kittie on the road and was overcome with a desire to have sex with her. Though she cried out for him to stop, he admitted to paying no attention, but said he was sorry that he didn't cease when she begged him to.

The men arrived in Asheville around 3:15, with the deputies and fifty horsemen protecting Brackett. Hundreds of people who'd heard about the rape and the posse gathered outside the jail. Once Brackett was placed in a temporary cell, Brown, the Special Term Chairman, sent a wire to Judge Ewart, requesting a special court term in Asheville to try Brackett immediately.

The throng surrounding the jail eventually left, but there would be no peace in the cells that night.

By order of the sheriff, Deputy Sheriff McDonald removed Brackett from his cell and left to take him to a safer place. Meanwhile, White men who wanted to lynch Brackett had spies around the jail. Their aim was to learn about any plan to remove

Brackett and transfer him elsewhere. The spies, however, gave conflicting reports: one said Brackett was still in the jail, the other that he'd been spirited away. Two hundred enraged men gathered in the vacant lot near the Banner warehouse to discuss the matter. Passionate speeches whipped the mob into a frenzy. Eventually, they decided that the information that Brackett had been taken out and moved elsewhere was just a ruse to prevent the men from storming the jail.

A few blocks away on Court Square, another group of men had assembled and began talking about setting up a lynch party. Local churchman Reverend J. T. Betts tried to cool them down, but his words did little to stifle calls for vigilante justice. At a little after eight o'clock in the evening, the men who'd been congregating in the vacant lot began marching. As they did, more and more men and teenage boys joined the mob. Some had guns; all were fired up and out for blood.

Suddenly, every street leading to the jail was filled with irate White men. They stopped at the gate to the jailhouse yard, where the chief of police was stationed, but he did not see the extent of the danger. Sheriff Worley came out and tried to deputize every other man in the crowd, but they spurned the duty.

Worley realized that no one would stand with him against the mob, but he still refused to yield; he backed against the jailhouse door to prevent anyone from getting through. The mob demanded the keys to the jail, but he refused to hand them over. Worley yelled to the crowd that Brackett had been moved and offered to allow two or three men to come inside and see for themselves. But they quickly shoved him aside, and with a heavy timber as a battering ram, smashed the jail's solid wooden door. The door at last gave way, and the maddened men flooded the jail. City Attorney Locke Craig and Solicitor McCall were there and tried to stop the riot, but their voices were drowned out.

Using hammers and crowbars, the men smashed open the locked cells, but when they saw that Brackett was not there, they indiscriminately freed six White prisoners. None of the Black prisoners were released. Disappointed and infuriated at not finding Brackett, they took out their rage on the jail, smashing up the place.

Eventually, around 11:00 p.m., the mob abruptly stopped the wanton destruction, lit candles, and again searched through the jail. Once they realized for sure that Brackett was gone and Worley had been telling the truth, they became furious all over again and cursed aloud those who had taken Brackett away.

Meanwhile, Deputy McDonald and another lawman were in a carriage with Brackett heading over Beaumont Gap for Swannanoa to catch an early train to Raleigh. Around 1:40 a.m., Brackett and Deputy McDonald were at the train station in the community of Terrell, twelve miles from Asheville. Just as they were starting to board the Number 16 train, suddenly they were shocked to see a horde of men rushing toward them. "Hang the officers and the Negro!" the mob yelled. The officers were overawed and fled the scene. The mob seized Brackett. The gang "swarmed on him like yellow jackets," one report said. McDonald tried to send a wire message about the mob, but "the operator at Terrell refused to wire a message from the officer to Biltmore, as it was not a Western Union office."

Once the vigilantes had Brackett in their clutches, they could not agree on when and where to kill him. As was common in lynchings, the mob took him back near the scene of the crime, to the Henderson home. But just as they did, they got wind that militiamen were on their way to prevent the lynching, so they decided to take Brackett elsewhere.

Governor Russell, who'd been informed that the mob had overwhelmed the officers and made off with Brackett, called out the Asheville Light Infantry to assist Sheriff Worley in preserving law and order.

At 11:15 on Tuesday morning, August 10, the bell rang summoning the infantry. A company of forty-three men and Sheriff Worley left the armory and set out in carriages for Weaverville.

The governor sent a telegram to Colonel Virgil S. Lusk, stating that if Brackett was *not* lynched, but convicted by a jury, the governor would personally guarantee he would be hanged within two weeks. However, the mob, numbering about a hundred, finally had its hands on Brackett, and they were determined to take satisfaction for the crime. They hauled Brackett four miles northeast of Weaverville to the Hemphill schoolhouse. One newspaper described the atmosphere as an enthusiastic assembly, not unlike an "old Methodist camp meeting."

Kittie was there to hear Brackett's last words. He admitted to being the man who'd assaulted her. He made no protest. Once a rope had been placed around his neck, Brackett was "listed up, the rope was fastened to a limb, and the Negro dropped." He died quickly. Souvenir hunters swooped in. With a voracious appetite for anything connected with the hanging, they cut pieces from Brackett's clothes and pulled cords from his hanging rope. Women pulled down branches and cut bits of the large oak limb that had held the rope. Women were later seen wearing twigs from the hanging tree as relics, pinned to their dresses.

Sheriff Worley and the state troops arrived at the Henderson home, but never caught up with the lynchers. Instead, they were confronted by two hundred armed men who claimed to have no knowledge of where the lynching party had taken Brackett.

The 1930 lynching of Thomas Shipp and Abram Smith, two African-Americans accused of robbery, murder, and rape. An angry mob broke them from jail and lynched them in Marion, Indiana.

The militiamen got back in their carriages, but the mob, many of whom were drunk, gathered around the troops, blocked their way, and said they would die rather than let them pass. The militiamen countered by forming battle lines. Eventually, the men blocking the road gave way, but they had accomplished their purpose in delaying the militia. As the troops pulled out, the mob "jeered and hissed." By the time the troops reached the Hemphill schoolhouse, the body of Bob Brackett was hanging lifeless from a tree.

By then, some of the vengeful men had left. Captain Bookhart of the NC State troops sent the governor a telegram: "I arrived on the scene 14 miles from the city at 2:50 and found the Negro hanging to a tree, dead. All is quiet and the sheriff has dismissed the company."

After the hanging, Sheriff Worley called for an inquest with a jury of six men. While a number of witnesses were examined, none could or would give testimony about who actually strung Brackett up and hanged him. The inquest was not accepted as final. Worley gave out that efforts would be made to prosecute those who released the federal prisoners from the Asheville jail.

Brackett's body was cut down by Sheriff Worley and taken to Asheville undertaker Jesse R. Starnes. At his office, Coroner Reed summoned a jury of six men to hold his own inquest. There were two issues: Who hanged Bob

Lynching and Lynch Mobs

Lynching is an extrajudicial act of pre-meditated murder carried out by a mob. In early nineteenth-century America, victims of lynching were typically White men, but after emancipation, Blacks became targeted. With a single accusation from one woman, a man could be hunted down and hanged, thereby depriving both the victim and society of due process of law. In North Carolina alone, there were one hundred and sixty documented lynchings, a few of which occurred in the state's mountain region. North Carolina's attorney general began keeping track of crime statistics in 1889, and in the years that followed, there were more lynchings than legal executions in the state.

Nationwide statistics on lynching vary, since at the time few people were keeping track of the victims. In 1869, a Black man in Orange County, North Carolina named Wright Woods was lynched after being accused of assaulting a White woman. When his body was found hanging from a tree, a note was found attached to his foot that said: "If the law will not protect virtue, the rope will." The practice of lynching eventually died out after the civil rights movement. Where did the term "lynch" originate? During the American Revolution, a popular phrase called the "Lynch Law," which meant penalty without trial, came into use. Eighteenth-century Virginians Charles Lynch and William Lynch are credited with having coined the term.

Brackett, and who had freed the prisoners from the Asheville jail? Reed took testimony from several witnesses.

W. E. Brees Jr. testified that Sheriff Worley had summoned him to go with a posse to Reems Creek "where the Negro was found hanged."

Chief of Police W. A. James, who along with Worley had been shoved aside by the mob storming the jail, testified that in the crowd he recognized Milt Ledford. J. F. Austin testified that men named Smith and Ross were threatening to "tear down the jail" to find Brackett. At the lynching, there were an estimated one hundred spectators, and fifteen men who "brought the Negro up." The man who climbed up in the tree to tie the rope to a limb, afterward "slid down the rope, stamped on the Negro's head, and then kicked him in the face."

Mrs. Samuel Davidson testified that about thirty strangers had stopped by her house early Wednesday morning. Some of the men carrying guns asked her to cook breakfast for them. In the crowd of White men, she saw one "Darkey." The men said "they were going to lynch the Negro." She fed them and they left.

Though they gave details about the break-in at the Asheville jail, only W. T. Herritage spoke about the hanging party. He claimed fifteen men, who'd also been part of the mob on the train at Terrell, had brought Brackett to the hanging site. They had bound his feet and hands and strung up the rope.

Sheriff Worley testified in his own defense against fierce criticism for having protected the prisoner and the jail, but he'd been directed to do so by Solicitor McCall and other local officials.

Four days after the rape, the verdict of the inquest was rendered on August 12, 1897. Although Governor Russell considered issuing warrants for those responsible for the lynching, Brackett had been lynched by men whom no one was willing to identify. The state's adjutant general telegrammed the governor: "Warn the mob orally of its peril, but uphold the law at all hazards and fire with ball cartridges to kill, if necessary. If you need more troops telegraph me." Since rape was punishable by death, if Brackett had benefited from a trial he'd have no doubt been convicted and hanged. But justice had not been completely denied. Eventually, a grand jury in Hendersonville found three separate true bills of indictment against the violators of the law. One bill was against Delbert "Dell" Ross for "breaking into jail at Asheville to lynch Bob Brackett, rapist." Another bill was against Will Huntley and George Bryant, and a third found against J. W. Morris, Dell Ross, Milt Ledford, and W. P. Black. Ross was charged with murder, and was said to have been the ringleader in the lynching.

Two years after the violent horde had stormed the jail, Deputy Sheriff Reed arrested George Bryant for "breaking into the Buncombe jail on the night when the mob was searching for Bob Brackett." Bryant paid a $100 bond and was released. How Ross's murder charge was resolved, no newspapers reported. But it does appear that Ross got away with murder.

A final editorial in the *Asheville Citizen* stated:

> Lynching is always wrong, but it is because it is not the greatest wrong and because it is, after all, a rough form of justice, as well also as because of the delays and uncertainties of legal procedure, that it can be tolerated by public sentiment in an otherwise law-abiding community.

CHAPTER NINE

Murder in Big Bend

Bound down in transgression no hope to be free.
If they were back at the Big Bend how different they'd be.
Their drinking and wild hogging would come to an end.
Perhaps they would make better women and men.
SARA RATHBONE, APRIL 5, 1936

G EOGRAPHY CAN BE DESTINY.

Some places in the Smoky Mountains have shed more blood than others. Perhaps your ancestors lived into old age, but up in the Big Bend, young lives were cut short by the ravages of indwelling hatreds, unfettered feuds, and drunkenness; herein lies a story of all three.

The Big Bend area sits in the northeast corner of Haywood County. By 1993, a local newspaper described the settlement, just four miles from the Madison County line, as "almost extinct." One hundred fifty years ago, however, a cluster of moonshining families lived in this extremely remote mountain settlement. Established in the mid-nineteenth century on a large bend of the Pigeon River, Big Bend's history is filled with traumatic events.

Big Bend was originally settled by the McGahas of Crosby, Tennessee. In February 1857, Samuel and Sarah McGaha obtained the first deed for one hundred acres in Big Bend. They were followed by the Hicks, Packetts, and Yarboroughs. Merritt Hicks and Nancy McGaha were the first children born to the original Big Bend settlers. By the dawn of the twentieth century, eight families were living in the area, and most had intermarried with the other Big Bend families. Cousins, second cousins, double cousins, and who-was-married-to-whom wove the pattern of life in this remote moonshiner clan.

Sadly, from the time of its settlement until 1934, Big Bend had neither church nor school to serve the needs of its people. What it did have—in abundance—was moonshine and unresolved inter-familial conflicts that often resulted in bloodshed. The lack of schooling or organized church life but easy access to guns and alcohol led to high levels of emotion, quick arguments, and tragedy. Feuds continued for generations, frequently creating heartbreak over murdered loved ones. These mountaineers held grudges, and lingering hatred all too often led to violence. And it seemed that nearly everyone carried a gun. Few of the men in Big Bend lived into old age.

The Big Bend story that remains strongest in the memory of old Haywood County mountaineers is the story of Oma Hicks. Nicknamed "Omy," her history with men and marriage, and the violence that swirled around her, characterized her young life.

Born in December 1896 to Merritt Linville Hicks and Nancy McGaha Hicks, Oma was the third of six children. Like other girls in her area, Oma spent her childhood in and around Big Bend's sprawling valleys, deep creeks, and thick woods. In the beautiful Smoky Mountains, her moonshiner relatives carried on an ancient practice of producing homemade brew, using the caves and coves to hide and protect their enterprise. Prohibition or not, folks wanted their liquor, and these families had the skill to make it. It was in their heritage—a tradition brought over from Europe generations earlier. Moonshining was their way of life, and in a moonshiner family, Oma grew up learning every step, from corn to quart. Oma's childhood was not recorded, but she emerges in the historical record as a bride at the age of seventeen. In November 1914, Oma married Benjamin "Parker" Naillon in Haywood County. He was thirty-eight and had for a time been restless and on the move.

Ben was born in May 1876, in Cocke County, Tennessee. The second-youngest child of ten, he grew up in the fertile hills of East Tennessee with a short-lived education that left him with few marketable skills.

By 1900, at age twenty-four, Ben was living with his brother, "Doc" Lafayette Naillon, in Wise County, Virginia, where they boarded with the Owens family. Ben worked as a day laborer. The Owenses had a daughter, Rosa Dove "Rose" Owens, who was about eighteen at the time. She and Ben began a relationship that grew into marriage.

But by 1910, Ben is recorded as being a widower living in a boarding house in Wasatch County, Utah. He'd ventured West to work as a teamster engaged in ditch construction. Ben had by then suffered the deaths of his beloved wife, father, mother, sister, and half-sister, all passing away within a six-year span. Parentless, Ben must have keenly felt his loneliness as he labored at his low-paying job in Utah.

Sometime after his stints in Utah and then Montana, he returned east, to North Carolina, where he met Oma Hicks in Big Bend.

Oma was at that time a vivacious seventeen-year-old who was apparently ready to strike out on her own. Though she had no formal schooling, she did have friends, especially the young men she'd grown up with who thought she was quite fetching. She likely enjoyed all their attentions, but especially Ben's. On November 11, 1914, Oma and thirty-eight-year-old Ben were married in Waynesville, North Carolina. On their marriage license, signed one month shy of her eighteenth birthday, she claimed to already be eighteen, perhaps in order to avoid needing her parents' permission to marry. Ben also fudged his age, stating that he was thirty-two. Married in a civil ceremony by a justice of the peace, they had three witnesses, all from Waynesville. Oma's family did not attend the ceremony. She likely announced it to them afterward, as a *fait accompli*.

Had she persuaded Ben to marry her by telling him she was pregnant? How else could a girl half his age coax him into marriage? Or was he lonely and eager to marry again? The historical record is silent, and the old ones have taken what they knew to their graves.

Oma and Ben began a new life together in Big Bend. He continued as a day laborer, and she kept house. She'd also hang out with her lifelong friends, including Sylvester "Vester" Brown, a teenager with a serious crush on her. Another of her admirers from the Brown family was Vester's double first cousin, Joel Canary "Scott" Brown.

Oma apparently enjoyed keeping a crowd around her that most husbands would not have appreciated. It's likely they had words—or worse than that—on more than one occasion. Men in Big Bend didn't tolerate much backtalk from their women. Oma would have understood that a sassy-mouthed girl could get slapped or punched by these proud men with roaring tempers and hard-drinking ways.

Oma and Ben had been married just a year when a dispute turned into tragedy.

In July, 1915, Vester Brown, aged fifteen, showed up at the home of Oma's father, Merritt Hicks. His first cousin Scott Brown, twenty-one, and John McGaha accompanied him. Loudly and angrily, Vester called Merritt to come out. Vester, liquored up and holding a shotgun, had a few words with old man Hicks, and then opened fire. Merritt fell, fatally wounded, but managed to tell his family who'd done the shooting. The following day, Oma's father passed away at the age of fifty-four.

Vester, Scott, and John were arrested. In October of the same year, they were all tried for murder. The jury deliberated until the next morning before agreeing on a verdict.

On October 5, 1915, at just fifteen years old, Vester was convicted of second-degree murder. Had he been convicted of murder in the first degree, he'd have received the death penalty; instead Vester was sentenced to thirty years in the state prison.

Scott Brown and John McGaha were acquitted.

Oma's life with Ben went on.

Then, in 1916, after being married less than two years, Ben suddenly disappeared.

Oma didn't claim he'd abandoned her, or that he'd made plans to move away. He was just inexplicably gone. For a long time it was presumed, in whispers and gossip, that Oma's family had murdered Ben and buried his body in the woods around Big Bend. The same woods that would one day figure large in Oma's life.

After Ben's disappearance, Oma returned to her family. Had he been abusive, she might have asked her family for help. Despite their two-year marriage, Oma had not borne a child. If she had tricked Ben into marrying her by pretending to be pregnant and then later confessing her deceit, he may have become violent at learning the truth. Or perhaps Ben had felt insecure in his marriage because Oma socialized with friends while he was at work. If he had turned unreasonably violent toward her, it would have made sense that her family might intervene. Did she show up at her family home, making Ben out to be a monster? Or, as they say up in Big Bend, did Ben just "need killin'"? To these North Carolinians, blood was thicker than water, and you didn't abandon your own when they were in trouble. It was a principle they lived by.

The thread that runs through all this violence is the uneasy feeling researchers get that Oma may have purposely played the victim, like a femme fatale. Perhaps she persuaded others that Ben had been violent and that she feared him. In the case of her father's murder, had she pulled on the sympathies of Vester Brown, convincing *him* that her father had said or done something cruel? Was it something she said that got Vester so fired up that he exacted revenge by murdering her father? While the historical record is silent, most any theory is plausible.

Ben Naillon was never declared legally dead in any public document. After he went missing, he was simply presumed dead.

However, according to North Carolina law back then, if a husband disappeared, his widow was unable to remarry for seven years. Because Ben's body was never found, no death certificate was ever issued.

Meanwhile, life went on in Big Bend much the same, except that in 1920, Prohibition became law. Hard-drinking men did not take kindly to the idea that the government could forbid their one indulgence in this impoverished country. It seemed that everyone drank—and wanted to keep on drinking. The folks in Big Bend seized the opportunity to make, bottle, and sell moonshine whiskey to their neighbors. Up on the mountain, a still was doing a booming business.

Not only was it unlawful to make liquor without paying the tax, Prohibition (1920-1933) brought another layer of illegality to the mix.

The photograph below shows a 1920s moonshiner and his still.

By 1930, Oma's life had again changed in Big Bend. With Prohibition raging on, the still on the mountainside continued producing moonshine to satisfy steady customers. Oma helped bottle and deliver the liquor. She'd also married again—a man she'd known for years, Scott Brown.

The marriage must have taken place sometime after 1920, although no record of the marriage was found in Haywood County, North Carolina, or Cocke County, Tennessee. If Oma had waited the seven years, as was the law in missing-spouse cases, she and Scott would have married in 1923 or later.

In June 1917, Scott had enlisted to serve in World War I as a private in the US Army. He signed his registration record as a twenty-three-year-old White male with blue eyes and light hair. Photos of him in uniform show he served in Company D, 4th Infantry, 3rd Division. He rose to the rank of sergeant, was wounded, and on April 15, 1918, returned home.

By late August 1930, Scott and Oma had been married several years. Scott and his friend Mims White picked up their paychecks after work at a lumber yard in Sunburst and headed home toward Big Bend. On the way, they spent the night at the home of Joe Packett.

Oma may have been lonely, with Scott working out of town for long periods of time, but she didn't stay lonely, since she could easily beguile other men in Big Bend. At this time, Oma was busy with Vester Brown, who had been granted early release from his thirty-year sentence for the murder of Oma's father.

On August 22, Scott and Mims started out of Big Bend on their way to the still located up a rough ridge, a long climb to the gap. After hiking up the Cataloochee Road, at the top of the ridge, folks would stop for a breather at what was called the "resting log." But it had also become a popular place for lovers.

On that bright summer day, Scott Brown and Mims reached the resting log, but were surprised to find Oma and Vester "trysting." Scott angrily demanded of Vester, "What are you doing up here with Oma?"

Cataloochee, a neighboring settlement to Big Bend, in Cherokee, means, "In the shelter of the tall trees."

That question began a heated argument. As it grew hotter, Oma became frightened and scurried down the mountain to summon help from the men working the still.

As she hurried off, Scott called out to her, "There goes that Bobbed-haired hussy to Cataloochee now. Bet you're going to Carl Miller!" He hollered for Oma to tell Carl he was there. Oma, scared, didn't answer but continued down the mountain.

When she reached the still, she found Frank McGaha and Vester's half-brother, Varnell Gates, Big Bend men she'd known all her life. Agitated and terrified, Oma yelled, "Scott's up there in the gap and he might kill Vester!"

Gates grabbed a .41-caliber Swiss rifle belonging to McGaha and said, "Well, he won't hurt Vester if I can help it!"

They hurried away from the still and headed up toward the gap. A few minutes later, shots rang out—two from the rifle and three from a pistol.

Scott Brown and Mims White were never seen alive again. Their families made frantic inquiries that turned up nothing.

In October, Mims's family went looking for help to find the men. They paid a visit to attorney M. G. Stamey. This led to the

By this time, the Roaring Twenties had seen women evolve. Perhaps enjoying this new freedom for women, Oma had bobbed her hair. Men found her desirable, and her husband, Scott, was probably painfully aware of this.

involvement of Chief Deputy Sheriff Arthur Ledbetter, but the lawmen failed to find any trace of the men.

And there the matter stood—until the following year.

Meanwhile, a raid by federal revenue agents led to surprising events in the murder case. Arrests came as a result of a tip that led to a dramatic offensive by a federal "dry agent" about a still in Big Bend. After wading in freezing water three feet deep in the Pigeon River, agents then tramped for miles in a heavy snow until they found a moonshiner's outpost. Moonshiners would post guards to stay on the lookout for approaching federal agents, the revenuers. That night, the guard was captured, and the raid continued until they finally arrested Vester Brown and Varnell Gates and took them to the Asheville jail. No one had yet suspected Vester or Varnell in the disappearance of Scott Brown and Mims White. Both men languished in jail for months.

Then something quite unusual happened.

This 1886 *Harper's Weekly* engraving, "Moonshiner's Home," features a sentinel (often a child) who kept a lookout for the revenue man.

A Chicago detective named J. J. O'Malley decided to take a much-needed vacation. After perusing various maps in search of a destination, he hit on Waynesville, North Carolina, nicknamed "the land of the sky." On a whim, he decided to travel down there, to a place he'd never been.

When he arrived, O'Malley found the Waynesville townsfolk friendly and conversational. Someone asked, "What do you do in Chicago?" He said, "I'm a detective." Then someone chuckled and jokingly said, "Then you oughtta try and find out what happened to those men who disappeared in Big Bend." This chance remark, though said in jest, piqued O'Malley's interest, which ignited a firestorm of activity and discovery. O'Malley began searching for clues in the case of the missing Mims White and Scott Brown, and he enlisted Stamey and Ledbetter in the investigation.

By mid-March, O'Malley's persistent detective work had begun to pay off. The two brothers, Frank and Cass McGaha, while still in jail for moonshining, were arrested for the murders of Mims and Scott. By April 3, the *Charlotte Observer* reported that Frank had made some strange remarks. He claimed that three friends who'd visited him in jail had told him that Mims and Scott were both in Mexico. The friends said the fuss over their whereabouts was a great joke, and that the pair would likely return to Waynesville after the trial of the McGaha brothers. Frank, in his defense, claimed he hadn't seen Scott Brown in two years, and that he'd never met Mims White.

On April 5, Sheriff Lowe unexpectedly announced that he was dropping murder charges against Frank and Cass McGaha, who'd been in jail on liquor charges, but whose attorneys had earlier threatened to apply for a writ of *habeas corpus*. Since the prosecuting attorney hadn't shown up in court, Lowe couldn't continue to hold them in jail.

On April 15, 1931, Vester Brown and Varnell Gates, still in jail for moonshining, were also charged with murder.

Both McGaha boys could be released from jail, the sheriff said, provided they made bonds on other cases (aside from the liquor charges) on which they were being held. Frank was in default on a $1,000 bond on a charge of assault with a deadly weapon. Cass was $200 in default on a charge of carrying a concealed weapon. Cass made bond and was released. Frank, unable to make bond, remained in jail.

The following week, a stunning development emerged.

J. J. O'Malley, Arthur Ledbetter, and M. G. Stamey spent hours interrogating Frank McGaha. Under the weight of his guilt, Frank finally broke down and confessed, while also implicating Vester and Varnell.

On a cloudy afternoon in April, Frank led O'Malley, Ledbetter, and Stamey to the side of the mountain where Scott Brown and Mims White had disappeared eight months earlier. A huge chestnut tree, blown over by strong winds, marked the spot, and the men began digging. Soon, a macabre sight emerged: a human foot.

Immediately, the men sent for others to come help and to bring heavy digging equipment.

In a leaf-strewn sinkhole created by the uprooted tree, they found two bodies in an advanced state of decomposition. The evidence mounted: friends identified the corpses, dental work yielded their identities, and bits of the victims' clothing were recognized. The bodies were Scott and Mims. Scott's skull had a bullet hole in it. Mims's skull had been battered into sixteen fragments. A piece of paper lay inside the makeshift grave, linking Carl Miller to the crime. After Scott Brown and Mims White were killed, Carl had sold his car to Frank. Vester Brown later testified that he'd seen "some papers left in the pocket of the car," and that Frank looked at him "and winked," saying, "I know what to do with them," and they took the papers with Carl's name on them and put them in the graves.

Carl was arrested while walking down the street in Waynesville, and jailed as a material witness. Authorities also arrested Oma on a charge of murder. Another report said she was being held as a material witness. By that time, officials had begun to believe that she "played a leading role in the mountain tragedy, and was really at the bottom of it all."

As the investigation progressed, Frank testified that at the time of the killings, he heard five or six shots. Frank said he had rushed to the top of the ridge, where he found Scott and Mims lying dead on the ground, their shoes and hats off. When he asked what was going on, Vester said, "Nothing, and if you tell, I will kill you!"

Frank originally denied being part of the shooting, but eventually admitted he'd shot Scott Brown. He testified that Varnell Gates had killed Mims White.

On Sunday, April 12, at one o'clock in the morning, the jailer yanked Vester from his jail cell. He was relentlessly grilled. Vester denied everything. Finally, his interrogators informed him that they had found the bodies. At that moment, he cracked under the pressure. He confessed to being a witness to the murders and accessory who helped bury the bodies. He told police he'd seen Scott and Mims fighting their assailants with their bare fists, as they had no weapons.

Varnell Gates was next. Taken from his cell around 4:30 in the morning, he too denied all knowledge of the men's disappearances. But then O'Malley confronted him with Frank's and Vester's signed statements. O'Malley asked Varnell if he'd robbed the dead bodies, and if he'd said, "Dead men tell no tales." Varnell, like his cohorts, broke down and agreed to sign a confession.

Varnell told them, "Oma came to me and Frank, saying Scott Brown was at the restin' log. She was scared Scott and Mims were gonna jump on her."

O'Malley asked, "And then what happened?"

Varnell replied, "We finished our run of liquor, and decided to see what was goin' on." He went on to say that he and Frank had charged up to the top of the mountain. There, they found Scott and Mims at the resting log, complaining that their shoes had been stolen. As it turned out, the night before, Varnell and Frank had snatched Scott and Mims's shoes. (In that rough mountain country, a lack of shoes was no joke, especially during the Depression.)

Frank tried to pass off the shoe stealing as a joke, but Mims didn't see it that way. Frank whispered to Varnell to hit Mims, who was unarmed. Varnell struck Mims over the head and the blow cracked his skull. Frank then pistol whipped Scott, who jumped into the middle of the road, and Frank shot him. Scott fell to the ground, and Frank shot him twice more. He then walked over to Mims's motionless body and shot him with the pistol. Varnell frantically searched through their pockets for money, but found nothing but Scott's old watch. Vester corroborated Varnell's statement and added that they'd stolen the men's shoes while at his mother's house. He then stood by while Frank shot Scott dead. He also told the police that Oma had been terrified of Scott Brown, and that he'd threatened to kill her.

Frank had come up with the idea for Varnell to put the paper with Carl Miller's name on it in the grave, so that suspicion would fall on Carl who had been released from suspicion.

The bodies of Scott Brown and Mims White, which had laid hidden for seven months, were taken to town. Even though in a state of advanced decomposition, hundreds of townspeople came to the undertaker's parlor to view the remains.

O'Malley had achieved success with the confessions of Frank, Vester, and Varnell, but he also wanted to clear up the mysterious disappearance of Oma's first husband, Ben Naillon.

In the end, however, O'Malley was never able to solve Ben's disappearance, though he felt that Oma knew more than she was saying—not just about Ben, but also about the double murders. He likely thought that she'd at least been an accessory. In every statement given by Varnell, Frank, and Vester, however, they testified that Oma had nothing to do with the killings. One newspaper reported:

> The public imagination was fired. Was Vester the girl wife's lover, and what part had she taken in this tragedy? Her origin and early romance with the man she had married were dug up. Glamorous stories of those chapters were told. It seemed evident that there had been a family feud going on for some years among the double first cousins, half-brothers, and their clans; and that Oma, like some Helen of Troy, had been in some way the pawn in it all.

At their July trial, the three men, Varnell Gates, Frank McGaha, and Vester Brown, pleaded guilty to murder in the second degree, bringing the court proceedings to a swift conclusion. Frank and Varnell drew sentences of fifteen to thirty years for each of the murders, and were remanded to the state prison. Vester Brown, who pleaded guilty to murder in the second degree in the death of Mims White, was sentenced to fifteen years in prison.

Oma, who was tried for murder at the same time, entered a plea of not guilty, which was accepted by the state. However, she was sentenced to twelve months in the Haywood County jail on illegal liquor charges.

Frank McGaha, aged twenty when sentenced for thirty years was later paroled. In 1952, he was working in Canton, where he fell into a rock crushing machine. He was forty-one.

After serving her sentence, Oma was released. Was she the inspiration for the double murders in August 1930? Or was she an innocent witness who simply—and all too often—was in the wrong place at the wrong time?

In July 1932, she quietly married Carl Alton Miller. Born in Haywood County in 1887, Miller

Sheriff And Victim's Widow

This April 15, 1931, newspaper photo features Oma Hicks-Brown with Sheriff Jake Lowe.

was forty-five when he married Oma, who was thirty-five. They remained married until his death in 1960 at the age of seventy-three. Oma never had children, but she and Carl took in and raised her brother Oliver's daughter.

Oma Hicks Naillon Brown Miller died on April 18, 1974, at the age of seventy-seven.

She is buried in the Garrett-Hillcrest Cemetery in Waynesville, NC, next to Carl Miller. Her grave is simply marked "MILLER." It seems clear that of all the names she carried throughout her life, Miller suited her best.

Oma's story inspired a poem, "Up on Big Pigeon," composed in 1936 by Sara Rathbone (edited for spelling, punctuation, and meter by Nadia Dean, May 15, 2021).

Up on Big Pigeon up at the Big Bend
Perhaps you have heard of that rough bunch of men.
Their latest conduct, oh it was a sight,
by taking Mims White and Scott Brown's life.

Upon the north mountain not far away,
Vester and Oma went to pass time away,
At the rest log just sitting around,
Up came Mims White and Oma's husband Scott Brown.

Oma ran off on down the hill,
To Varnell and Frank at the moonshine still.
She said to them in an awful fright,
"I'm afraid Scott and Mims will take Vester's life."

They went up the mountain in nearly a run,
Both armed to their teeth with a pistol and gun.
They said they had come up to hear the news,
But Scott and Mims demanded their stolen shoes.
There at the rest log the trouble begun,
By beating and shooting with their guns.

Varnell said to Frank, "We may go to jail,
But I've often heard dead men tell no tales."
Little did they think that in the end,
It may be their death or life in the pen.

After they were buried forgotten and gone,
Scott's widow would have married, she would have lived on,
But Frank McGaha in the Waynesville jail
Told Detective O'Malley their awful tale.

Bound down in transgression no hope to be free.
If they were back at the Big Bend how different they'd be.
Their drinking and wild hogging would come to an end.
Perhaps they would make better women and men.

CHAPTER TEN

Fugitive Justice

CHARLEY HOOD WAS JUST TWENTY-SIX years old in 1885. His thick wave of light-brown hair and boyish face made him look years younger than his days. This was to his advantage, since he could make himself whatever age he required when beginning a new life with a new name. Charley was especially charismatic and could easily win people over. Some said he was truthful and honest but had a hot temper. Others described him as "a violent and dangerous man." Another said he was "a man of few words but dangerous when in a row."

Charley had escaped jail in the North Carolina mountains, having been convicted of murder. One of Charley's in-laws, an attorney and later US Senator, advised the hotheaded, fast-drawing Charley to stay out of trouble and live an honorable life, with the hope that in years to come, he could apply for a pardon. Although that had been his aim, now and again, he'd find himself in the midst of conflict.

Eventually Charley made his way to the American Southwest in the closing days of the Old West. Wyatt Earp's famous shootout, the death of Cochise, and the initiation of the Transcontinental Railroad were already history. But Charley would soon make his own history, leaving his mark on the times and places that continue to awaken public curiosity and imagination.

In October 1885, Charley arrived in El Paso, Texas. Checking in at the Windsor Hotel, he signed the register as "C. R. Hood from Erwin, Tennessee." He had been determined to flee more than 1,500 miles. In that long journey, Charley had likely taken the following routes from Tennessee to Texas: He may have caught the East Tennessee & Western NC Railroad (the "Tweetsie" line) at Hampton or Roan Mountain and proceeded to Johnson City, Tennessee. Or, he may have traveled by horse directly to Johnson City. From there, he could have taken the East Tennessee, Virginia, & Georgia Railroad to Knoxville, down to Chattanooga, and across Tennessee to Memphis. Next, he could have caught the Memphis & Little Rock Railroad to Little Rock, Arkansas. He could then have boarded the St. Louis & Iron Mountain and gone to the border town of Texarkana. At Texarkana, Charley may have taken the Missouri, Kansas & Texas (the "Katy Line") to Dallas. Six different lines from Dallas went farther west or south.

The East Tennessee & Western NC Railroad.

Near El Paso, Charley began work as a line rider, thought to be the loneliest job in the West. Before the advent of barbed-wire

This 1887 photo shows a typical Southwest cowboy with his leather chaps and gloves, bandanna and wide brimmed hat.

fencing, these cowboys kept the cattle within the ranch's boundary lines. Cattle were notorious for wandering off, and it was the line rider's job to drive them back.

Each day he'd ride along the property line, back and forth, checking to see that no cattle were grazing on the neighboring ranch. Sometimes Charley would catch the lost, unbranded calves from other ranches that turned up now and then. He was also tasked with keeping watch that no cattle thieves were lurking nearby. In every kind of miserable weather, while evading coyotes and rattlesnakes, Charley labored to protect the herd.

Texas ranchers built small, extremely isolated cabins for the line riders. Charley worked, hunted, cooked, ate, and slept alone. It was a solitary existence, but for Charley, it must have seemed like a small price to pay for not having someone breathing down his neck or threatening his life.

After a long stint in this harsh, secluded life, Charley determined he'd had enough of laying low. Surely, by now, it would be a safe bet that the hunt for him had ended. The time had come to move farther west. By 1888, Charley was in Boca, California, a settlement along the railroad, a few miles west of Reno, Nevada.

In April 1888, while working in a lumber mill, Charley got caught up in the tense atmosphere prevailing in Boca. Violence erupted among workers at the Boca brewery and the Boca Sawmill Company, which were located on opposite sides of the Truckee River. The problem started between two men who were vying for the affections of two women who lived on River Street. The violence spread, and a mob formed and divided into two groups—the "Dutch," who worked for the brewery, and the "Irish," who were the "mill-hands and lumbermen."

One night, the brewery bunch crossed the river and started a fight with the mill hands. Pistols were fired, and brewery worker William Beck was "shot by Charles Hood, a mill-hand." Beck ended up with "an ugly scalp-wound." Infuriated, Beck went to the town of Truckee and "swore out a warrant for Hood's arrest on a charge of assault to commit murder." After the shooting, Beck's buddies went hunting for Charley and found him "in the barroom of the Boca Hotel."

> The Boca Brewing Company began producing California's first lager in 1875. Boca was ideal because of its below-freezing winters, natural spring waters, and nearby railroad.

Beck's drunk and infuriated buddies attacked Charley. By the time "desperate efforts" were made by his friends to prevent him from being killed, Charley was "badly cut and bleeding." But Charley was just one of the many men who were bruised and beaten that night. The next day, the brewery workers sent word over the river that they'd soon take the town. Constables James Reed and C. A. Green were working hard to preserve order. Charley had yet to be arrested, and his friends defended him, saying, "He shall not be taken."

The next morning, Charley surrendered. He admitted to the judge that he had hit Beck on the head with his pistol, and that the strike had discharged his gun. The judge released Charley on personal recognizance but ordered him "to appear for examination" at ten o'clock the next morning. Charley did not show up; he "left the state to avoid arrest."

Charley headed east into Nevada. He checked in at the Palace Hotel in Reno, a short train ride from Boca. He signed the register as "C. R. Hood of Boca," but he didn't stay there long, either. Soon, he headed south to Arizona Territory.

This 1888 photo of the Boca Hotel depicts a bustling community with seasonal ice and lumber workers as well as tourists.

The Land of Second Chances

In those days, Arizona was the place where a man with a dark past could go to forget who he'd been, what he'd done. Folks in the Territory understood that it was best never to ask a man too much about his history. It had become the land of second chances, of unlikely fortunes to be made, and of lives in peril.

In late August 1889, Charley registered as a guest at the Cosmopolitan Hotel in Tucson. Accompanying him was his in-law, David A. Bowman, who gave his address as North Carolina; Charley signed as "C. R. Hood from El Paso." Years had been put between Charley and his yesterdays and, being grateful for that, Charley was eager to see what came next.

The Southern Pacific Railroad had reached Tucson a decade earlier, ushering in a new economic era and facilitating the expansion of mining efforts in southeastern Arizona. This was good for Charley, since he'd long had an interest in mining; so much so that from time to time he'd disappear into a mining camp somewhere in Arizona, California, or Mexico.

Charley never stayed in any one place for very long.

By September 1892, Charley had begun running a gambling establishment called the Silver Lake Resort. When it was announced that Charley would take over the club's management, one newspaper predicted, "Mr. Hood will conduct the place in a first-class manner."

The resort, near Tucson, also served as a venue for private parties, such as one given in 1891 where the guests were "accompanied by a string band and a wagon load of the comforts of life . . . merry dancers were gliding to sweet music, while the bright-colored lanterns distributed among the large trees threw their light on boating parties passing gracefully over the water." But as pleasant as that all might have been, within just a few months,

Charley was headed out on a mining adventure in San Bernardino County, California. There, Charley lived for several months at the Vanderbilt mining settlement where miners were yielding plentiful gold finds.

The Silver Lake Resort as it appeared in 1888.

Months later, not long after his return to Tucson, Charley got himself into another fight. He could be a bit touchy, easily offended, and was hot to brandish his gun. His propensity for carrying concealed weapons and pulling them out when angry had become a lifelong habit.

On a Saturday night in March 1894, a row broke out at a Tucson "uptown saloon." A man named Mike Sullivan had words with Charley, and commenced punching him. Charley could hold his own in a scuffle, and he gave back as good as he got. The authorities showed up and arrested Sullivan for assault and battery. Charley was arrested for carrying concealed weapons. Charley's trial took place the following Tuesday in Pima County court. After giving Judge Culver his version of events, Charley was acquitted of the charges.

In late October 1894, the *Arizona Weekly Citizen* reported on several civil cases, including one for Charles Hood. Although

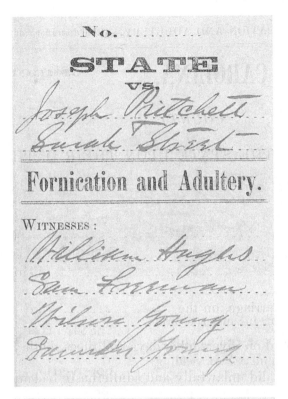

Mitchell County, North Carolina case, 1874. In the nineteenth century, the criminal offense of fornication often accompanied a charge of adultery.

the historical record remains silent as to the particulars of the case, it does show he was arrested for fornication. Had he been caught with an unmarried woman or someone else's wife? The record doesn't say, but the charge was later ignored.

Around March 1896, Charley left Tucson and moved to Nogales, a one-street border town between Arizona Territory and Mexico.

John T. Brickwood, an early settler of Nogales, became friends with Charley, and they attended Republican Party meetings together in Tucson. In 1897, Brickwood built the notorious Exchange Saloon in Nogales on the line between the US and Mexico. In her book *Nogales: Life and Times on the Frontier*, Jane Eppinga writes, "A fugitive could stop in the Exchange Saloon on the United States side, fortify himself with a glass of red-eye, and sneak out the back door into Mexico." Perhaps, in a poetic sense, the saloon became a metaphor for Charley's life. A bit of a trickster, he was a man always at the line (line rider), near the line (Nogales), or sometimes shifting back and forth across the line dividing law and outlaw.

In Nogales, Charley bought the GEM Saloon, "on the other side of the line," meaning on the Mexico side, on the corner of International Street and

By 1895, the bicycle was becoming wildly popular. During the bicycle boom, Charley came up with a clever idea. In Tucson, he announced that he would be selling chances for people to try their luck at winning a bicycle, which cost $113. But since he kept a chance for himself, and won, he got to keep the bike *and* the $113.

At left, a circa 1900 photograph of a young man and his bicycle.

Calle de Elias in Sonora, on the border between Nogales and Sonora. In his newspaper advertisements, he boasted being able to offer a "fine line of wines, liquors, Mexican cigars, and tobacco." A newspaper editorial said Charley's stock of French liquors "is especially an excellent one." But after a while running a Nogales saloon, Charley began missing the wild-hogging nightlife of Tucson, so he decided to pay a visit there.

Cowboys at the bar in Old Tascosa, Texas, circa 1907.

On a January night in 1897, Charley went drinking in Barrio Libra. Located near Tucson, the neighborhood had been settled by laborers and ranchers who loved to drink and have a wild time. That night, Charley had for some time been imbibing at a saloon when he suddenly became sleepy. Someone took him to a back room and put him to bed. A little later, he woke up. Getting his

The game of Farro was popular in saloons throughout the Southwest.

bearings, he searched his pockets and realized that he'd been robbed. His $200 was gone. One newspaper reported that the thieves had likely been "the light-fingered sons of the land of *manyana*." Charley swore out a complaint, but nothing came of it.

By August 1897, Charley decided that being in the saloon business suited his warm, friendly nature, as well as his propensity for drinking and fighting. After owning the GEM Saloon for eight months, Charley resolved to buy the Senate Saloon in Nogales at the corner of Congress and Meyer Streets.

US Field Deputy Marshal in Arizona Territory

On April 18, 1898, Charley must have felt a deep sense of pride. He took the oath and was sworn in as a US Field Deputy Marshal in Arizona Territory. Being a lawman in the Territory meant he had to be a skilled gunman. Charley, who loved to hunt, became active in the Tucson gun club, often competing in pigeon shooting "on the wing." The *Oasis* reported that Hood once "killed two bears in Peck canyon."

It was never recorded whether or not he'd ever killed a man in the line of duty.

About that time, the notorious outlaw Tom Ketchum, aka "Black Jack," was thought to be living with a gang of about fifteen men, including Indians and Mexicans. Their hideout was in the Sierra Madre Mountains, and the desperate characters were all good with a gun.

In early December 1897, Charley was called upon to join Deputy US Marshal Finley's posse to try and capture men thought to be part of Black Jack's gang.

Newspapers reported that they rode out of Tucson anticipating that Black Jack's gang was planning to hold up the Southern Pacific Railroad near Stein's Pass in New Mexico Territory. The posse included Deputy Marshal Lee Matney, Deputy Sheriff Benata, and Deputy Sheriff Bill Hildreth, of Tombstone. After capturing several men suspected of being part of the gang of outlaws, the posse sent them under guard to Tucson.

Charley and the others in Finley's band rendezvoused with Colonel Kosterlitzy and eighteen soldiers, who escorted them one hundred fifty miles into Sonora to Dos Cabezas. From there they

Form No. 10.

DEPUTY U. S. MARSHAL'S OATH OF OFFICE.

Territory District of *Arizona*

I, *Charles R. Hood*, do solemnly swear that I will faithfully execute all lawful precepts directed to the Marshal of the *Territory* District of *Arizona*, under the authority of the United States, and true returns make, and in all things well and truly, and without malice or partiality, perform the duties of the office of *Field* Deputy United States Marshal of the *Territory* District of *Arizona*, during my continuance in said office, and take only my lawful fees; and that I will support and defend the Constitution of the United States against all enemies, foreign and domestic; and I will bear true faith and allegiance to the same; that I take this obligation freely, without any mental reservation or purpose of evasion; and that I will well and faithfully discharge the duties of the office upon which I am about to enter; So HELP ME GOD.

Chas. R Hood

Sworn to and subscribed before me, this *Eighteenth* day of *April*, 1898

Charley may have carried a Colt single-action Army revolver.

Thomas Edward "Black Jack" Ketchum (1863 – 1901) was a New Mexico cowboy who became an outlaw. Marshal Finley called Ketchum's gang "The most dangerous band of organized outlaws which has ever infested the Southwest."

For a time, Ketchum joined Butch Cassidy's Hole in the Wall gang. He was hanged April 26, 1901, for attempting another train robbery. His execution (photo below) didn't go well. When the trap door opened and he fell, his head snapped off. Executions always drew a crowd of spectators who saw these hangings as a venue of entertainment.

went to Chuichupi and then Colona Juárez, two hundred miles south of El Paso, in the Sierra Madre mountains in the Mexican state of Chihuahua. The posse spent six weeks in the saddle. During that time, "they ascertained beyond any question of doubt that Black Jack is living and has a gang ranging from six to sixteen freebooters of the very worst character." The posse returned without Black Jack, but three years later, the outlaw met his fate.

Wells Fargo & Co.

Sometime after returning from the Black Jack posse, Charley was appointed to the position of railroad express guard. He worked for the Wells Fargo company to protect the train's strongbox. Upon his assignment to the Denver & Rio Grande Western Railroad, Charley received this letter of appointment from the Wells Fargo division chief Frederick J. Dodge:

In placing you on this run, I have put you on the most responsible run that we have in this section of the country. It will take you away from the hot, burning desert of New Mexico and Arizona, where smallpox and general cussedness run rampant, and will give you a touch of life over the Rockies. . . . I am directly responsible for your actions, and I am certain that my confidence

WELLS, FARGO & CO.'S EXPRESS BOX, on SONORA AND MILTON STAGE ROUTE, was ROBBED this morning, near Reynolds' Ferry, by one man, masked and armed with sixteen shooter and double-barreled shot gun. We will pay

$250

for ARREST and CONVICTION of the Robber.

JNO. J. VALENTINE, Gen. Supt.

San Francisco, July 26, 1875.

Wells Fargo began service with stage coaches and later used trains to transport money and valuables, making them a target for outlaws.

has not been misplaced, and that these trains will be guarded and guarded right. I hope that we don't have any trouble, but if we do, well, guard the trains on the Colorado-Midland and Rio Grande Western railroads, between Colorado Springs, Colorado and Helper, Utah.

Photo of Hagerman Pass at the time Charley was a train guard. His route between Colorado Springs and Helper, Utah, took him through this pass (elevation, 11,925 feet).

Along Charley's route, the train crossed Hagerman Pass, elevation 12,000 feet, where even in summer it could be bitterly cold and packed with high snow drifts.

Charley worked hard to make a name for himself as "one of the most courageous men in the employ of the company." One newspaper wrote that Wells Fargo would do well to treat Charley right, since they'd never had a "more nervy man in their employ." During his tenure with Wells Fargo, he "played an important part in the frustration of two train robberies."

Hot Headed & Trigger Happy

In 1899, Charley again found himself on the wrong side of the law. Not in any deliberate way, but every now and then Charley just seemed to fall into trouble. A man named Layton said something that offended Charley, and it touched off his violent temper. Charley drew his pistol and started shooting. On that fateful February night, Charley was charged with assault

Charley was arrested for assault with intent to kill.

In the Justice Court

First Precinct, County of *Pima*, Territory of Arizona.

THE TERRITORY OF ARIZONA,
Plaintiff

vs.

Charles R Hood } **Warrant of Arrest.**

Defendant

IN THE NAME OF THE TERRITORY OF ARIZONA:

To any Sheriff, Constable, Marshal or Policeman in this Territory. A Complaint upon oath having been this day laid before me, by *A V Spicer* _____ that the crime of *Assault with intent to kill E. E. Layton*, has been committed, and accusing *Charles R Hood* thereof, you are therefore commanded forthwith to arrest the above-named *Charles R Hood,* and bring *him* before me at *Tucson, Pima County*, or in case of my absence or inability to act, before the nearest and most accessible magistrate in this County. Dated at *Tucson* this *27th* day of *February* 189*9*

W H Culver

Justice of the Peace of said Precinct.

No. 136.—WARRANT OF ARREST—The H. H. McNeil Company's Red-Line Blanks, Phœnix, Arizona.

with intent to kill. He pleaded not guilty. At his trial in Tucson, Charley said he'd been drunk at the time and argued that it was precisely because he'd been intoxicated that he'd shot E. E. Layton in self-defense. After the judge heard arguments from both parties, Charley was acquitted.

Three months later, Charley looked to make another change. In May 1899, he left Nogales for a new post in Yuma. As a result of a petition to the superintendent of the Territorial Penitentiary "asking appointment of Charley Hood," he was hired to work as a guard at the prison. He worked there from May 14, 1899 to October 14, 1899.

Five months of guarding the prison was enough for Charley, and he was ready for another change. He then became the deputy collector and inspector of customs at the Yuma port. By then, Charley had become "well and widely known throughout Arizona as a very capable business man and officer." With Charley's new position came new dangers. Given the Indian and Mexican troubles in the Territory, customs officers "were in constant danger." Smuggling Chinese people into Arizona was a persistent problem at the time of Charley's tenure with US Customs. Eventually, Charley testified in the case of his superior, William M. Hoey. Charley thought that Hoey was innocent and should be cleared of the charges of trafficking illegal Chinese migrants into Arizona Territory.

Among the infamous characters imprisoned at Yuma was Frank Leslie, who'd worked for Wyatt Earp at the Oriental Saloon in Tombstone. Leslie was sentenced for murdering his girlfriend in a drunken rage, as well as for killing the Clanton Gang's Billy Clairborne.

Shooting at the Saddle Rock

Charley was fearless, even when he wasn't hunting outlaws. He could exhibit dark moods, and once in a while, it spilled over into violent acts, like the Old West tradition of shooting up the town. One day in Tucson, at the Saddle Rock restaurant, Charley ordered up some ham and eggs. He was hungry, and he thought the cook was taking too long. In a fit of rage, Charley drew his .45 Colt and fired at the cook, who "nervously finished preparing the ham and eggs." The marshal heard the shooting and came running. He escorted Charley to the justice of the peace who heard the complaint and gave Charley a firm lecture and a fine of $10 for disturbing the peace.

George Smalley, editor of the *Tucson Daily Citizen*, thought his readers would like to learn about the restaurant shooting. Eager to write the story, he went looking for Charley, who was sometimes referred to by folks as the "express car guard," and found him "in one of the saloons where he was having a drink." Smalley explained to Charley that his antics would soon find their way into his newspaper. Incensed, Charley lambasted Smalley, saying he'd shoot him if he printed a story like that. Charley finished his drink. Still infuriated, he then followed Smalley out into the street, threatening him further.

A short time later, Charley showed up at the *Citizen* newspaper office. Smalley had already written the story, and it was in type and ready for publishing. Charley continued repeating his threats. Smalley got up from his desk, went to the back room, and got his gun. He came back and put it on his desk and went back to work. Charley left in a huff, but a little later came back to the office, "waving a telegram from Herbert Brown," a friend of Charley's who happened to own the *Citizen*. The message: "Advise Smalley not to write anything about you." Smalley had no choice but to kill the story.

Cochise and Fairbank Train Robberies

In 1899, Charley was again called on to join an Arizona posse. Authorities had received information about a planned train robbery. Burt Alvord was constable of Willcox, as well as deputy sheriff of Cochise County. Alvord, who was not the smartest guy in town, would later use both his position and his stupidity to get away with robbery. Alvord formed a gang to rob trains, and enlisted Billy Stiles, along with Bill Downing and Matt Burts. Stiles, "a Mexican half-breed" with a "volatile temper," had once been a deputy sheriff under noted lawmen Jeff Milton and John Slaughter and eventually became Alvord's deputy. Nearly every member of the gang at some point had served as an officer of the law.

Since Stiles was also the Wells Fargo & Co.'s agent at Willcox, his inside knowledge of the company's procedures aided in planning the robberies.

Before joining the gang, the notorious "Three-Fingered Jack" Dunlap had been on the run. A Texas cowboy turned outlaw, he'd been hunted down and captured in Cripple Creek, Colorado, and forced back to Cochise County "to answer a charge of highway robbery." Although he was branded as a terrorist of southern Arizona, territorial authorities failed to establish a case against Dunlap, and he was released. That's when he joined Burt Alvord's gang.

John Slaughter was a Texas Ranger during the Civil War and later became an Arizona cattleman.

On September 11, 1899, Alvord's gang set in motion their plan to rob the Southern Pacific Railroad at Cochise. To create an alibi, Alvord's scheme included bribing a saloon porter. The gang was holed up in a private back room of Schwertner's bar, playing cards. The porter brought them drinks from time to time, and when returning to the saloon, would make remarks like, "Boy, those men sure are drinking a lot tonight," or "They've got a serious poker game going, and they don't want anyone bothering them."

Meanwhile, the gang put down their cards and slipped out the back of the saloon. They hopped on their horses and took off, heading for the Southern Pacific Railroad near Cochise. Along a certain stretch of the railroad, a steep incline forced the train to move slowly; that's when Stiles jumped on the train. Climbing into the engineer's cabin, he stuck a gun in the engineer's face and ordered him to stop the train. The express rider, responsible for protecting the strongbox in the Wells Fargo car, realized the train was being robbed and jumped off and ran away. Stiles commanded the engineer and fireman at gunpoint to remain quiet, while other gang members separated the engine from the cars. All the while, he sat "complacently smoking a cigarette and joking with the trainmen."

An explosion blasted open the Wells Fargo & Co.'s strongbox. The express car was shattered, and the bandits took off with "more money than they could carry," estimated at $30,000, although it was likely not that much. Charles Adair, the express messenger, later testified in court that the bandits stole thousands of dollars in gold coins, some Mexican money, and the passengers' jewelry. Richardson, the train's engineer, told of the explosion of the safe and damage done to the express car. Charles Bircher, the fireman, said he did what Stiles had demanded he do, because he always obeyed orders "when backed up behind a gun."

The outlaws returned to town after Alvord stashed the money. To throw off suspicion, Alvord warned the gang not to spend a lot of their shares around town. However, Stiles was afterward seen in Casa Grande showing off "a great deal of coin," his share in the robbery, estimated at $5,000.

Meanwhile, the train eventually rolled into Willcox. The railroad employees went looking for Constable Alvord to report the theft. They barged into the saloon's back room and saw him sitting there playing poker.

"The train's been robbed!" they announced. Alvord responded, "Oh, my God! We need to raise a posse!" He pointed to Bill Downing and Billy Stiles and said, "Come on, boys. Let's go get 'em," and they rode out. The next day, the three men came back and said, "Well, the robbers got away." When suspicion about his involvement with the holdup was aroused, Burt Alvord remarked, "Well, you know I'm not smart enough to pull something off like that."

The gang's next robbery didn't go as well.

Months later, on February 15, 1900, the train robbery they'd spent six weeks planning was set in motion. The gang had sworn to each other that "whoever should prove false or cowardly in the enterprise should be killed by the others." The gang put their plan to hold up the train at Fairbank, a stop between Benson and Tombstone, into action. Bob Brown, Billy Stiles, "Bravo Juan" Tom Yoas, "Three-Fingered Jack" Dunlap, Matt Burts, and the Owens brothers (George and Louis) were all in. The outlaws wanted to be sure and had confirmed that the fearsome former Texas Ranger Jeff Milton would *not* be the Wells Fargo express messenger, the man guarding the money box. However, at the last minute, Milton replaced the originally scheduled messenger.

This did not bode well for the gang.

On the platform at the depot, the criminals started acting like drunk cowboys, playing the fool.

The train coming up from Nogales slowly rolled in to Fairbank. Jeff Milton was standing in the open doorway of the express car. The outlaws, who'd been pretending to be drunk, suddenly sobered up. They took aim and began firing. Brown shot Milton twice, seriously wounding him in the shoulder. Milton slumped over onto a trunk, and Brown thought he'd killed him. Some of the gang then charged toward Milton, who suddenly rose up with a ten-gauge sawed-off shotgun and fired, scattering the bandits. When Bravo Juan turned to run, he got a butt load of buckshot. Milton then shot "Three-Fingered Jack," who fell, Winchester in hand, severely wounded in the abdomen. One bandit managed to get into the mail car and seize a bag. As he was leaving the train, he found Milton bleeding, and stole his "six-shooter and forty-two Mexican dollars."

Jeff Milton

Railroad Depot, Fairbank, Arizona, circa 1900.

The robbers, getting away with only a small amount of booty, took off on their horses, heading for the Dragoon Mountains.

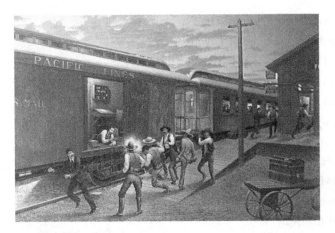

Charley, who'd by then been sworn in as a deputy sheriff of Cochise County, joined the posse to pursue the outlaws. As a "well-known line rider," he rode 300 miles with the posse in their efforts to seize the bandits. He then rode with Sheriff Tom Broderick and Sid Mullen to capture Jack Dunlap in the Dragoon Mountains. In their hunt, the posse found Dunlap.

This painting of the Fairbank Train Robbery by Cal Peters was commissioned by the US Postal Service.

Billy Stiles and the others thought Dunlap, being badly injured, was slowing them down, so they left him in the wilderness to die. When the posse found Dunlap bleeding out, he was all too eager to confess and give the names of the other members of the gang. Charley was credited in an Arizona newspaper as "the officer to whom Dunlap told his story before dying." Dunlap confessed to Charley not just about the heist at Fairbank, but also the Cochise robbery months earlier.

Dunlap was taken to Tombstone and the posse returned to the Dragoons in search of Robert E. "Bob" Brown, who'd not only been part of the hold-up at Fairbank, but was credited with having been the "chief conspirator." Charley and the others seized Brown, who then piloted the posse to the Owens brothers' hideout. They apprehended George and Louis Owens and hauled them off to the Tombstone jail. The *Los Angeles Times* reported on the Fairbank bandits, saying that Charley, "one of the sheriff's posse," had helped capture the Owens brothers near Pearce, Arizona. Sheriff Scott White of Cochise County credited the arrest of the gang to Charley, "for it was through his staying qualities and information that he became possessed of that which made the capture of the robbers possible."

Jack Dunlap's testimony led to the arrest of Billy Stiles, Burt Alvord, and Bravo Juan. All were put in the Tombstone jail. Stiles, in exchange for his freedom, volunteered to become a government witness. He was released and hired as a detective for Wells Fargo & Co. A month later, he returned to the Tombstone jail to visit his gang, having asked the sheriff if he could take Alvord and Bravo Juan "some dainties." At the jail, Stiles suddenly shot and wounded the jailer, George Bravin, and then liberated Alvord and Juan. They left behind Bill Downing, who started cussing up a storm while he watched the rest of his gang flee the jail.

Charles Hood Sues Wells Fargo & Co.

The Cochise robbery, otherwise known as the Southern Pacific Train Hold-up, spawned fresh trouble for Charley. He'd weathered the perils of running with the posse, and had endangered his life to apprehend Billy Stiles, Bob Brown, and the Owens brothers. Charley had cut a deal with Wells Fargo, and they'd agreed to pay $1,000 for the apprehension of Billy Stiles.

On July 7, 1900, the *Oasis* newspaper reported on the arrest of Stiles:

> Last Saturday Officer Charles Hood was summoned to Casa Grande by telegraphic information that Billy Stiles, the bandit, would surrender to him. He took the train, went to Casa Grande, and Stiles delivered himself into custody, Hood taking him to Tombstone and lodging him in jail Sunday evening.

The *San Francisco Call* reported, "No one thought that the capture would be made without bloodshed, but Hood is a clever trailer and got his men where he wanted them before he threw down his guns on them." Charley and Burt Grover brought Stiles in under guard on a stagecoach. One newspaper would later call Stiles, "The Ishmael of the Southwest. His hand was against every man and every man's hand against him." The folks in Tombstone got a surprise when they heard that Stiles, "the self-confessed

Tucson Citizen newspaper editor George Smalley feigns surrendering to Billy Stiles.

train robber and outlaw," was again "in the hands of the law," having given himself up. After being taken into custody, Stiles unburdened himself while Charley listened. Stiles said he surrendered because "he was tired of being an outlaw and had reason to fear that his life was in danger, not only from officers, but his friends in crime, and therefore wanted protection."

All those events were now a year past, and Wells Fargo still hadn't paid Charley what he was owed. He and Burt Grover had joined forces to bring in the outlaws with the expectation they'd be paid what the Wells Fargo company man had promised. In the District Court of Tombstone, Charley and Burt Grover filed suit against Wells Fargo & Co. The complaint claimed that Wells Fargo had never paid the $1,000 promised for the arrest of Billy Stiles. The historical record is silent as to the outcome of the suit, but it's likely that Charley and Burt were never paid. Charley's case was just one among others in which agents of Wells Fargo had promised to pay rewards and then reneged. In letters written to his relatives back east, Charley called Billy Stiles and Burt Alvord "two of the most desperate and notorious outlaws in this or any other country," and said that he'd put many more like them behind bars.

A Governor's Pardon

By 1900, fifteen years had passed since Charley first arrived in the Southwest. In September of that year, the *New York Times* reported that an application for a pardon had been presented to the North Carolina governor. The case was "not only of great interest throughout this State, but is also National in character because of the man for whom pardon is asked." The article stated that a murderer, who'd escaped and never been caught, had been living out West under an assumed name.

Charley's in-laws, US Senator Jeter Pritchard and former Mitchell County Sheriff George Pritchard, had filed the pardon request with a third North Carolina governor. In late October

1897, one newspaper reported that the two Pritchard brothers had "returned from their trip West," which was likely to visit Charley in light of his third pardon request. Charley had written a cousin to say he was glad to hear that the incoming governor might approve his request for a pardon. Eager to present letters of recommendation, Charley wrote, "I have a commission at present from the governor of Arizona and also have other commissions as deputy US marshal, deputy collector of customs, and deputy sheriff and have recommendations from most all the members of our last legislature, which I can send to show the governor that I have been upholding the law in this country. . . . I can also get letters from the president and general superintendent of the railroad company which I am working for at present, and from every officer almost in the state in regard to my life in this country." Charley's appeal argued that the pardon should be granted because he'd paid his debt to society by serving as "an efficient peace officer, fearless in hunting down outlaws."

Several months passed while Charley waited to hear from the governor to whom he'd applied. Even though it had been years since his first pardon request, Charley was still holding out hope, waiting for news that might change his fate. For years, he'd longed to return to the lush, green hills of the Appalachian south, a far cry from the parched, hot desert of the American Southwest. His children by then were grown, and his wife had never remarried; both had maintained hope that he'd be pardoned and return home for the last years of his life.

It must have been early September 1901 when Charley received the distressing news. His third request for a pardon had been rejected. Perhaps the governor had been moved by the emotional plea of the mother of the man Charley had killed, begging him not to grant the pardon. Whatever the case, now it seemed he'd never return home.

On that September afternoon Charley became so distraught that he did things he later regretted. Drinking until he became "much under the influence of liquor," he boarded a train at the Yuma station, supposedly looking for illegal Chinese migrants. But when he attempted to enter a sleeper car, the train conductor restrained him. The two began bickering. Charley pulled out his pistol and started firing. The conductor jumped aside to dodge the bullets, which lodged in the wood panels of the train car. Charley then staggered off the train. At the depot, he "went on a rampage," shoving his gun in peoples' faces. He then made everyone he met "waltz to his music." Eventually, a sheriff's deputy showed up and "tried to reason" with him, but Charley poked a gun "of large caliber" in the deputy's stomach. Charley continued his drunken foray, but soon disappeared. Ironically, given his shooting of the train car, Charley had once written home to say, "Either the Yankees or the revolutionists shoot up our trains every few days, and we are constantly on the lookout for trouble."

After this episode, Charley resigned as the collector of customs. A warrant for his arrest was sworn out, but before it could be served, he headed for Mexico, where he'd spend the next few years prospecting and mining. (See maps, pp. 160-161. Also see a map of Charley's travels, Appendix 2.)

From Grand Jury to Barroom Brawl

By early 1905, Charley was back in Nogales. In April, he served on a grand jury in Santa Cruz County in the district court of the Territory of Arizona. Some of the cases in which Charley was tasked with discerning guilt or innocence included murder, assault with a deadly weapon with intent to commit murder, robbery, burglary, and grand larceny.

Soon, Charley managed to get himself into another fight. This time, it was with two men at the Monte Carlo barroom in Nogales. A man named Anthony Joyce punched Charley, and then William O'Brien joined in the fray. In the brawl, Charley pulverized O'Brien, punching him until he went "on a journey of several days to the land of visions"; in other words,

O'Brien was knocked unconscious and remained that way for several days.

The *Oasis* newspaper reported:

> William O'Brien, night bartender at the Palace Saloon, was badly beaten up in a fight in the Monte Carlo barroom this morning. O'Brien, who was very drunk, got into an altercation with Charles Hood, an ex-line rider, who knocked him down and beat him up badly. Dr. Purdy was called to attend the injured man, at his room, where he was taken by friends. O'Brien's nose is broken and his head and face are a mass of cuts and bruises. It will be several days before he will be able to leave his room.

In the hearing of the case, the judge fined Anthony Joyce $12 for assaulting Charley. The judge dismissed charges brought against Charley for assaulting O'Brien and for disturbing the peace.

On May 5, 1910, a US census taker in Nogales paid a visit to the boarding house where Charley was living at the time. The taker noted that Charley Hood was forty-six and unmarried. He gave his place of origin as North Carolina, and his occupation as mining—in Mexico.

1901 First National Bank of Nogales Territorial issue.

Toward the end of 1910, Charley got a new job in Nogales. Maybe he missed his old friends, or maybe he wanted a break from all the mining and prospecting he'd been doing over the

years. In a more settled life, he took the post of guard at the First National Bank of Nogales. But a few months later, he apparently tired of the mundane labor and headed south again. This time, he went to work for the railroad in Mexico.

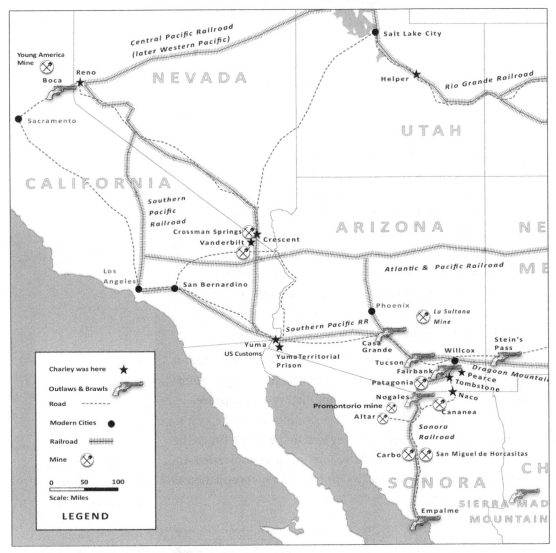

These maps illustrate Charley's adventures as a miner, train guard, and outlaw hunter in California, Colorado, Utah, Nevada, Arizona Territory, Mexico, and New Mexico Territory.

TWO OF THE ARIZONA DESPERADOES CAPTURED.

A Brace of Bandits, the Owen Brothers, Run to Earth Near Pearce by a Posse.

NOGALES (Ariz.), February 17.—Word was received at this place to-day from Charles Hood, one of the Sheriff's posse, saying that the Owen brothers, two of the bandits who held up and robbed a Wells-Fargo express car at Fairbank Thursday evening, had been captured near Pearce, Ariz., by the posse.

TAKEN BY SURPRISE.

Arizona Desperado and Fugitive From Justice Captured at Casa Grande.

TUCSON (Ariz.), July 1.—William Stiles, train robber and fugitive, was arrested at Casa Grande last night by Charles Hood and Burt Glover. It is reported that Alvord was also arrested and was concealed by officers when they passed here this morning, for fear that friends would attempt to take him from the officers. This cannot be verified. Stiles talked with a number of friends, and seemed unconcerned. He was arrested near the home of his mother as he was going into Casa Grande. It has been known for some time that he has frequently visited his mother and wife at Casa Grande. Stiles was taken by surprise, and was powerless to resist the officers. He is known a desperate man, and the officers here are surprised that he was arrested without a fight. He was taken to Tombstone. Stiles is the man who released Alvord and Bravo Juan, and he has been in the mountains with them since.

Salt Lake City

COLORADO

Helper

Rio Grande Railroad

Denver

Colorado
Springs

Pueblo

UTAH

ARIZONA

NEW

Atlantic & Pacific Railroad

MEXICO

Rio Grande Railroad

Phoenix

*La Sultana
Mine*

Southern Pacific RR

Casa
Grande

Willcox

Stein's
Pass

a Territorial
on

Tucson

Fairbank

Pearce

Dragoon Mountains

El Paso

TEXAS

Patagonia

Tombstone

Nogales

Naco

Promontorio mine

Altar

Cananea

*Sonora
Railroad*

CHIHUA

Carbo

San Miguel de Horcasitas

SONORA

Empalme

SIERRA MADRE
MOUNTAINS

BILLY STILES

*Remarkable
Audacity of
Train-Robber
Stiles*

By October 1912, Charley, considered "one of the old timers along the border," had for some time been living in Empalme, near Guaymas, Mexico. Jim Finley of the Southern Pacific Railroad of Mexico had hired Charley as a night watchman for the Southern Pacific Railway Club. The Club accommodated railroad executives, not unlike the upscale members-only lounges in airports today.

In the early hours of March 5, 1913, Charley had been drinking on the job. "At half past three in the morning," he began arguing with J. H. McCahon, the night clerk. The argument got so heated that in a fit of anger, Charley pulled out his pistol, and "snapped his gun" at McCahon. But before Charley could squeeze the trigger again, McCahon whipped out his gun and shot Charley through the heart. He died almost instantly. McCahon immediately fled to a US warship stationed in the Guaymas harbor. Because of the red tape involved in transferring the body from Mexico to the US, Charley was buried in the common graveyard in Empalme.

One obituary stated that Charley "had a reputation as a gunman, but it is not known that he ever killed a man while serving in any of his dangerous positions. . . . He had a wide reputation, however, as a peace officer and was well known over the entire Southwest."

Another obituary reported that Charley had come to Arizona from Asheville, NC. Charley had not been completely bereft of familial fellowship. Charles Bowman, whom he called a cousin, had moved West to Tucson and eventually became a lawyer in Tombstone. Charles's father, David Bowman, had also migrated to Arizona. Charles Bowman notified Mrs. Nora Anderson of Bakersville, NC, whom the newspapers assumed was Anderson's sister, but of course, this was his wife.

Indeed, Charley was, in fact, the infamous Waightstill Avery Anderson, the convicted murderer who in 1885 had escaped from the Buncombe County jail in Asheville, North Carolina. For nearly three decades he'd eluded his captors and lived as Charles R. "Charley" Hood.

For Anderson to have pulled off his escape, remained hidden, and lived successfully under an alias reveals that he received support from his powerful legal, judicial, and political relatives. Asheville attorney Melvin Carter, who had defended Anderson, signed a petition stating that "the conviction of Anderson was a great miscarriage of justice, and that he ought to be pardoned." George Pritchard, former sheriff of Mitchell County, along with solicitor Adams, who'd prosecuted the murder trial, also asked Governor Russell to pardon Anderson. Pritchard had "hunted up" five of the jurors who signed the petition. Sadly, all these efforts were not powerful enough to gain him a pardon.

In 1900, when news broke of his application for a pardon, several newspapers published false claims about Anderson. The *Gastonia Gazette* announced that John C. L. Harris, chief of staff to NC Governor Russell, reported that a fugitive from justice had asked for a pardon. Harris's disinformation asserted the far-fetched notion that Anderson had been working in the secret service under President William McKinley. There were no follow-up newspaper articles.

Clearly, this was one of the many disinformation stories that friends of Anderson planted. Another one claimed that on the night Anderson escaped, it was accomplished by "500 sturdy mountaineers, armed with pistols, knives, and Winchester rifles," who stormed the jail and set the men free. North Carolina state records pertaining to rejected pardons are not available, but it is certain that Anderson's third request for a pardon had been refused.

According to newspaper accounts, Charley, aka Anderson, had applied for a pardon to the administrations of governors Carr, Russell, and Aycock. What is so telling about Anderson's case is that Aycock held to a generous clemency policy, granting more pardons than any other governor in North Carolina history, and yet, he passed over Anderson's request. One newspaper reported that the governor would not consider Anderson's application because Anderson had been "in the woods." Judge Avery, who presided over Anderson's murder trial, joined his voice with other leading attorneys who pointed out to Governor Aycock precedents set by other governors who'd pardoned criminals who'd been "in the woods."

Throughout his life, Anderson demonstrated extraordinary resilience and tenacity, able to reinvent himself whenever necessary. Clearly, he was a charismatic and complex man. Sadly, he risked his life as a lawman, thinking it would gain him a pardon so he could return home. He'd maintained a correspondence with a cousin in North Carolina, and once described his deep longing:

> God knows what a pleasure it would be to me to once more see the dear ones who are left, and once more feel like a free man before I quit this land of trouble. As you know, we are getting to be old men and at the most it will not be many years before we will have to pass over the river.

At the time of his conviction of murder, Anderson had been a US Deputy Marshal in North Carolina. He continued that legacy in the American Southwest, not just to curry favor with the governor, but as a way to exonerate himself. His story—a convicted murderer who'd escaped death, only to cheat death while upholding the law—became a great irony. Charley Hood, former peace officer, died as recklessly as Waightstill Avery Anderson had lived: with gun in hand and finger on the trigger.

Appendices

Appendix 1: Forty Women Indicted

During the Civil War, a "tithing officer" collected tithes of grain from farmers. Provisions were dealt out to people in need until authorities in Asheville ordered tithes to be reserved exclusively for Confederate forces. One afternoon, the tithing officer went home "to avoid the pitiful appeals of half-starved women and children for a little corn." Moments later, forty women in Yancey County showed up to ask for corn, and were dismayed to find that the officer had left. The women "held a council of war and agreed to break open the door of the tithing house and supply themselves with corn." The forty women forced open the door and seized a total of twenty bushels of tithed corn; each of them got a half of a bushel.

Judge Merrimon, solicitor of the mountain district, sent a bill to the grand jury which included the names of the women. A true bill was found, and the women were indicted. After warrants were issued, the sheriff "arrested and held in custody" the women named in the indictment.

At the time, the husbands, brothers, and fathers of these women had not deserted the army, and were "in the trenches around Richmond and Petersburg fighting while their wives, sisters, mothers, and children were starving at home." After the bill was found, William Ray, "a prominent man and a staunch friend of the Confederate cause" appealed to Judge Merrimon, saying the women should not be prosecuted, since their men were still fighting for the South. He argued that "it would be an outrage to prosecute and convict" the women, especially under the circumstances. Merrimon agreed not to prosecute the indictments as long as the solicitor's fees were paid. "Out of his own private purse," Ray paid Merrimon $560, and the women were discharged from the sheriff's custody.

Appendix 2: Map Detail of Charley Hood's Adventures (see legend p. 160)

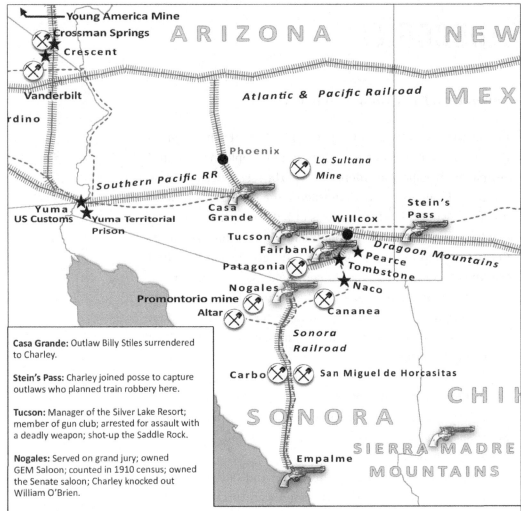

Casa Grande: Outlaw Billy Stiles surrendered to Charley.

Stein's Pass: Charley joined posse to capture outlaws who planned train robbery here.

Tucson: Manager of the Silver Lake Resort; member of gun club; arrested for assault with a deadly weapon; shot-up the Saddle Rock.

Nogales: Served on grand jury; owned GEM Saloon; counted in 1910 census; owned the Senate saloon; Charley knocked out William O'Brien.

Dragoon Mountains: Charley & posse found outlaw "Three-Fingered" Jack Dunlap.

Vanderbilt: Charley lived for months in the gold mining camp.

Tombstone: Charley put Billy Stiles in jail; Charley sued Wells Fargo; Charley's relative Charles Bowman became lawyer.

Young America Mine: Charley prospected.

Altar district: Charley mined for gold.

Cananea: Charley prospected.

Promontorio Consolidated Mining Co: Charley prospected 6 miles north of Las Planchas de Plata, Sonora.

Patagonia Mountains: Charley did assessment work on his mining claims.

La Sultana Mine: Charley prospected for copper.

San Miguel de Horcasitas: Charley invested in five Mexican mines with veins of copper, silver & gold:
- *The Booster*
- *The Corker*
- *Joe Dandy*
- *Cerro de Plata*
- *Juanita*

Carbo: Charley worked as a railroad guard.

Crossman Springs: 20 miles N of Vanderbilt, Charley prospected for ore.

Naco: Charley worked as a guard for the Cananea, Yaqui & Pacific Railway.

Sierra Madre Mountains: 200 miles S of El Paso, TX, Charley & posse hunted Black Jack's gang here.

Empalme: Charley is shot and killed March 5, 1913, and buried in Empalme's common graveyard.

Appendix 3: Rutherford County Ku Klux Klan, aka the White Brotherhood and the Invisible Empire

Those Arrested for Whipping Biggerstaff and Two Trials

All secret political societies—Leagues and Ku Klux alike—must be broken up, and those who prowl about at night committing depredations must expect punishment sooner or later, whether they be white or black.
—THE CHARLOTTE DEMOCRAT, OCTOBER 3, 1871

First Trial. In US Circuit Court on September 23, 1871, the case began of *US vs. Amos Owens* and twenty-five others indicted on three counts, including conspiracy (an agreement to do an unlawful act) and assault on Aaron Biggerstaff for voting for Congressional candidate A. H. Jones in 1870.

Charges within the Three Counts of the Indictment (Greensboro Patriot, *October 5, 1871):*

> 1. Conspiring to beat Aaron Biggerstaff to prevent him from exercising his right of suffrage.
>
> 2. Beating Aaron Biggerstaff for having exercised his right of suffrage.
>
> 3. Conspiracy to prevent the execution of the 1st section of the act to enforce the right of citizens of the United States to vote.

Jury Rendered Verdicts September 28:

> Not Guilty: Benjamin Gould, Joseph Wilson, Daniel Gould, Alfred Early, Joseph DePriest, James McDaniel, Joseph McDaniel, Achilles Durham, and John W. Calton.
>
> Guilty on all three counts—Amos Owens
>
> Guilty on the third count only: James Sweezey, Jason Witherow, Wm. DePriest, Taylor Carson, Owen Carson, Benjamin Fortune, Thomas Fortune, Joseph Fortune, Adolphus DePriest, Lloyd Early, Leander Toms, Daniel Fortune, Samuel Biggerstaff,

Alfred Biggerstaff, Barton Biggerstaff, and Lawson Teal.

A *nol pros* was entered for Amos Harrell and Joseph Fortune. (*Nol Pros*, Latin for "to be unwilling to prosecute," is the abbreviation of *nolle prosequi*, indicating a prosecutor's decision to abandon prosecution of a person under indictment.)

Second Trial. Of Randolph Abbott Shotwell and others who were charged with conspiring to deprive James Justice "of the natural rights of a lawful citizen, as to the privilege of franchise, and, on the 10th day of June, 1871, attempting to hurt and intimidate Mr. Justice by beating his body and otherwise brutally maltreating him." (*Tri-Weekly Era*, Raleigh, September 19, 1871.)

Those Charged in the Indictment:

Randolph Shotwell, Frederick A. Shotwell, Adolphus DePriest, Amos Owens, James Edgarton, Calvin Teal, William Tanner Jr., George Holland, William McIntire, William Teal, Spencer K. Moore, David Collins, William Scoggins, D. B. Fortune, and William Alexander.

Witnesses for the Prosecution (* indicates he was a KKK member who became a witness for the prosecution)*:*

James M. Justice, *M. M. Jolley, *Alfred Harris, Joseph Fortune, *Julius Fortune, Thomas Tate, *John B. Harrill.

Summoned to Testify:

J. R. DePriest: initiated into the Invisible Empire February 1870; Chief of Den No. 3 in Rutherford County; claimed never to have been on a raid. Testified that there were 400-500 members of the Invisible Empire in Rutherford County.

*J. H. Withrow: initiated into the Invisible Empire March 1870; was on the Biggerstaff raid and the beating of Ibby Jenkins, a young Black girl, along with Alfred Bridges, Amos Owens, William McIntire, Alex McIntire, William Teal, Spenser Moore, Thomas Sweezy. Testified that when they raided Biggerstaff for the second time, "We were all drunk." Before becoming a witness for the prosecution, Withrow had been under indictment. (*Tri-Weekly Era*, Raleigh, September 21, 1871.)

T. J. Downey: took the oath of the Invisible Empire because he wanted "to expose it, but never went on a raid." The KKK plans had been to murder Federal Judge Logan and James Justice and to skin alive J. B. Carpenter. The KKK accused Downey of betrayal and whipped him severely with over one hundred lashes.

On the Jury:

J. W. Bell, Joseph Ward, Madison Pace, George W. Charles, B. F. Beckerdite, Jesse F. Grubbs, Joseph Miller, John Bryant, Joseph Motsinger, Edward Teasley, James Smith, W. P. Wetherell.

No Trial. Plato Durham, a leader of the KKK in Cleveland County, was arrested on September 6, 1871. (*Carolina Watchman*, September 15, 1871.) The case of Plato Durham and forty-one other defendants charged with Ku Kluxing was set for trial the second Wednesday in December.

Durham was arraigned in federal court in Raleigh on a charge of being a member of the Ku Klux Klan, but filed for a continuance; his case was called for and then postponed until December. On October 3, 1871, the *Charlotte Democrat* reported that, "The case of the *United States vs. Plato Durham* and others was not called."

Plato Durham never stood trial.

Appendix 4: Those Who Testified before Congress in 1871 Who'd Also Been Indicted in the Biggerstaff Case

Wm. C. DePriest

Attended one meeting. Sentenced to two years in jail and a fine of $100.

Taylor Carson

Never was in a meeting or on a raid; was sworn in, but was never in disguise; fined $50.

Olin Carson

Was in the McGaha raid and at three meetings; quit the order in November 1870; knew nothing of the Biggerstaff whipping; fined $50.

Joseph Fortune

Judgment suspended, he having been used as a witness for the prosecution.

Leander Toms

Attended four meetings, was on no raids, claimed to know nothing of the Biggerstaff whipping. One year in jail and $1 fine.

Amos Owens

Judgment not prayed, he being already under sentence for the James Justice raid. Pardoned by President Grant in 1872.

Daniel Fortune

Claimed he was in two meetings but heard nothing of the Biggerstaff raid until it was over; sentenced to six months in jail.

Samuel Biggerstaff

Convicted or submitted in the second Aaron Biggerstaff raid. Judgment not prayed at the instance of Aaron V. Biggerstaff, on account of a reconciliation, they being half-brothers.

Alfred Biggerstaff

Claimed he was in two meetings and then quit; knew nothing of his uncle (Aaron) being whipped until it was over; convicted in the second Aaron Biggerstaff raid; sentenced to one year in jail.

Barton Biggerstaff

Claimed he was never on a raid or at any meeting; convicted in the second Aaron Biggerstaff raid; sentenced to two years in jail.

Lawson Teal

Went on two raids; convicted in the second Aaron Biggerstaff raid; sentenced to two years in jail.

James Sweezy	Joined the White Man's Brotherhood and attended two meetings; convicted in the second Aaron Biggerstaff raid; sentenced to two years in jail.
Adolphus DePriest	Convicted or submitted in the second Aaron Biggerstaff raid; judgment not prayed, as defendant was already sentenced to two years.
Thomas Fortune	Submitted and confessed to Judge Logan; convicted in the second Aaron Biggerstaff raid; sentenced to six months in jail.
Benjamin Fortune	Claimed never to have belonged to any order; convicted in the second Aaron Biggerstaff raid; judgment not prayed, as defendant was already sentenced to six months in jail.
N. T. Thorn	Submitted and pleaded guilty; sentenced to one year in jail.
Isaac Padget	Submitted and pleaded guilty; sentenced to six months in jail.
David Holland	Submitted and pleaded guilty; judgment not prayed, defendant being under sentence for two years for the James Justice raid.
Stanly Hanes	Submitted and pleaded guilty; sentenced to six months in jail.
Mike Grigg	Submitted and pleaded guilty; sentenced to six months in jail.
Watt Grigg	Submitted and pleaded guilty; sentenced to six months in jail.
Samuel Goforth	Submitted and pleaded guilty; sentenced to six months in jail.
Mike Grigg	Submitted and pleaded guilty; judgment not prayed.
Alvin Johnson	Submitted and admitted to helping whip Aaron Biggerstaff; sentenced to one year in jail and $50 fine.
Peter Baxter	Submitted and pleaded guilty; sentenced to one year in jail and $50 fine.
J. A. Lingerfelt	Submitted and pleaded guilty; sentenced to six months in jail.

John Sainey	Submitted and pleaded guilty; sentenced to six months in jail.
Jacob Wilson	Submitted and pleaded guilty; sentenced to six months in jail.
Henry Baxlie	Submitted and pleaded guilty; sentenced to one year in jail and a $50 fine.
T. O. Lackey	Submitted and pleaded guilty; sentenced to one year in jail and a $50 fine.
William McIntire (aka McIntyre)	Submitted and pleaded guilty; convicted in the James Justice case; sentenced to two years hard labor; fined $500.
William Teal	Submitted and pleaded guilty; convicted in the James Justice case; sentenced to three years hard labor; fined $500; pardoned by President Grant in 1872.
Jason Withrow	Submitted and pleaded guilty; judgment not prayed, as he had been used as a witness.
D. H. McCown	Judgment not prayed, as he had been a witness for the prosecution.
William Scruggs	Pardoned by President Grant in 1872.
David Collins	Pardoned by President Grant in 1872.
Thomas Toms	Indicted for Biggerstaff's second whipping.
James Hunt	Not guilty of Ku Kluxing Aaron Biggerstaff.
James Scruggs	At the trial for Biggerstaff's second whipping, the indictment had charged assault as well as the charge "to intimidate Biggerstaff away from his political principles."

Appendix 5: Cases of Execution by Hanging in North Carolina

On the morning of a public hanging in North Carolina, throngs of spectators would gather to get a glimpse of the person, "about to make earthly atonement for the violation of the laws of God and man." At times, the governor would respite the condemned, allowing a little more time to prepare for death.

RALEIGH REGISTER.

FRIDAY, MAY 7, 1824.

This day, between the hours of 12 and 3, the unfortunate *Lemuel Lewis*, convicted at our last Superior Court of the murder of Hinton Pugh, is to make earthly atonement for the violation of the laws of God and man. "Blood for blood" has been the law of nature, from the period when the first living, mourned over the first dead.

1820   A man named Fitzpatrick—hanged for horse stealing.

1824   Lemuel Lewis—hanged for the murder of Hinton Pugh.

1830   Elijah W. Kimbrough—hanged for the murder of his stepfather.

1833   Frankie Silver—hanged for the murder of her husband.

1836   John Calhoun—hanged for the murder of his wife.

1847   Daniel Angel Jr., son of a Yancey County sheriff—hanged for murder.

1850   Coonrod Creasman—hanged for rape.

1859   Bill, a slave—hanged for burglary, but escaped.

1859   A "Negro girl," aged nine—sentenced to hang for nearly killing her owner.

1859   Erastus Hogue—sentenced to hang for murder; governor respited.

1860s   Hangings for desertion was not uncommon during the Civil War.

1868   Thomas Dula—hanged for the murder of a pregnant woman, Laura Foster. (Tom Dula inspired the song "Hang Down Your Head Tom Dooley.")

1870   Jennie Greene—sentenced to hang but imprisoned for life after governor commuted.

1870   Josiah Henderson—hanged for the murder of Burwell Hilton.

1872   Govan and Columbus Adair—hanged for the murder of a biracial family.

1873   Bayliss Henderson—hanged for the murder of Nimrod S. Jarrett.

1873   Joe Baker—hanged for the murder of Newton Wilfong.

1874   Austin Hill and Cornelius Williams—hanged for murder.

1879   Bob Boswell—hanged for the murder of Nannie Blackwell and child.

1884   Estimated date Buncombe County jail was built, with a death-drop that was never used.

1885   US Deputy Marshal Waightstill Anderson—sentenced to hang for murder, but escaped.

1886   Andrew Jackson Lambert—the only man hanged in Charleston (later renamed Bryson City).

1890   James P. Davis, alias William S. Shackelford—hanged for the murder of his children.

1891   Orange Page— hanged for the murder of Rosa Haywood.

1893   Murder was divided into first and second degrees; first degree was punishable by death.

1893   John Curprew and Abram Williams—hanged for the murder of a man named Umphett.

1894   Peter DeGraff—hanged for the murder of Ellen Smith, his sweetheart.

1899   Avery Kale—hanged for the murder of George Travis.

1902   James Wilcox—killed his sweetheart Nellie Cropsey and was sentenced to hang; given a second trial and sentenced to thirty years in the pen.

1902   Ben Foster and Frankl Johnson—two of the Emma Burglars gang, hanged.

1907   John Mathis—hanged for the murder of Tom Merritt, his step-father.

1910   The last judicial hanging in North Carolina and the institution of the electric chair.

Appendix 6: Transcription of the Sentencing of John M. Williams

Judges who were compelled to pronounce the death penalty often gave compelling speeches to the condemned. This 1824 speech—made in Georgia—reflects the judge's sensitivity to the gravity of the moment that many judges must have felt when declaring to a prisoner the sentence of death. The following is a transcript of an article in the *Raleigh Register*, January 27, 1824. This domestic violence murder was especially gruesome; reader discretion is advised.

> The following affecting sentence was passed by Judge [Augustus Baldwin] Longstreet on John M. Williams, convicted of the murder of his wife, at the late Superior Court in Jones County, Georgia—which has been furnished for publication by the Judge, at the solicitation of the Bar and a number of citizens who attended the trial.
>
> John M. Williams – When I heard the history of your case from the lips of those who testified on your trial, I thought it was such an one as would reconcile me to the painful task I am now about to perform. But all the disgust and horror which I then felt at the enormity of your crime, have now given way to a succession of kind, but conflicting emotions, that almost overpower me; and I meet you upon this occasion, no better prepared to pronounce, than you are to hear, the awful sentence which awaits you. But it is vain to shrink from a duty which the law compels me to perform.
>
> Hear me then for a few moments, and forgive me for prolonging your suspense, while I once more rehearse the sad story of your guilt. Believe me, the piteous tale is not again repeated to shoot another pang into your agonized bosom. I would not wantonly sport with your feelings or mock your calamity. It is directed to the throng which presses around you, to witness our last sad interview. By them it will be long remembered, and may hallow the rude and turbulent passions that would hurry them into crime, which the stern mandate of the law would be

forgotten. Perhaps too, it may touch some tender chord of your own heart that remains yet unbroken, and awaken you to such a sense of your perilous situation, as will induce you to make a successful appeal to that Being, whose arm alone can snatch you from the ruin which threatens you.

It appears that some years since, you wooed and won the heart of an amiable, lovely, affectionate and fatherless female – you lead her to the altar, and there, in the presence of that Being, before whom you must shortly appear, you inter-changed with her vows of perpetual love and fidelity. She kept her vows amidst the severest trials; she did not forget it. The marks of your brutal violence disclosed your cruelty to the world, before her own lips whispered it to her nearest friend.

When her wounds awakened the sympathies of the only male connection she had on earth, and forced him to step forward in her defence, she interceded in your behalf, quelled the rage of her defender, palliated the offence of her husband, forgave him, and with manifestations of unabated love, again received him to her bosom. With each revolving month your cruelties were repeated, and as often as they were repeated, so often were they forgiven.

At length your conduct assumed a more alarming character, and she foresaw the fell purpose you have now executed. She appealed to the laws of her country to avert the ruling which menaced her; but ere she could experience their efficacy; one kind word from you dissipated all her fears; she again relented, withdrew her complaint, again forgave, and again received you to her embrace. All this could not melt your locked and frozen heart—it served only to embolden you to iniquity.

Her friends expostulated with you, she besought you, and her mother, trembling under the weight of years, implored you to deal more kindly with her daughter. That mother addressed herself to your feelings in language, that I should have thought even a demon could not resist. When she repeated it here, the sternest heart in this vast multitude could not withhold from her the tribute of a tear. Behold, she said, I am a weak and aged woman; I can neither protect nor defend my child—her father is dead; if you discard her, where is she to seek protection? This eloquent appeal could not find its way to your heart.

Your inhuman treatment continued, and was borne by your companion with unexampled fortitude for more than five years; during which period, she presented you four children. It was the ninth day of the age of your youngest, when its mother had not yet left the room of her confinement, you selected to execute your hellish purpose. Then, when she clasped to her bosom her helpless innocent, with this instrument, a knife, still covered with her blood, you commenced the work of death. Nay, her life was not sufficient to appease your vengeance – her mangled corpse gave unequivocal proofs that many of her wounds could've been inflicted only to try the strength of her nerves. The keen edge of the knife made her forget her infant and her weakness; she fled; you pursued her and dealt to her a blow that arrested her feeble flight— You then dropped the knife, went to your trunk and drew from it this instrument of keener edge, a razor, and with it, you severed her head from her body. For all this, what is your defence? A plea that would deprive her of all that she has left behind her, her reputation. Happily, for her memory, this lies beyond the reach of your vengeance. Your efforts to tarnish it have only given to it additional lustre. If there was one in this vast assembly who witnessed your trial, that harbored for a moment a suspicion dishonorable to her, his conscience now rebukes him for his cruelty.

After five months separation, after producing the inmates of your family, you have not been able to extort from one, a single word that could alarm even jealousy itself. All attest that she was constant, artless, meek, submissive and kind. Oh, she would have been a prize to any man but you; had you permitted her to live, she would've been a blessing to your children. Poor helpless orphans, what is now to be their destiny—who is left to watch over their dawning intellects, to chasten their morals, to lead them to virtue's shrine. Father of Mercy, be thou their protector, guardian and friend-Spirit of their murdered mother, hover over and direct them through the dangers and devious windings of life!

Williams—I have now faintly sketched the picture of your guilt. If it be not faithful to the original, it is only because the coloring is not deep enough. With all this weight of sin upon your head, you have but 20 days to live. The hour is at hand when you must leave us, and hasten into the presence of a Being, whose frown is far more dreadful than the sentence which now consigned you to the tomb. Are you prepared for the interview or have you wrought yourself into the belief that there is no futurity? And will you rest satisfied in this belief, until you are aroused from your torpor by the signal for your appearance at the bar of the Most High?

Oh, sir, you are risking too much upon your opinion. Should you err in this particular, the anguish which now rends your bosom, is peace when compared to the misery that awaits you. When you reflect that the wisest, ablest and best of men are against you, does it not sometimes occur to you that you may be in error? When you open the sacred volume, are you not sometimes startled with the thought, that it may be true? If it be, how dreadful are its denunciations against you.

But amidst its thunders, it breathes a whisper of consolation, even to the most hardened offender.

Yes, Williams, even you, all bloody as you are, may be yet within the reach of its kind promises. Fly then, I beseech you, to the last stay of the sinner's hope for a happy eternity. You have nothing to bind you to this life—there is not a being upon earth whom you can call your friend—not one who would dare to acknowledge you as a friend. You have arrested the throbbings of the only bosom that could now be in unison with your own—You have silenced the only lips that could speak a word of consolation to your drooping spirits but there is an all ruling Power above who may not forsake you, when your kinsmen, countrymen disown you. While the light of life yet gleams upon your short and dreary path to the grave, catch the fleeting moment to bespeak the intercession of your Redeemer, whose power is equal to your necessities. He may yet wash out the foul stain that renders you loathsome to the world, and raise you to mansions of bliss, where you may again be greeted and once more be forgiven by the kind compassion of your bosom.

Hear now the sentence of the law, and then farewell for ever. You, John M. Williams, will be reconducted to the place from whence you came, where you will be kept in close and safe custody until Friday, the seventh day of November next, when you will be taken to some convenient place of execution, and there, between the hours of 10 in the forenoon and 2 in the afternoon you will be suspended by the neck until you are dead. And may the Lord have mercy upon your soul.

Endnotes by Chapter

CHAPTER ONE

Burgess S. Gaither was related to Avery's uncle by marriage.
Daily Journal, November 24, 1851.
Gass, W. Conrad. *North Carolina Historical Review* (NCHR).
North-Carolina Star, November 26, 1851.
Raleigh Register, November 19, 1851.
Republican and Patriot, December 18, 1851 also reported Erwin giving Avery a small pistol.
North-Carolinian, November 29, 1851.
Saga of a Burke County Family, Edward William Phifer, North Carolina Historical Review.
The History of a Southern State: North Carolina, third edition, Hugh Talmage Leffler and Albert Ray Newsome, The University of North Carolina Press, Chapel Hill, p. 419.
"The Misfortune of a High Minded and Honorable Gentleman: W. W. Avery and the Southern Code of Honor," *The North Carolina Historical Review* 56, no. 3 (1979): 278-97.
Tri-Weekly Commercial, November 20, 1851.
William Lenoir was a soldier in Brig. General Griffith Rutherford's 1776 military campaign against the Cherokee Indians. Lenoir kept a diary on the campaign. Read *A Demand of Blood: The Cherokee War of 1776*, by Nadia Dean.

CHAPTER TWO

An 1886 Act of Congress for the Relief of Nancy Franklin.
Asheville News, June 24, 1869.
Bayliss and James served in Co. E, 2d NC Mounted Infantry, and Josiah belonged to Co. G, 3d NC Mounted Infantry.
Case of Nancy Franklin, February 10, 1875, including exhibits.
Case of Nancy Franklin, September 24, 1883, including exhibits and deposition H, case number 176.751, October 4, 1883.
H. Baker, commissioner of pensions, report February 17, 1875.
M. E. Weeks, report to the commissioner of pensions, February 17, 1875.

Drury Norton probate file described the home as a "mansion house."

Indictment for murder, tried before his Honor Judge Saunders, at Spring Term, 1855, Buncombe Superior Court.

In Drury Norton's Probate file, Nancy and Drury's children were listed in order of their birth: Catherine Norton, Bayliss Norton, James Norton, George W. Norton, and Delaney J. Norton.

Captain H. A. White gave an affidavit in Nancy's pension case in 1885. On September 20, 1864, Colonel Kirk sent White to make a raid into Madison County to arrest Union deserters. Bayliss, James, and Josiah Norton had been cut off from their own company and regiment and were serving in White's cavalry regiment instead. The Confederates captured a drunken soldier who betrayed White's plans and movements. White testified that "immediately the rebels surprised and captured me," carrying him to Salisbury, North Carolina. That same day, he was informed that the Norton boys had been captured and killed.

Mr. O'Hara, the committee on invalid pensions, in the Act for Relief of Nancy Franklin document, quoting Howard Miller and quoting L. E. Payne.

Nancy Franklin, biographical details: Three books have published fabrications about Nancy, a reflection of the authors' failure to conduct research in primary documents: *The Kingdom of Madison*, by Manly Wade Wellman, published in 1973, *Victims*, by Phillip Shaw Paludan, published in 1981, and *Bushwhackers* by William R. Trotter, published in 1988. These books contain serious errors about Nancy's life story, chief among them that she had been a Confederate sympathizer, but clearly she was not, as expressed in statements she made in her pension application. Unfortunately, these falsehoods have been re-published in newspaper articles and genealogy magazines, perpetuating the misinformation about Nancy. Wellman claimed that the stories he heard were "widespread and consistent" and said his sources were from folklorist Bascom Lamar Lunsford and others who lived many decades after Nancy's ordeal. The Probate file of Drury Norton stated the location of Nancy's farm as adjoining the lands of David Farnsworth.

North Carolina Madison County Court of Pleas in quarter sessions 1854.

Proof of widowed mother's dependence.

Single affidavit of Mr. John Shelton and John W. Ball.

CHAPTER THREE

A Saga of the Carolina Hills Being a True Story of the Naming of Mount Mitchell, a pamphlet with no date or publishing information, but estimated after 1900. https://archive.org/details/sagaofcarolinahi00math/mode/2up;

Asheville News, October 30, 1856; Amos Ray owned land near Styles Valley and the Green Mountains. *Yancey Record*, November 8, 1851.

Charlotte Democrat, April 26, 1864.

Center of the Mountain Heartland: A Historical Profile of Yancey County, Jerry L. Cross, Lloyd Bailey, and David Moore, 1992.

Daily Confederate, April 28, 1864.

Deed, June 1836, from Joseph Shepherd to Amos L. Ray for seventy-five acres for $100.00, dated April 4, 1831.

Deed, June 1836, from Amos Lafayette Ray to Joseph Shepherd for thirty acres for $50.00, dated April 4, 1831.

Deed, June 1837, from William Dickson, Chairman of Yancey County Court, to Amos L. Ray for Lot # 4, Town of Burnsville, in consideration of $255.00, dated March 11, 1837.

Deed, June 1837, from William Silver to Amos Lafayette Ray for four acres in consideration of $50.00, dated October 24, 1836.

Estatoe is a Cherokee town name.

Montraville was one of nine children of Amos Lafayette Ray and Martha "Patty" Allen, per US Census records. In 1900, "Senator Pritchard introduced a bill to give a pension of twelve dollars per month to Martha Ray, widow [eighty-one years old] of Amos. L. Ray, who served in the Cherokee Indian war," meaning the forced removal of the Cherokee Indians from their ancestral homeland. Martha was born in 1809 and died in 1906. At age twenty, on April 17, 1853, Montraville married Mary "Polly" Elizabeth Austin. They had eight children, but Mary eventually divorced Montraville, and he went on to have children with Jane E. Styles. Styles is listed as divorced in US Census records, and died on January 18, 1922, in Yancey, age eighty, but she'd kept her maiden name. In the 1880 federal census of Jack's Creek, Yancey County, "Polly" Austin, age forty-nine, is listed as a widow, even though no divorce record was found and Mont was still alive.

National Archives and Records Administration (NARA), Washington, DC.

Private C. D. Young wrote in a letter to home: "I will give you the Boys names that started Home. It was Joseph Ray, Samuel Ray, Montraville Ray, Samuel Boone, Thomas Edge, Manning Sheapard, E. Z. Banks." *Our Young Family: The Descendants of Thomas and Naomi Hyatt Young*, Perry Deane Young, The Overmountain Press, 2003.

Raleigh Daily Telegram, February 17, 1871.

Rutherford Star, October 8, 1870.

The Blue, the Gray, and the Green: Toward an Environmental History of the Civil War, an anthology edited by Brian Allen Drake, University of Georgia Press, 2015, pp. 61-62. On Ray's desertion, see NC Troop Roster, 6:35, s.v. "Ray, Montreville." He deserted his Confederate troops during the Peninsula Campaign. Desertion was high in regiments mustered out of the mountains; [footnote in book: J. W. McElroy to Governor Z. B. Vance, April 12, 1864, in US War Department, War of the Rebellion: A Compilation of the Official Records of the Union and Confederate Armies (Washington, DC: US Government Printing Office, 1898), 53:326-27].

Farmer and Mechanic, March 7, 1911.

The governor's proclamation, Raleigh, February 15, 1871.

Union Provost Marshals' File Relating to Individual Civilians, National Archives and Records Administration (NARA).

Western North Carolina; a History, John Preston Arthur, p. 329.

Wilmington Morning Star, October 12, 1870.

Yancey County was a violent place where folks indulged in drinking and fighting, as demonstrated in early court records. During the 1837 spring term, the Superior Court in Burnsville heard fourteen cases. Ten were for assault and battery or for disturbing the peace in a public brawl. By 1840, thirty-one out of fifty-five criminal cases were for these offenses. Alcohol had always been a part of mountain life. As a service to the community, some preachers made and sold whiskey, and even some sheriffs did, too, including Mitchell County's Adam Wiseman. Liquor was sold in every country store, and alcohol consumption became so widespread that drinking was common at "all public occasions." In 1854, while holding court in Burnsville,

Judge Merrimon "spoke very bitterly against the prevalence of drinking among the office-holding class in Yancey County." The judge said that he couldn't hope for improved social conditions as long as men persisted in being so drunk "that they were unable to perform their duties." "The Toe River Valley to 1865," Jason Basil Deyton, *The North Carolina Historical Review*, v. 24 (October 1947), pp. 423-466, North Carolina Office of Archives and History.

Yancey County Criminal Actions Papers, North Carolina State Archives.

CHAPTER FOUR

Congressional testimony; "Conditions of Affairs in the Southern States."

Govan Adair had enlisted in the Confederate Army at age seventeen but deserted six months later; the Adair boys had been fingered as the arsonists who had recently burned Black churches and barns.

Henderson was charged with murder, jailed in Rutherford County, and brought before Judge Logan. The court records, however, are incomplete and the handwriting in them made it impossible to decipher the outcome of Henderson Adair's charge of murder.

North Carolina Confederate soldiers who'd managed to survive disease, warfare, or being taken prisoner, and who also hadn't lost a limb, were the exception. Fathers, husbands, and sons perished, and many who did return were too maimed to perform farm labor. This fact alone was a root cause of widespread alcoholism.

Shotwell, Randolph Abbott, 1844-1885. *The Papers of Randolph Abbott Shotwell*, Rebecca Cameron, and Joseph Grégoire de Roulhac Hamilton. Raleigh: North Carolina Historical Commission, 1929. See also, "The Klan in the Southern Mountains: The Lusk-Shotwell Controversy," Gordon McKinney, *Appalachian Journal*, vol. 8, no. 2, 1981. Along with Shotwell were arrested: his brother Frederick Shotwell, Adolphus DePriest, Amos Owens, James Edgarton, Calvin Teal, Wm Tanner, Jr., George Holland, William McIntyre, William Teal, Spencer K. Moore, David Collins, William Scoggins, D. B. Fortune and William Alexander. The prosecution expected "to prove that Randolph Shotwell conspired with and guided a desperate body of men to the residence of James M. Justice for the purpose of beating and killing him." Henderson County North Carolina Superior Court, Criminal Action Papers, 50.326.31, North Carolina office of Archives and History, Raleigh. See also: North Carolina Reports: Cases Argued and Determined in the Supreme Court of North Carolina, vol. 66, January term, 1872. See also *Carolina Era* newspaper Raleigh, November 18, 1871; The *Charlotte Democrat*, July 30, 1872; and November 12, 1872; *Southern Home* newspaper, October 28, 1872; the *Western Vindicator*, January 12, 1899.

Shotwell was arrested on July 5, 1871. The Horn Creek Bend den was involved in the James Justice beating.

Years earlier, Sallie and Sheriff Taylor had been romantically involved. When the relationship ended, she later married Baynard. Sallie and Martin had three children.

CHAPTER FIVE

Aaron Vanzant Biggerstaff Jr., son of Aaron Vanzant Biggerstaff Sr. (1780–1861) and Jane Carter (1774-1861), was born on November 29, 1811, in Rutherford, North Carolina. Aaron V. Jr. married Margaret Gold (aka Gould) on October 25, 1830. They had seven children. One newspaper reported that Margaret died November 22, 1872 (The *Daily Era*, Raleigh, November 29, 1872); another noted she died of cancer on November 27, 1872. Aaron died in 1880 in Rutherford, North Carolina, at the age of 69. Aaron's half-brother Samuel P. Biggerstaff, born in 1823, married Nancy Toney, November 2, 1842, and died May 16, 1889.

Collett Leventhorpe, *The English Confederate: The Life of a Civil War General, 1815-1889*, J. Timothy Cole, Bradley R. Foley, 2014.

Cowhiding dates back to Roman *lictors*—those trained to scourge prisoners in what was called the "half death." A lictor would stop and check the pulse of the captive; if he still had a strong pulse, the whipping resumed. Similarly, in modern vernacular, Aaron had been whipped "within an inch of his life," a KKK trademark punishment likely borrowed from the Romans.

Congressional testimony of Plato Durham.

Congressional testimony of James M. Justice.

Greensboro Patriot, October 5, 1871.

Klan Oath, *New Berne Times*, September 23, 1871.

Mary Ann Biggerstaff, born August 12, 1841, married William A. Norville, December 12, 1861; Logan Store, Rutherford County. The Civil War made her a widow, and she remarried a man with the last name Ramsey.

New York Herald, May 20, 1871.

President Grant ordered pardons in 1872 for several men convicted in the whipping of Biggerstaff, including David Collins, William Teal, Amos Owen, and William Scruggs after they'd been found guilty one year earlier of violating the Enforcement Act.

Raleigh Sentinel, September 13, 1871.

Rutherford Star, April 29, 1871.

Rutherford Star, July 22, 1871. North Carolina's 1868 Constitution granted suffrage to Black men and eliminated property requirements in order to vote for state senators. Amendments such as these were passed because the constitutional convention was presided over by a biracial coalition of Republicans. Democrats opposed changes to their constitution, and sought to hold another convention to undo the changes made in 1868. It was this convention that legislative member James Justice and other North Carolina Republicans opposed.

Testimony of T. J. Downey, said the initial plan was to kill Logan and skin Carpenter alive.

The Ku Klux Bill, April 29, 1871.

The Union Leagues were private clubs established to induce loyalty to the Union and the policies of President Lincoln.

United States Congressional Serial Set. United States: US Government Printing Office, 1872.

CHAPTER SIX

Asheville Advance, June 12, 1886; the paper says Dick Wilson "lingered some days" but the court document says he lived until 2:00 a.m. the next day, and the *Asheville Weekly Citizen* (July 15, 1886) says he "died within a few hours."

Asheville Weekly Citizen, July 15, 1886; Note that Carden's account has him shake the sheriff's hand.

Carl G. Lambert Sr., grandnephew of Jack Lambert, January 31, 1975.

Indictment for Murder, tried before Judge John A. Gilmer of the 5th District, at Spring Term, 1885, of Swain.

Lambert's July 8, 1886, letter to his wife and family, courtesy, Museum of the Cherokee Indian.

Lambert's second wife of only eight months, was the second great-grand-aunt of the author.

"Madison Found a New Life in WNC," a blog article by Gary Carden.

News and Observer, July 29, 1886.

New York Times, July 31, 1886, "Did They Revive Him?"

State v. Lambert, 93 NC 618 (NC 1885), Supreme Court of North Carolina, October 5, 1885.

Wilmington Morning Star, July 4, 1885.

CHAPTER SEVEN

Title from the *Asheville Citizen* headline, July 22, 1885.

1st Lt. was C. A. Moseley; 2d Lt., T. A. Jones.

The Charlotte News, May 14, 1901. There were incidents in which angry mobs busted through the jail to lynch a prisoner. See "The Lynching of Bob Brackett" of this volume.

1884 Annual Report of the Adjutant General. Anderson and Ray were in the Henderson County jail from March 24 to April 21, when they were moved to the Mitchell County jail. Governor Jarvis would only sanction use of the military "in extreme cases," but since the state did have "an efficient Guard," with their help, he thought "any lawlessness can be easily put down." Jarvis instructed Adams to tell Judge Shipp that he'd provide any support necessary; April 1, 1884, Governor Jarvis to Solicitor Adams (8th judicial district), Adjutant Report; online: https://digital.ncdcr.gov/digital/collection/p249901coll22/id/28029/

Anderson was born in June 1859. Horton lived on land adjacent to the mine. Ray lived in Madison County, forty miles from the mine. Ed Horton married Lodimia Demaris Woody on November 28, 1880. They had one daughter.

Charlotte Democrat, April 19, 1889. On March 30, 1887, the *Lenoir Topic* reported: "The old case against Ray and Anderson, convicted of murder, is kept continued on the docket in anticipation of the capture of these fugitives at some time in the future." Several cases were tried in absentia: State v. E. W. Ray, Caldwell County, 1886; *State v. E. W. Ray and W. A. Anderson*, 97 NC 510 (February 1887); State v. Ray 1 S.E. 876 (NC 1887). North Carolina Civil Action Court Papers, 1878 to 1880, NC Archives & History.

Anderson's father, the Rev. Jesse Woodson Anderson, testified in court and said Waightstill had been born in June 1858, however, census records date his birth at 1859. *Lenoir Topic*, January 29, 1885.

Anderson had also been in altercations with W. B. Councill and Tode Councill.

Anderson and Ray surrendered on Friday, March 7, 1884; The *News and Observer*, March 14, 1884.

Anderson worked under Republican and Internal Revenue Collector John James Mott.

Andrew Jackson Lambert was the 2nd great-grand-uncle of the author's husband. Just hours before the jailbreak, Lambert had been in the same cell block with the other men who escaped, but he and Anderson had been in an altercation, and the jailer moved Lambert to a different cell.

Aramaic Bible in Plain English.

Asheville Weekly Citizen, April 24, 1884. The costs for prosecuting Anderson and Ray were reportedly considerable, and later a motion was filed to recoup costs by a tax against Mitchell County.

Asheville Weekly Citizen, May 1, 1912; special article to the Citizen by P. C. Cocke; Anderson and Ray surrendered to Bowman on March 10, 1884. *Carolina Watchman*, March 20, 1884. The following eight attorneys were retained for their defense: Honorable R. F. Armfield, of Statesville; Colonel G. N. Folk, of Caldwell; Major A. M. Irwin, of McDowell County; Colonel J. S. McElroy, of Madison; and J. H. Merriman, M. E. Carter, and Johnstone Jones, of Asheville.

Bible, English standard version.

Bowman, Jacob Weaver, b. July 31, 1831, Mitchell County; d. June 8, 1905, Bakersville, NC. Superior Court Judge Bowman's daughters were Honora "Nora" Bowman-Anderson and Malissa "Lizzy" Matilda Bowman-Ray. Ray's family had a history of mining. In Yancey County in the late 1860s, Garrett Ray started the Ray Mica mine on Hurricane Mountain.

Cabins in the Laurel, Muriel Earley Sheppard, Chapel Hill Books, 1935.

Carolina Watchman, July 16, 1885.

Charlotte Democrat, April 25, 1884.

Charlotte Democrat, July 17, 1885. The day after the jailbreak, "the jail building was visited by hundreds to see the hole in the wall, and the excitement has not abated at all."

Bowman had served as Captain in the CSA, Co. B, 58th Infantry.

Charlotte Democrat, April 25, 1884.

Charlotte Home-Democrat, May 9, 1884.

Charlotte Observer, November 12, 1933.

Charles York murdered John York on May 21, 1885.

March 20, 1884, Mitchell County Sheriff W. C. Hickey to General Johnstone Jones, 1884 Annual Report of the Adjutant General.

March 22, 1884, G. S. Ferguson, Solicitor to the Governor, to Governor Jarvis, 1884 Annual Report of the Adjutant General.

March 23, 1884, Governor T. J. Jarvis to Capt. W. T. Weaver, 1884 Annual Report of the Adjutant General.

March 29, 1884, General Jones to Sheriff Hickey; April 1, 1884, Governor Jarvis to Gen. Johnstone Jones. The Governor requested that the Statesville and Asheville companies stay in readiness; 1884 Annual Report of the Adjutant General.

Daily News, New York, January 6, 1929.

Edward W. Ray (b. 1843, Yancey) married Malissa "Lizzy" Matilda Bowman on December 21, 1876, in Mitchell County. Ed's father was the Reverend Thomas Washington Ray. His mother was Hannah Louisa Carter. Augusta Louise Ray, Ray's sister, married Jeter Pritchard. After her death, Pritchard married Ed's ex-wife, Malissa Bowman, the sister of Anderson's wife.

Ed W. Ray became the focus of a sensational murder in Ashe County, North Carolina, in 1877. For the story of Edward W. Ray, read "Dealing in the Crooked," in *Moonshine Wars* by Nadia Dean (to be published 2023).

Gastonia Gazette, October, 18, 1900.

Governor Jarvis called out Company B of the Third Regiment of State Troops.

Hutson Byrd and William Haynie were witnesses.

Jesse Woodson Anderson was a Baptist minister in the French Broad Association. He served as a Confederate soldier in the 64 Regiment, NC. He began ministry at age forty. At the beginning of the Civil War, he was well-to-do, but most of his wealth was in slaves, and emancipation "left him broken." Anderson became a strong preacher, and was a pastor for years. He was ordained by Mars Hill Church, and became its pastor. He was also a pastor at Bakersville (Mitchell County), Burnsville (Yancey County), and Morgan Hill and Gash's Creek (Buncombe County). He was described as "a powerful preacher and one of the best known and beloved Baptist ministers in that section of the state." *Charlotte Observer*, May 29, 1907. Rev. Anderson died in Asheville on June 2, 1907. He was nearly ninety; History of French Broad Association. Sadly, while Waightstill was on trial, his only sister, the wife of James M. Ray, Ed Ray's brother, died just days before the trial began. Waightstill's mother, Elizabeth Caroline Carter Anderson, died in Raleigh on August 1, 1881. In 1877, Elizabeth had become ill and "her mind clouded," and she "lost her reason." In February 1878, she was taken to a hospital for the insane in Raleigh, under the care of Dr. Grissom, who attempted to treat her mental illness, but to no avail; *Biblical Recorder*, August 24, 1881.

John G. Heap pioneered the industry of manufacturing stove doors made from mica, which was found in abundance in western North Carolina.

Judge Avery was the younger brother of William Waightstill Avery, who was mortally wounded in an engagement with Col. Kirk's men in 1864. Waightstill Avery was a North Carolina Revolutionary War patriot. His grandson William Waightstill Avery was Anderson's namesake. Read Avery's ordeal in Chapter 1, "Emotional Insanity." Ironically, Judge Alphonso Calhoun Avery, grandson of the Revolutionary War patriot and brother to Anderson's namesake, presided over Anderson's trial.

Lenoir Topic, March 19, 1884.

Lenoir Topic, May 28, 1884.

Lenoir Topic, January 21, 1885.

Lenoir Topic, January 29, 1885.

Lenoir Topic, July 22, 1885. "The jail at Asheville contains 52 prisoners, with the capacity for 96." *Lenoir Topic*, May 13, 1885.

Newton Enterprise, December 6, 1884.

North Carolina State Supreme Court Case Files, 1884-1885, NC Dept. of Archives & History.

North Carolina Supreme Court Decision, *State v. W. A. Anderson*.

News and Observer, Raleigh, October 24, 1882, identifies David A. Bowman as Anderson's uncle, but he was actually the brother of Anderson's father-in-law. In 1868, Bowman had been appointed postmaster at Bakersville, and in 1877 he was the United States Commissioner to Bakersville in the Western District, Fourth Circuit. Bowman was Clerk of Court and later Justice of the Peace. The 1910 Federal Census shows Bowman born about 1846, died 1910, in Black Butte, Crook County,

Oregon. David A. Bowman's son, Charles, born 1870, became a lawyer in Tucson, married Frances Cook in 1904, and eventually moved to Los Angeles, where he died.

News and Observer, Raleigh, February 24, 1884.

News and Observer, March 2, 1884.

News and Observer, March 4, 1884.

North Carolina Civil Action Court Papers, 1878 to 1880, NC Archives & History. *State v. W. A. Anderson*, July 22, 1880. Hutson Byrd and Wm. Haynie were witnesses.

North Carolina Reports, vol. 92, Cases Argued and Determined in the Supreme Court of North Carolina, February Term, 1885, Google Books, p. 691.

North Carolina State Supreme Court Case Files, 1800-1886, NC Dept. of Archives and History.

On March 30, Reuben and Hardy Sparks, who'd been arrested as accomplices in the shootings of Horton, Miller, and Burleson in the Flat Rock mica mine homicides, escaped from the Bakersville jail. With help from friends on the outside, they escaped by cutting through the floor.

Ray was represented by R. F. Armfield and G. F. Folk.

Richmond Dispatch, August 20, 1885.

Semi-Weekly Asheville Citizen, Saturday, May 23, 1885.

Semi-Weekly Asheville Citizen, July 22, 1885 (headline). In the 1880 US census, Anderson was living in a boarding house. Charles Stewart "kept a public house in Bakersville," and Anderson boarded with him for several months.

State v. W. A. Anderson, Mitchell County Justice's court, NC Dept. of Archives and History.

The author began research on the murder in 1990, and when she inquired as to the location of the old jail records, she was told, "The records were interred in the rubble when they tore down the old jail."

The death certificate for Eveline's daughter Molly states that Charles York was her biological father, and the informant on the certificate was her son, so surely he would have known the identity of his grandfather. Could this have been the cause of their argument?

The guard constituted of Captain W. T. Weaver, commanding; First Lieutenant C. A. Mosley, Second Sergeant W. L. Murphy, Third Sergeant W. R. Israel, Third Corporal J. A. Campbell, Fourth Corporal E. Weddin, privates; and W. R. Byrd, J. W.

Speares, J. O. Howell, C. H. Miller, T. W. Pulling, Walter Allen, James Young, and H. C. Jones.

The old Asheville jail was located on Eagle Street.

Until the railroad was completed in 1879, Cooper's Station in the Swannanoa Valley, ten miles east of Asheville, was an old stagecoach stop near the Alexander Inn.

William Samuel York is the great-grandfather of the author. In an interview with D. D. York, the author's grandfather, in 1989, he related the story of the murder and the ill effects it had had on his father, William.

York, Eveline "Vicey" (nee Reece), is the author's 2nd great-grandmother; Vicey was a daughter of William Samuel Reece. Her sister, Louisa Jane "Jennie" Reece, married Andrew Jackson Lambert just eight months prior to his arrest.

Weekly Raleigh Register, January 18, 1885.

Weekly Raleigh Register, February 18, 1885. The award money of $4,300 would be about $129,000 in today's economy. Anderson and Ray spent eight months in the Lenoir jail before being transferred to the Buncombe County jail, and the cost of boarding and guarding Anderson and Ray in the Lenoir jail cost Mitchell County $1,653; *Lenoir Topic*, February 18, 1885.

Weekly Star, May 29, 1885. The Supreme Court of North Carolina rendered its decision on May 23, 1885.

CHAPTER EIGHT

Asheville Citizen-Times, August 9, 1897.

Asheville Citizen-Times, August 10, 1897.

Asheville Citizen-Times, August 11, 1897.

Asheville Citizen-Times, August 12, 1897.

Asheville Citizen-Times, August 13, 1897.

Asheville Citizen-Times, September 12, 1899; prosecuting attorneys aimed to prosecute under an act of 1893, and Bryant would have been the first to be tried under the Act.

Asheville Citizen-Times, September 27, 1897.

Goldsboro Headlight, August 19, 1897, reported that they'd lynched Brackett "at Terrell Station on the Southern Railroad, eighteen miles east of Asheville."

Hangings were usually ordered to occur ninety days after sentencing, so two weeks would have been unusually quick.

James S. Coleman was a wealthy lumber dealer in Buncombe County.

Kittie/Kitty Emma Henderson, b. September 28, 1871 (or 1872); d. May 3, 1953. She was the daughter of John Heatherly Henderson and Mary Aiken. Kittie had been engaged to be married at the time she was assaulted, but apparently that marriage never took place. In the 1900 census, Kittie was listed as being single and twenty-seven years old. Although no marriage record has been found, Kittie married James Robert Settle (b. November 21, 1866; d. January 3, 1953). They had one child listed in their census records, a son, Millard E., who was likely a child of Settle's first marriage.

Messenger, October 1, 1897.

Old Testament law saw no such thing as a prosecuting attorney. The accusers in a crime essentially became the prosecutors, and in similar manner, Kittie Henderson had become Brackett's prosecutor.

Press-Visitor, August 12, 1897.

Press-Visitor, August 13, 1897.

Reverend Sandy Ray of the Big Ivy community organized Mount Olive Baptist Church on July 15, 1917.

Tarborough Southerner, September 30, 1897. Bryant was arrested on September 11, 1899.

The jurors were J. E. Henderson, T. I. VanGilder, J. A. Nichols, G. S. Powell, W. A. Blair, and C. H. Miller. Brackett was buried in an unmarked grave in an Asheville cemetery. The record of his death can be found in the Buncombe County Register of Deeds office and online at Book DTH, page 73.

The jury was made up of F. A. Fanning, Dr. A. B. Ware, W. P. Brown, A. W. Fullman, Clarence Ledford, and D. G. Noland. John M. Campbell, H. C. Jones, and William H. Deaver were the magistrates.

The mob liberated James Payne and George Hensley, both arrested for killing a woman in Madison County. Hensley was recaptured before he could exit the jail yard. Payne escaped. Another prisoner, Clay McCarty, put on a messenger's Western Union hat and managed to get out without being recognized, but later was captured and returned to jail. Three federal prisoners, D. H. Brandell, J. D. Sheppard, and James Kilpatrick, escaped and were never recaptured.

The precedent for a mob storming a jail was established in 1891, when tens of thousands of angry men took part in the largest lynching in American history; they stormed a Louisiana jail with a battering ram, and then massacred and tore apart the bodies of Italian immigrants.

CHAPTER NINE

Asheville Times, April 15, 1931.

Asheville Citizen-Times, April 16, 1931.

Ben and Oma signed their marriage certificate with an "X," indicating they were illiterate.

Charlotte Observer, April 22, 1931. Deputy Prohibition Administrator Ed Kanipe led the raid. Assigned to the case was Charlie Braton of Bryson City, in Macon County.

Charlotte Observer, August 2, 1931.

Mims White was married to Letha Pace, and his brother-in-law, Henry Pace, and Scott's mother went looking for answers to his disappearance.

Oma's death certificate lists the cause of death as cerebral vascular thrombosis (stroke) with a complication of hypertension, and further noted there was a "post-op fractured hip."

Rile McGaha and his son Arnold were arrested and held as material witnesses to the murders.

Scott came home aboard the military transport ship Madawaska, just ten months after enlisting. He had listed his mother as next of kin, indicating that he was not married at the time.

Sunburst is now a campground located in Pisgah National Forest.

"Up on Big Pigeon" was originally written April 5, 1936, by Sara Rathbone.

Varnell Gates (newspapers also spelled his name Vornelle), just a few months after being incarcerated, escaped from the Caledonia Prison Farm with eighteen other prisoners on November 4, 1931, but was recaptured the next day.

Vester shot Oma's father Merritt on July 12, 1915.

CHAPTER TEN

Albert "Burt" Alvord was sent to the Yuma Territorial Prison from December 8, 1903 until October 9, 1905. Arizona Prison records.

Alma Enterprise, June 7, 1901.

Arizona Daily Star, January 17, 1894.

Arizona Daily Star, January 30, 1897.

Arizona Daily Star, January 16, 1898; Charley checked in to the
    Grand Central Hotel in El Paso, signing as someone from
    Colorado. *El Paso Daily Herald*, September 16, 1898.

Arizona Daily Star, April 11, 1899.

Arizona Daily Star, April 21, 1899; February 24, 1889, *Arizona v.
    Charles R. Hood*, case no. 1046, Pima County, the Honorable
    Judge Culver presiding.

Arizona Weekly Star, April 27, 1899.

Arizona Daily Star, February 18, 1900.

Arizona Daily Star, February 21, 1900.

Arizona Daily Star, August 30, 1901.

Arizona Daily Star, February 6, 1912.

Arizona Daily Star, March 6, 1913.

Arizona Daily Star, March 7, 1913.

Arizona Daily Star, June 22, 1950.

Arizona Republican, June 16, 1891.

Arizona Republican, March 3, 1900. The old newspapers were not
    always consistent or clear with information that they shared
    with other newspapers. I am indebted to my friend and fellow
    historian Marshall Trimble for helping me sort out the series
    of events of the Alvord train robberies.

Arizona Republican, October 18, 1900. Brown admitted to Billy
    Stiles that he'd shot Milton. Brown was given two trials. In the
    first, one man hung up the jury for fifty-two hours, but Brown
    was eventually sentenced to ten years in the penitentiary; hav-
    ing turned states' evidence. George and Lewis Owens were
    each sentenced to four years.

Arizona Republic, October 8, 1901.

Arizona Sentinel, January 2, 1901. Charley took the place of Albert
    Behan, who had held the position for the previous four years.

Arizona Sentinel, September 11, 1901.

Arizona Weekly Citizen, May 21, 1892.

Arizona Weekly Citizen, September 17, 1892. Charley was a member
    of the Tucson gun club, which held shooting competitions at
    the Silver Lake Resort.

Arizona Weekly Citizen, October 27, 1894.

Arizona Weekly Citizen, March 14, 1896.

Arizona Weekly Citizen, May 16, 1896.

Asheville Citizen-Times, Friday, October 29, 1897.

Bisbee Daily Review, May 1, 1903.

Border Vidette, September 24, 1910.

Border Vidette, March 8, 1913.

Charles Bowman was the son of David Alexander Bowman (brother of Anderson's father-in-law Jacob Bowman). Charles was appointed by Governor Kibbey, March 1907, for Cochise County for the Second Judicial District. Bowman had first settled in Tucson, where he worked as clerk of court before moving to Tombstone.

Charley fudged his age by five years when interviewed by the census taker in 1900.

Charley's advocates included US Senator Jeter Pritchard and his brother the former sheriff of Mitchell County, George Pritchard, as well as Judge A. C. Avery, who in 1885 had presided over Anderson's murder trial.

Charley's two friends posted bail. One was Alexander Rossi, president of the Old Pueblo Mining & Milling Company in Tucson, which owned nine claims five miles west of Tucson, mining copper, silver, and gold. W. P. Woods, Charley's other friend, was a member of the Tucson City Council.

Charlotte Observer, November 12, 1933.

El Paso Herald, November 19, 1900.

Daily Times, November 1, 1885.

Daily Alta California, April 11, 1888.

Florence Tribune, July 7, 1900.

Florence Tribune, September 14, 1901.

Holbrook Argus newspaper of Holbrook, Arizona, December 29, 1908, reported the death of Billy Stiles: "News comes from Nevada that Billy Stiles is dead; shot down like a dog for some wrong, either real or fancied. While living in Arizona, Stiles betrayed his friends, robbed right and left, stole and committed murder, and made for himself a reputation that any outlaw might well be proud. He was the Ishmael of the Southwest. His hand was against every man and every man's hand against him. As he lived he died, with none to mourn his loss and no one to envy him his fame; the day of the outlaw is passed, and forever."

Hood was buried in the common grave land in Empalme Municipality, Sonora, Mexico.

I am indebted to historian Matthew Bumgarner for his knowledge of the railroads and for suggesting the numerous trains that Charley likely took when he escaped to the American Southwest.

In his book *Until He Is Dead*, author and former district attorney
Tom Rusher relates conversations he had with Anderson's
grandson, Milton A. Anderson, who remarked, "My father
was conceived in jail." Milton also confirmed Anderson's alias
as Charley Hood. This discovery was the key to finding over
170 newspaper articles about Charley Hood that became the
framework for this story.

John Slaughter had once pronounced Alvord as "fearless."

Lenoir Topic, January 29, 1885.

Los Angeles Times, September 3, 1895.

Los Angeles Times, February 17, 1900. Tom Broderick was Sheriff
of Santa Cruz County.

New York Times, September 23, 1900.

Tom "Black Jack" Ketchum should not be confused with another
outlaw named William "Black Jack" Christian. Stein's Pass was
an 1880 settlement built along the Southern Pacific Railroad.

Oasis, March 21, 1896.

Oasis, October 3, 1896. In 1890, the US Census counted 1,194
people living on the United States side of Nogales.

Oasis, August 21, 1897.

Oasis, August 13, 1898.

Oasis, May 13, 1899; *Arizona Sentinel*, May 20, 1899; *El Paso Daily
Herald*, May 27, 1899. The *Arizona Sentinel*, September 2, 1899,
reported that Charley's guard salary for third quarter 1899
was $80.00. His dates of employment are per Yuma Territorial
Penitentiary records, Greater Arizona Collections, Arizona
State University.

Oasis, January 27, 1900.

Oasis, September 15, 1900.

Oasis, April 29, 1905. In 1905, Charley was appointed deputy
assessor of Santa Cruz County territory, and held this position until 1908, per *Charlotte Observer*, November 12, 1933.

Oasis, May 6, 1905.

Oasis, April 15, 1911.

Oasis, October 19, 1912; Empalme is on the south-central coast of
the Mexican state of Sonora.

Morning Union, April 13, 1888.

Named for Jack Hagerman, made wealthy though mining silver
near Aspen, Colorado; he joined the railroad. Mining became
an impetus for developing the railroad in the West.

Reno Gazette-Journal, December 22, 1888.

San Francisco Call, July 2, 1900. Charley Hood, "well known throughout Arizona," was running for sheriff of Santa Cruz County against Tom Broderick, who became deputy sheriff. *Arizona Republic*, Phoenix, August 22, 1900. *Arizona Daily Star*, September 4, 1900.

San Jose Mercury-News, April 13, 1888.

Second Judicial District Court Records of the Territory of Arizona, Cochise County, Book 11, pp. 9 and 172, the Honorable Fletcher Doan presiding.

Semi-Weekly Messenger, January 18, 1901, reported that Governor Russell, whose term ended in January 1901, had refused to grant Anderson a pardon. "Ex-Judge Avery made another attempt yesterday to get a pardon, but failed."

State v. Anderson, February 1, 1885, Evidence, Declarations, Conspiracy, Res Gestae, Removed, Record, North Carolina.

Billy Stiles's home was in Pinal County.

"The best way to describe Trickster is to say simply that the boundary is where he will be found – sometimes drawing the line, sometimes crossing it, sometimes erasing or moving it, but always there." Lewis Hyde, *Trickster Makes This World*, 2010.

The film *Sergeant York* depicts a type of saloon similar to Brickwood's Exchange Saloon in Nogales; in the film, the saloon was between Kentucky and Tennessee.

The origin of the secret service employment story is unknown, but it is certain that Harris communicated this to the press, as numerous newspaper articles surfaced with that false information. Harris was a correspondent for the *New York Times* and would have been considered a reliable source for the story. His motivation for planting this disinformation is unclear. It is also possible that Pritchard submitted the disinformation in the pardon application in order to protect Anderson. In Anderson's application, had he asserted this misinformation? After all, had he told the truth of his whereabouts and doings for the past decades, and the pardon had been refused (as it was), then he'd have divulged his whereabouts, making himself a target for the law after blowing the cover he'd spent so many years cultivating in order to stay alive.

The word "marshal" comes from an old German word meaning "master of the horse." Marshals and sheriffs could deputize men from the county and assemble a posse comitatus, which means "power of the county."

Tombstone Weekly Epitaph, December 16, 1900.

Tucson Citizen, August 26, 1889. David Alexander Bowman had
served as postmaster in 1868 in Burnsville and eventually
became a "special land and timber agent" in Arizona. *Arizona
Daily Star*, Tucson, September 10, 1889. His son Charles W.
Bowman also migrated west with Charley, eventually becoming an attorney in Tombstone. In 1896, the *Arizona Weekly
Citizen* in Tucson reported: "D. A. Bowman leaves for his house
in the east in the morning. Chas Bowman and Chas Hood have
gone on a short visit to the Silver Bell district."

Tucson Citizen, March 19, 1894; *Arizona Daily Star*, March 21, 1894;
trial was on March 20.

Tucson Citizen, September 9, 1901.

Tucson Citizen, April 27, 1955. Re-printed December 3, 2012.

United States district attorney Robert E. Morrison prosecuted
the Fairbank train robbery case in Tucson. The Los Angeles
Times, February 1900; *Arizona Daily Star*, February 22, 1900.

US Marshals, Arizona Territory, 1864–1912; Oath/1 page, Library
of Congress. Hood was placed under Colonel William Griffith.

Charley Hood's death was reported on March 10, 1913, by
Empalme Police Commissioner L. L. Aguirre; translated from
Spanish: "In the city of Guaymas, state of Sonora at five o'clock
in the afternoon of the tenth day of March, 1913, I, Manuel
Castañeda, Judge of the Civil Registry of this place, attest to
have in sight and to be filed, 3 copies of death certificates sent
today to this court by the police commissioner of Empalme,
one of said copies reading as follows: *In the Precinct of Empalme,
District of Guaymas, municipality of the same name, on the fifth
day of March of nineteen hundred and thirteen, the undersigned
Commissioner states, that: at half past three in the morning of said
day, was killed by a bullet in the heart on the premises of the Hotel
of this station the American Charles H. Hood of fifty-five years of
age, of trade watchman, single, not having knowledge of the rest
of his identifying information.*" [Hood's correct initial (his alias)
was R, not H.]

Sources by Chapter

1. Emotional Insanity

Daily Journal, November 24, 1851.
North-Carolina Star, November 26, 1851.
North-Carolinian, November 29, 1851.
Raleigh Register, November 19, 1851.
Tri-Weekly Commercial, November 20, 1851.
United States Congressional Serial Set, 1872 (Google Books).

2. Bloody Madison

Asheville News, June 24, 1869.
Case of Nancy Franklin, September 24, 1883.
Deposition H case of Nancy Franklin number 176.751, October 4, 1883.
Exhibit in the case of Nancy Franklin, February 10, 1875.
H. Baker commissioner of pensions report, February 17, 1875.
M. E. Weeks report to the commissioner of pensions, February 17, 1875.
Mr. O'Hara, the committee on invalid pensions, in the Act for relief of Nancy Franklin.
North Carolina Madison County Court of Pleas in quarter sessions 1854.
Probate file of Drury Norton, NC State Archives.
Proof of widowed mother's dependence.
Single affidavit of Mr. John Shelton and John W. Ball.

3. The Tragedy of Montraville Ray

Asheville Citizen-Times, December 10, 1933.
Asheville Messenger, June 19, 1850.
Asheville News, October 30, 1856.
Asheville News, August 12, 1858.
Charlotte Democrat, April 26, 1864.
Daily Confederate, April 28, 1864.

Eleventh Census of the United States Special Schedule of Surviving
 Soldiers, Jack's Creek.
Farmer and Mechanic, March 15, 1911.
Fayetteville Weekly Observer, May 2, 1864.
New York Herald, July 29, 1870.
Raleigh Daily Telegram, February 17, 1871.
Raleigh Post, April 5, 1900.
Rutherford Star, October 8, 1870.
Township, Yancey County, enumerated June 1890.
Tri-Weekly Era, August 31, 1872.
Union Provost Marshals' File Relating to Individual Civilians,
 National Archives and Records Administration.
Western Sentinel, February 4, 1921.
Wilmington Journal, October 7, 1870.
Wilmington Morning Star, October 12, 1870.
Yancey County Criminal Actions Papers, North Carolina State
 Archives.
Yancey Record, June 15, 1950.
Yancey Record, November 8, 1851.

4. The Weston Family Massacre

Carolina Watchman, May 5, 1871.
Carolina Era, November 18, 1871.
Charlotte Democrat, July 30, 1872.
Charlotte Democrat, October 29, 1872.
Congressional Testimony; Conditions of Affairs in the Southern
 States, *United States Congressional Serial Set*, 1872.
Monmouth Democrat, June 1, 1871.
New York Daily Herald, May 3, 1871.
New York Times, December 25, 1898.
Rutherford Star, November 18, 1871.
Southern Home, May 9, 1871.
Southern Home, October 28, 1872.
State v. Columbus Adair, 66 NC 298 (NC 1872) Supreme Court of
 North Carolina.
Tri-Weekly Era, November 18, 1871.
Western Vindicator, June 3, 1872.
Western Vindicator, January 12, 1899.

5. The Whipping of Aaron Biggerstaff

Congressional Testimony of Plato Durham.
Congressional Testimony of James M. Justice.
Greensboro Patriot, October 5, 1871.
New Berne Times, September 23, 1871.
Raleigh Sentinel, September 13, 1871.
Rutherford Star, April 29, 1871.

6. The Hanging of Jack Lambert

Asheville Weekly Citizen, July 15, 1886.
Asheville Advance, June 12, 1886
News and Observer, July 29, 1886.
New York Times, July 31, 1886.
State v. Lambert, 93 NC 618 (NC 1885), Supreme Court of North
    Carolina.
Wilmington Morning Star, July 4, 1885.

7. "Buncombe's Boasted Bastille Busted"

1884 Annual Report of the Adjutant General, State of North
    Carolina, https://digital.ncdcr.gov/digital/collection/p249
    901coll22/id/28029
Asheville Citizen-Times, May 23, 1885.
Asheville Citizen-Times, July 22, 1885.
Asheville Citizen-Times, July 23, 1885.
Asheville Weekly Citizen, April 24, 1884.
Asheville Weekly Citizen, May 1, 1912.
Biblical Recorder, August 24, 1881.
Charlotte Democrat, May 9, 1884.
Carolina Watchman, March 20, 1884.
Carolina Watchman, July 16, 1885.
Charlotte Democrat, April 25, 1884.
Charlotte Democrat, July 17, 1885.
Charlotte Democrat, April 19, 1889.
Charlotte Home-Democrat, May 9, 1884.
Charlotte Observer, May 29, 1907.
Charlotte Observer, November 12, 1933.
Daily News, January 6, 1929.

Evening Visitor, March 2, 1880.

Gastonia Gazette, October 18, 1900.

Lenoir Topic, March 19, 1884.

Lenoir Topic, May 28, 1884.

Lenoir Topic, January 21, 1885.

Lenoir Topic, January 29, 1885.

Lenoir Topic, February 18, 1885.

Lenoir Topic, May 13, 1885.

Lenoir Topic, July 22, 1885.

Lenoir Topic, June 27, 1888.

News and Observer, October 24, 1882.

News and Observer, February 24, 1884.

News and Observer, March 2, 1884.

News and Observer, March 4, 1884.

News and Observer, March 14, 1884.

Newton Enterprise, December 6, 1884.

North Carolina Civil Actions Court Papers, 1878 to 1880, NC Archives.

North Carolina Reports, vol. 92, Cases Argued and Determined in the Supreme Court of North Carolina, NC Archives.

North Carolina State Supreme Court Case Files, 1884-1885, NC Archives.

North Carolina State Supreme Court Case Files, 1800-1886, NC Archives.

Richmond Dispatch, August 20, 1885.

Semi-Weekly Asheville Citizen, May 23, 1885.

Semi-Weekly Asheville Citizen, July 22, 1885.

State v. W. A. Anderson, Mitchell County Justice's court, NC Archives.

State v. W. A. Anderson, North Carolina Supreme Court, February 1, 1885, 92 NC 732 (NC 1885).

State v. W. A. Anderson, July 22, 1880, NC Archives.

Weekly Raleigh Register, February 18, 1885.

Weekly Star, May 29, 1885.

8. The Lynching of Bob Brackett

Asheville Citizen-Times, August 9, 1897.

Asheville Citizen-Times, August 10, 1897.

Asheville Citizen-Times, August 11, 1897.

Asheville Citizen-Times, August 12, 1897.

Asheville Citizen-Times, August 13, 1897.
Asheville Citizen-Times, September 27, 1897.
Asheville Citizen-Times, September 12, 1899.
Goldsboro Headlight, August 19, 1897.
Press-Visitor, August 12, 1897.
Messenger, October 1, 1897.
Tarborough Southerner, September 30, 1897.
Tri-Weekly Examiner, October 1, 1869.

9. Murder in Big Bend

Burlington Daily Times, April 6, 1931.
Asheville Citizen-Times, April 7, 1931.
Asheville Citizen-Times, April 14, 1931.
Asheville Citizen-Times, April 15, 1931.
Asheville Citizen-Times, April 16, 1931.
Asheville Citizen-Times, April 17, 1931.
Asheville Citizen-Times, April 19, 1931.
Asheville Citizen-Times, April 21, 1931.
Asheville Citizen-Times, July 15, 1931.
Asheville Citizen-Times, July 22, 1931.
Asheville Citizen-Times, November 5, 1931.
Burlington Daily Times, April 14, 1931.
Charlotte Observer, April 4, 1931.
Charlotte Observer, April 17, 1931.
Charlotte Observer, April 22, 1931.
Charlotte Observer, August 2, 1931.
Statesville Record, April 20, 1931.
Statesville Record, July 23, 1931.

10. Fugitive Justice

Alma Enterprise, Kansas, June 7, 1901.
Arizona Republican, June 16, 1891.
Arizona Daily Star, January 17, 1894.
Arizona Daily Star, March 21, 1894.
Arizona Daily Star, January 30, 1897.
Arizona Daily Star, January 16, 1898.
Arizona Daily Star, April 11, 1899.
Arizona Daily Star, April 21, 1899.

Arizona Daily Star, February 18, 1900.
Arizona Daily Star, February 21, 1900.
Arizona Daily Star, February 22, 1900.
Arizona Daily Star, August 30, 1901.
Arizona Daily Star, May 18, 1902.
Arizona Daily Star, April 28, 1905.
Arizona Daily Star, February 21, 1906.
Arizona Daily Star, August 6, 1907.
Arizona Daily Star, February 6, 1912.
Arizona Daily Star, March 7, 1913.
Arizona Daily Star, June 22, 1950.
Arizona Republic, October 18, 1900.
Arizona Republic, October 8, 1901.
Arizona Republican, March 3, 1900.
Arizona Republican, October 18, 1900.
Arizona Sentinel, May 20, 1899.
Arizona Sentinel, September 11, 1901.
Arizona Sentinel, January 2, 1901.
Arizona Weekly Citizen, May 21, 1892.
Arizona Weekly Citizen, September 17, 1892.
Arizona Weekly Citizen, October 27, 1894.
Arizona Weekly Citizen, March 14, 1896.
Arizona Weekly Citizen, May 16, 1896.
Arizona Weekly Star, April 27, 1899.
Bisbee Daily Review, May 1, 1903.
Border Vidette, May 2, 1903.
Border Vidette, June 13, 1903.
Border Vidette, September 17, 1904.
Border Vidette, February 4, 1905.
Border Vidette, October 26, 1907.
Border Vidette, September 5, 1908.
Border Vidette, September 24, 1910.
Border Vidette, March 8, 1913.
Charlotte Observer, November 12, 1933.
Daily Alta California, April 11, 1888.
Daily Times, November 1, 1885.
El Paso Daily Herald, September 16, 1898.
El Paso Herald, November 19, 1900.
Florence Tribune, July 7, 1900.
Lenoir Topic, January 29, 1885.
Los Angeles Herald, December 11, 1893.

Los Angeles Times, September 30, 1895.
Los Angeles Times, February 17, 1900.
Morning Union, April 13, 1888.
Oasis, March 21, 1896.
Oasis, October 3, 1896.
Oasis, August 21, 1897.
Oasis, August 13, 1898.
Oasis, May 13, 1899.
Oasis, January 27, 1900.
Oasis, September 15, 1900.
Oasis, September 13, 1902.
Oasis, January 16, 1904.
Oasis, January 14, 1905.
Oasis, April 29, 1905.
Oasis, May 6, 1905.
Oasis, August 11, 1906.
Oasis, January 26, 1907.
Oasis, May 18, 1907.
Oasis, April 15, 1911.
Oasis, October 19, 1912.
Periódico Oficial del Estado de Sonora, January 19, 1907.
Reno Gazette-Journal, December 22, 1888.
San Francisco Call, July 2, 1900.
San Jose Mercury-News, April 13, 1888.
Second Judicial District Court Records of the Territory of Arizona,
    Cochise County.
Tombstone Weekly Epitaph, December 16, 1900.
Tucson Citizen, August 26, 1889.
Tucson Citizen, March 19, 1894.
Tucson Citizen, September 9, 1901.
Tucson Citizen, April 27, 1955.

Miscellaneous Sources

United States Federal Census.
Death Certificates.
Records of Confederate Soldiers.

Illustration Credits

Title page and Acknowledgment page artwork: by Bryan Koontz.

Maps of Western North Carolina counties designed by Lamar Marshall and Nadia Dean.

Page before Chapter 1: Painting by Bryan Koontz.

Photo of William Waightstill Avery, courtesy of the North Carolina Collection Photographic Archives, Portrait Collection.

Early nineteenth-century engraving, "Cowhiding Slaves," stock photo.

Mountain Hotel newspaper advertisement as it appeared in the September 3, 1851, issue of the *Semi-Weekly Standard*.

Derringer pistol, private collection.

Sketch of Nancy Shelton Norton Franklin: Bryan Koontz, based on the only known surviving photograph of Nancy.

Photograph of Colonel George Washington Kirk and his wife Mariah; unknown Civil War-period photographer, public domain, from the collection of Leon Kirk.

Photograph in Shelton Laurel Massacre sidebar, courtesy of the Smoky Mountain National Park Foundation.

Flag of the 16th Regiment North Carolina Confederate troops, courtesy of John Woloski.

Newspaper clipping with the names of those who deserted the 16th regiment, as it appeared in the August 21, 1862, issue of the Asheville News.

Photograph of Montraville Ray, courtesy of the Ray family.

1862 illustration "Southern Volunteers," courtesy of the Library of Congress.

Montraville Ray's Provost Marshal Card, courtesy of the National Archives, Washington, DC.

1870 photograph of Colonel George Kirk, photographer unknown, public domain.

Pen and ink drawing "Egypt Township" (Yancey County) by Bryan Koontz.

Photograph of Rutherford County, Freemane Camp, Chimney Rock, two-story log building, courtesy of UNC Asheville Special Collections and University Archives.

1872 drawing "Visit of the Ku-Klux" by Frank Bellew, courtesy of the Library of Congress.

Photograph of Randolph Abbott Shotwell, courtesy of the State Archives of North Carolina.

Nineteenth-century engraving, "KKK Murder Prevented," stock photo.

1874 wood engraving, "The Union as it was; the lost cause, worse than slavery" by Thomas Nast, courtesy of the Library of Congress.

Photograph of Plato Durham, courtesy of D. Stoddard.

Photograph of Jennie Reece Lambert, the author's second great-grand aunt, courtesy of Nadia Dean.

Pen and ink drawing "A View of Bryson City" by Bryan Koontz.

The 1898 Hanging of James Fleming Parker in Prescott, Arizona, stock photo, public domain.

Photograph of an 1885 ticket to observe the last public hanging in Daviess County, Missouri, courtesy of Daviess County Historical Society.

Photograph, circa November 2, 1896, of Evelyn "Vicey" Reese York and Doc Gibson, probably on their wedding day, courtesy of Nadia Dean.

1880 Smith and Wesson advertisement, courtesy of Smith & Wesson, Inc.

Arrest warrant issued July 22, 1880, Mitchell County Superior Court records.

Recognizance Bond, Mitchell County Superior Court records.

United States Internal Revenue Stamp, courtesy of the US Treasury Department.

Newspaper clipping of the *Voice* newspaper masthead, November 5, 1880.

Photograph of circa 1870 Flaubert pistol, courtesy of Frédéric Dulyere.

Photograph of 1870 Webley .44-caliber pistol, public domain.

Pen and ink drawing "On the Banks of the Big Ivy River" by Bryan Koontz.

$800 reward newspaper clipping, *Asheville Citizen-Times*, July 23, 1885.

Photograph of a 1930 lynching, stock photo.

Photograph of a 1930s moonshiner and his still, stock photo.

Pen and ink drawing "Cataloochee" by Bryan Koontz.

"The Moonshiner's Home" by Julian Rix, published in *Harper's Weekly*, October 1886.

Digital image from a glass-plate photograph of Oma Hicks-Brown and Sheriff Jake Lowe, as it appeared in the April 15, 1931, issue of the *Asheville Citizen-Times*.

Photograph of the East Tennessee and Western North Carolina Railroad, public domain.

1887 photograph of an American cowboy by John C. H. Grabill, courtesy of the Library of Congress.

The Boca Brewing Company, courtesy of the Verdi History Center.

1880 photo Boca Hotel, courtesy of Truckee-Donner Historical Society.

Photograph of Arizona cowboy on his horse, stock photo.

1888 Photograph of the Silver Lake Resort by Leo Goldschmidt, courtesy of University of Arizona Library Digital Collections.

Arrest warrant for fornication and adultery, Mitchell County court records.

Photograph circa 1900 of a young man and his bicycle, stock photo.

1907 Photograph of cowboys in Old Tascosa, Texas, courtesy of the Library of Congress.

"Orient Saloon at Bisbee, Arizona, Faro game," courtesy of the National Archives at College Park, Maryland.

Charles R. Hood, Oath of US Field Deputy Marshal, April 18, 1898, courtesy of the National Archives at Washington, DC.

Photograph of Thomas Edward "Black Jack" Ketchum, author unknown, public domain.

1901 photograph of the hanging of Thomas Edward "Black Jack" Ketchum in New Mexico Territory, author unknown, public domain.

Wells Fargo robbery notice, courtesy of Wells Fargo Corporate Archives.

1899 photograph of Hagerman Pass, Beinecke Rare Book and Manuscript Library, Yale University, public domain.

Arrest warrant for Charles Hood, courtesy Pima County Arizona, courtesy of Arizona State Library, Archives and Public Records.

Photograph of Frank Leslie, photographer unknown, public domain.

Photograph of Texas Ranger John Slaughter, courtesy of the John Slaughter Ranch, Douglas, Arizona.

Photograph of Arizona lawman and pioneer Jeff Milton (1861-1947), public domain, Wikimedia Commons.

Photograph of Fairbank Railroad Depot, Arizona, circa 1900, stock photo.

Fairbank Train Robbery painting by Cal Peters, courtesy of the Postal History Foundation.

Photograph of Billy Stiles and George Smalley, courtesy of the Arizona Historical Society, Tucson.

First National Bank of Nogales Territorial note, private collection.

Charley Hood Maps designed by Lamar Marshall and Nadia Dean.

Map of Charley Hood's travels designed by Lamar Marshall and Nadia Dean.

Index

Bolded page numbers indicate photographs and illustrations.

A

Adair, Charles 152
Adair murderers/arsonists 42–47, 49, 184
adultery offense **142**
Aeschylus 8
Aiken, Mitchell 110
alcohol. *See also* saloons
   alcoholism 70, 84
   blockaders 40, 65
   brandy 42, 65
   bribes 2, 67
   common denominator xii, 70
   moonshiners **125, 128**
   production/sale 184
   Prohibition 121, 125
   Reconstruction 70
   spirituous liquor 27
   tax and Bureau of Internal Revenue 41, 65, 70, 90
   tax stamp 90
   Temperance Movement 70
   US Deputy Marshals 70
   whiskey 40, 56, 65, 174
Alexander Chapel 109
Allen (Colonel) 20
Allison, Bragg 70
Alvord, Burt 150, 152, 154, 156
Amendments 56
Anderson, Jesse Woodson (Rev.) 189
Anderson, Milton A. 197
Anderson, Waightstill "Wates" Avery
   assaults 87, 92
   Big Ivy River 106
   character 85, 98
   escapes 93, 103, 163
   deputy collector 90
   family 86, 87, 97, 101, 106, 162, 197
   gauger 90
   mine stake 88

    pseudonym 162

    reward **107**

    Until He Is Dead (Rusher) 197

Appalachia 30, **84**

Appomattox 65

Arizona Territory

    Arizona Weekly Citizen 141

    Casa Grande 152

    Cochise County 150

    cowboys 140

    Fairbank Railroad Depot **153**

    Frank Leslie **149**

    Oriental Saloon 149

    Saddle Rock Restaurant 149

    Silver Lake Resort 140

    smuggled Chinese migrants 149

    Tombstone jail 154

    train robberies 150, 153

    Tucson Daily Citizen 150

    Yuma Territorial Penitentiary 149

Arthur, John Preston 35, 39

Ashe, J. (Judge) 68

Aunt T. 105

Austin, J. F. 118

Austin, Mary "Polly" Elizabeth 182

Avery, Alphonso Calhoun (Judge) 190

Avery (Judge) 101, 163

Avery, William Waightstill "W. W." 2, **3**, 7, 11, 101, 180, 190

Aycock (Governor) 163

B

Baker, H. (Commissioner) 181

Ball, John W. 182

Ballman, John W. 24

Banks, W. B. 36

Battle, William Horn (Judge) 4

Baynard, Martin 41, 47, 51, 185

Beaumont Gap 115

Beck, William 138

Benata (Sheriff) 145

Betts, J. T. (Rev.) 114

bicycles **143**

Big Bend 120, 127

Biggerstaff brothers feud 57, 58, 185

Big Ivy River 105, 106
Big Ivy settlement 113
Big Laurel settlement 12
Bircher, Charles 152
Black Jack Gang 145, 146
Black Mountains 29
Black Mountains Boys 27, 28
Black, W. P. 119
Blalock, John 88
blockaders 40, 65
Bloody Madison 14, 20
*The Blue, the Gray, and the Green—Toward an Environmental History of
        the Civil* War (ed. Drake) 183
Boca Hotel **139**
bondsmen 89
Bookhart (Captain) 117
Bowman, Jacob Weaver (Judge) 83, 93, 105
Brackett, Bob 110, 116, 193
brandy 42, 65. *See also* alcohol
Bravin, George 155
Bravo Juan 153
bribes 2, 47, 67, 151
Broderick, Tom (Sheriff) 154
Brown, Andrew Jackson "A. J." 33, 35
Brown, Bob 153, 154
Brown (Commissioner) 111
Brown, Joel Canary "Scott" 126, 127, 131, 134
Brown, Sylvester "Vester" 123, 126, 131
Bryant, George 119
Buchanan, J. M. 98
Buchanan, Milton 92
Buchanan, Sherman 97
Bumgarner, Matthew 197
Bureau of Internal Revenue 41, 65, 90, 128
Burgess S. Gaither 180
Burleson, Bill 92
Burleson, Stephen 92
Burts, Matt 151, 153
Butch Cassidy Gang 146
Butler, John 97
Bynum, John 9
Byrd, Hutson 189

C

Caldwell, Tod (Governor) 34, 59
Calhoun, John C. 3
California 137, 138, 141, 155
Calloway, Lum 105
Carl Alton Miller 133
Carpenter, J. B. 61
Carr (governor) 163
Carter, Melvin 163
Cassidy, Butch 146
Cataloochee settlement 126, 127
cemeteries 8, 26, 39, 80, 133, 193
Chambers, Joe (Deputy) 110
Cherokees
    Cherokee Indian Reservation 80
    A Demand of Blood—The Cherokee War of 1776 (Dean) 180
    forced removal 182
    Old Cherokee Boarding School Campus Cemetery 80
    Quallatown Cherokee Indian Reservation 71
    scouts 29
    treaty 2
    Union sympathizers 11, 18
Chinese migrants 149
Civil War
    alcoholism 70, 175
    Black Mountains Boys 27, 28
    *The Blue, the Gray, and the Green—Toward an Environmental History of
        the Civil War* (ed. Drake) 183
    casualties 84
    Col. George Kirk, turncoat
        Col. George Kirk, turncoat 11
    Confederate Army
        16th NC Regiment flag 27
        attacks/captures 21, 30, 33
        burns Norton home 21
        Cherokee Indians scouts 29
        Cherokee Jack Lambert 65
        Col. George Kirk, turncoat 18, **32**
        Col. J. B. Palmer 30
        Collett Leventhorpe, *The English Confederate—The Life of a Civil War
            General, 1815-1889* (Cole & Foley) 185
        conditions 28
        deserters/defectors 28
        Gen. McElroy 30
        George Franklin enlists 23

   hoarding salt 20
   Home Guard raided 30
   horses stolen 53
   Maj. Gen. George H. Stoneman 19
   Red Strings (Heroes of America) 53
   Samuel Biggerstaff enlists 53
   secesh 41
   sympathizers 30
   terrorizes vulnerable 20
   thievery 21
   vs. Unionists 19, **29**
 conscription/drafting 19, 28, **29**
 deserters/defectors
   Confederate Army 11, 18, 23, 28, 183, 184
   roving marauder bands 21
   Union Army 181
 familial violence 53
 Union Army
   3rd NC Mounted Infantry 18, 35
   Burnsville sympathizers 30
   coffee 28
   Col. George Kirk, turncoat 11, 18, **32**
   Company D, 4th Infantry, 3rd Division 126
   horse thefts 53
   informants 56
   Norton boys betrayed 18
   pensions 24
   protects voting rights 56
   Provost Marshal oath **31**
   salt deprivation 20
   secession 11, 19, 53
   vs. Confederates 20, **29**
Clairborne, Billy 149
Clanton Gang 149
code of honor 10
Coleman, James S. 110
Collett Leventhorpe, *The English Confederate—The Life of a Civil War
    General, 1815-1889* (Cole & Foley) 176
Colorado 151
Congress 11, 61
conscription/drafting 19, 28. *See also* Civil War
Councill, Tode 99
Councill, W. B. 99
court week 99

cowboys **38, 137,** 140, **143**
cowhiding **5,** 185
Craig, Locke (Attorney) 114
Culver (Judge) 141

D

Davidson (Attorney) 75
Davidson, Mrs. Samuel 118
deathbed confession/testimony 16, 81
A Demand of Blood—The Cherokee War of 1776 (Dean) 180
Democrats 54, 57, 96, 186. *See also* votes; *See also* politics
Denver & Rio Grande Western Railroad 146
DePriest, Decatur 57
deputizing 198. *See also* US Deputy Marshals
Deputy Marshals 70
Derringer. *See* firearms
deserters. *See* Civil War
Dodge, J. F. 146
Downing, Bill 152
Dragoon Mountains 153
Dunlap, Three-Fingered Jack 151, 153
Durham, Plato **62**
Dutch vs. Irish 138

E

Earp, Wyatt 149
emancipation 31, 56, 117, 189
emotional insanity 9
Enforcement Acts 54
English Common Law 79
Eppinga, Jane 142
Erwin, John W. (Dr.) 5
Ewart (Judge) 113
Exchange Saloon 142

F

failure to appear 35
Fairbank Railroad **153,** 199
familial violence 14, 53, 121
famine/poverty 31. *See also* Civil War
Farmer and Mechanic newspaper 45
faro game **144**
Fifteenth Amendment 56

Finley (Marshal) 145
firearms
  .41-caliber Swiss rifle 127
  British bulldog pistol 103, **104**
  carry authorization 89
  Colt single-action Army revolver 144, **145**
  concealed weapons 141
  Derringer .50-caliber pistol **7**
  Flaubert 91
  Flaubert handgun **91**
  shotgun 153
  Smith & Wesson **86**, 92
First National Bank **159**
Fleming, Samuel 1, 2, 3, 7
fornication offense **142**
Fourteenth Amendment 56
Franklin, George W. 18, 23, 24, 25
Franklin, Nancy Shelton Norton
  family 12, 14, 21, 25
  fits of rage, divorce 23
  house fire 21
  husbands/lovers 13, 18, 24
  photograph and likeness **13**
  property independence 23
  Shelton Laurel Massacre 20
  sons murdered 21
  Union pension 24, 26, 180
  Union spy 22
free suffrage 2

G

Gaither, Burgess S. (attorney) 7
gambling house 140
Garrett-Hillcrest Cemetery 133
Garrison, W. T. 98
Gates, Varnell 128, 131, 185
gauger income 90
GEM Saloon **142**
Gibbs, James 37
Gibson, Doc **85**
Gill, James (Dr.) 110
Gilmer, John A. (Judge) 66
gold. *See* mines
Gouge, S. C. 98

governors, death sentence appeals 59, 69

Grant, Ulysses S. 45, 59, 186

Graves (Judge) 94

Green, Charles 98, 139

Greene, Thomas C. 87, 99

Greenlee (Fleming), Hannah 2, 4

Gregory (Captain) 71

Grover, Burt 156

guns. *See* firearms

Gunter, Mr. 14

H

Hagerman's Pass **147**, 148, 198

Hague, J. A. (Dr.) 35

Hammilton, Mose 62

handguns. *See* firearms

Hanes, Squire (Magistrate) 44

Hanging Dog Baptist Cemetery 39

hangings. *See also* Ku Klux Klan

  atmosphere 76, 79

  death penalty 79

  English Common Law 79

  gallows **78**, 79, 146

  Harper's Weekly 55

  Lambert's last request 79

  Shipp and Smith **116**

  souvenir rope 78, 116

  ticket **79**

  time line 184

Harris, John C. L. 163, 198

Haynie, William 189

Heap, John G. 87, 89, 99, 190

Hemphill schoolhouse 116

Henderson County 94

Henderson, Dan 102, 107, 184

Henderson, Kittie 109, 193

Henry, James L. (Judge) 48, 49

Hensley, Abe 105

Heroes of America (Red Strings) 53

Herritage, W. T. 118

Hester, Joseph G. (Marsha) 58

Hickey (Sheriff) 95

Hicks, Merritt Linville 123

Hildreth, Bill (Sheriff) 145

The History of a Southern State—North Carolina (Leffler & Newsome) 180
Hoey, William M. 149
Holden (Governor) 32
Home Guard 28, 30, 183
Hood, Charley
  arrests 141, 142
  assaults 138, **148**, 150, 158
  character 135, 149, 162
  Deputy Marshal firearm 145
  GEM Saloon **142**
  grand jury 158
  jobs 140, 144, 146, 149, 156, 159
  killed 162
  kills bear 145
  mining 160
    map **160**
  Nora Anderson, wife 162
  pardon requests 156, 157, 163
  pseudonym 162
  railroad **136, 147**
  robbed 144
  solitary life 137
  surrenders 139
  travels **161, 165**
Horton, Ed 91
House of Commons, North Carolina 1, 3, 10
human smuggling 149
Huntley, Will 119
Hyams, Wash 99

I

insanity, emotional 9
insurrection 32
Invisible Empire 54
Irish vs. Dutch 138
Ishmael of the Southwest (Billy Stiles) **155**

J

Jackson, Andrew (President) 1
Jackson, Mrs. 61
jails/prisons xii
  Bakersville County 68
  Buncombe County, the "Bastille" 68, 83, 94

Caldwell County 96
Henderson County 94
jailbreaks 103, 114, 135, 162
Marshall County 34
Mitchell County 95
South Carolina prison 53
Tombstone 154
Yuma Territorial Penitentiary 149
James Reed (Constable) 139
James, W. A. (Police Chief) 118
Jarvis (Governor) 93
John T. Brickwood 142
Jones, Bragg 65, 67, 69
Jones, E. P. 5
Jones (General) 95
Jones, T. A. (General) 186
Jones, Willie 70, 81
Joyce, Anthony 158
Justice, James M. 45, 59, 176, 186

K

Keener, Marshall "Marsh" 86, 99
Keith, James A. (Colonel) 20
Ketchum, Tom "Black Jack" 145, **146**
The Kingdom of Madison (Wellman) 181
Kirk, George (Colonel)
　3rd NC Mounted Infantry 18
　Kirk-Holden War 32
　Kirk's men 32, 35, 37
　lenient leave policy 24
　Norton boys killed 181
　photograph **18, 32**
　turncoat 11
Kosterlitzy (Colonel) 145
Ku Klux Klan 31
　Adair sons blame 48, 50
　arises 35, **54**
　attacks 57, 58, 59, 60, 61
　Decatur DePriest 57
　Democrats 50
　hearings postponed 58
　Invisible Empire 54
　Plato Durham 62
　Randolph Shotwell **45**

Samuel Biggerstaff 54
Visit of the Ku-Klux **43**
White League 55

L

Lambert, Andrew Jackson "Jack"
  kills R. Wilson 81
  last request 79
  legend 80
  Louisa Jane "Jennie" Reece, second wife **66**, 187, 192
  modern-day relatives xii
  saw Lee's surrender 65
  trials/sentences 66, **69**
  watches escape 104
  youth 65
Landers, Tilman 15
land of the sky 128
Layton, E. E. 148, 149
Ledbetter, Arthur (Sheriff) 128, 129
Ledford, Milt 118, 119
Lenoir, William (General) 8, 180
Lenoir, W. W. 8
Leslie, Frank **149**
Lincoln, Abraham 11
Lincolnites 19. *See also* Civil War: Union Army
liquor. *See* alcohol
Little Laurel settlement 12
Logan, George (Judge) 57, 58
Lowe (Sheriff) 129, **133**
Lusk, Virgil S. (Colonel) 115
lynching. *See also* Ku Klux Klan
  Brackett 113
  Governor Jarvis statement 95
  Lynch Law 117
  mob frenzies 113, 117, 186, 194
  Shipp and Smith **116**
Lyons, Captain 30

M

Madison, Robert Lee 77, 80
manslaughter vs. murder 16
martial law 32
Matney, Lee (Sheriff) 145

McCahon, J. H. 162
McCall (Attorney) 114
McClellan, W. H. 37
McDonald (Deputy) 111
McElroy, General John W. 30
McGaha, Frank 127, 129
McGaha, James 56
McGaha, John 123
Merrimon, Augustus S. (Attorney) 99
Mexico 142, 145, 159
Miller, Carl Alton 132
Miller, Ceborn "Cebe" 91, 97
Miller, Howard 24
Miller, J. C. 97
Miller, Oma "Omy" Hicks Naillon Brown
    arrested 130
    husbands/lovers 122, 124, 126
    parents 121
    photograph **133**
    Up on Big Pigeon 134
Milton, Jeff (Texas Ranger) 151, **153**
mines 160
    claim jumper 88
    Flat Rock Mine 88
    gold 141
    mica 181
    mine rights dispute 91
    Ray Mica mine 179
    silver 198
moonshine **125, 128.** *See also* alcohol
    Moonshine Wars (Dean) 189
Morehead (Avery), Mary Corrina 2
Morgan (Deputy) 102
Morgan, Mrs. 44
Morganton cemetery 8
Morris, J. W. 119
Moseley, Charles 105, 186
Mott, John 57
Mountain Hotel 6, **7**
Mount Olive Baptist Church 193
Mount Olive Cemetery 26
Mullen, Sid 154
murders profiled
    Andrew Jackson Brown 30, 33

Drury Norton 14
Ed Horton 93
lynching
   Brackett 113
   Governor Jarvis statement 95
   Lynch Law 117
   mob frenzies 113, 117, 186, 194
   Shipp and Smith **116**
Richard "Dick" Wilson 67
Samuel Fleming 8
Scott Brown & Mims White 131
vs. manslaughter 16
Weston family 42, 48

N

Naillon, Benjamin "Parker" 124
newspaper articles
   Asheville Messenger 9
   Asheville News 15, 28
   Asheville Weekly Citizen 65, 68, 77, 119
   Gastonia Gazette 163
   Harper's Weekly 55, 128
   Lenoir Topic 96
   Los Angeles Times 154
   Mountain Voice 87, **88**
   News and Observer 79, 80
   New York Herald 32, 49
   New York Times 79, 80
   North-Carolina Star 4, 6, 10
   North-Carolinian 9
   Oasis 145, 155, 159
   Oma Hicks and Sheriff Jake Lowe **133**
   Raleigh Register 4
   Rutherford Star 45
   San Francisco Call 155
   Tri-Weekly Commercial 5
   Tucson Daily Citizen 150
   Union and American 24
   Voice (Mountain Voice) 90
   Wilmington Morning Star 68
North Carolina. *See also* Ku Klux Klan
   16th Regiment NC flag **27**
   adultery/fornication offense **142**
   Alamance County 32

Buncombe County 68, 70, 83, 94, 107, 115
Burke County 19, 180
Caldwell County 96, 101
Caswell County 32
Cherokee County 39
Cleveland County 59, 62, 106
Deep Creek 80
free suffrage 2
Golden Valley 56
Halifax County 68, 69
Haywood County 120, 127
Henderson County 94
The History of a Southern State—North Carolina (Leffler & Newsome) 180
House of Commons 1, 3, 10
insurrection 32
Jackson County 66, 76, 80
land of the sky 128
Madison County/Bloody Madison
    The Kingdom of Madison (Wellman) 181
    Laurel River 12
    Marshall jail 34
    Marshall raided 20
    Pigeon River 120
    Ray brothers trial 34
    Shelton/Landers capture reward 15
    Shelton Laurel massacre 12
Mitchell County 94, 142, 157
mountain coves isolated 35
political divides 31
Prohibition early 70
railroad **137**
Rutherford County 44, 53, 56, 58, 59, 61
secedes from Union 11, 19
Smoky Mountains x, 12, 13, 93, 120
Swain County 80
Toe River Valley 28
Tuckasegee River 80
twenty-dollar rule 62
voting and land ownership 2
Waynesville, land of the sky 128
Webster 65
Western North Carolina
    history (Arthur) 183
    map of **vi–vii**

Yadkin County 80
Yancey County 30, 33, 35, 182, 183
Norton, Bayliss 21, 180
Norton, Delany Jane 21, 25
Norton, Drury 14, 180. *See also* Franklin, Nancy Shelton Norton
Norton, George 21, 25
Norton, James 21, 180
Norton, Josiah 21, 180

O

oaths 16, 31, 54
O'Brien, William 158
The Old Ship of Zion 71
O'Malley, J. J. 128, 129, 134
open-air market 99
Oriental Saloon 149
Owens brothers (George and Louis) 153
Owens, Rosa Dove "Rose" 122

P

Packett, Joe 126
Palmer, J. B. (Colonel) 30
Pearson, Mart 62
Penland homestead 93
Penland, Milt 30
Penland, Stokes 99
Peters, Cal 154
Piercy, W. E. (Sheriff) 34
pistols. *See* firearms
politics. *See also* Civil War
  Anderson/Ray trials 96
  Biggerstaff brothers 54
  Democrats 3, 41, 45, 50
  free suffrage 2
  Ku Klux Klan oath 54
  Republicans 41, 45
  widening divides **29**, 31
post-traumatic stress 48
poverty/famine 40. *See also* Civil War
prisons/jails
  Bakersville 68
  Buncombe County, the "Bastille" 68, 83, 94
  Caldwell County 96

Henderson County 94
jailbreaks xii, 103, 114, 135, 162
Marshall 34
Mitchell County jail 95
South Carolina prison 53
Tombstone 154
Yuma Territorial Penitentiary 149
Pritchard, George (Sheriff) 157
Pritchard, Jeter (Senator) 156
Prohibition. *See also* alcohol
becomes law 125
blockaders 40, 65
bribes 2
moonshiners 121, **125, 128**
tax and Bureau of Internal Revenue 41, 65, 70, 90
Temperance Movement 70
public executions 50, 79. *See also* hangings
Pumpkin Patch Mountain 93
Purdy (Dr.) 159
Putnam, William 97

R

railroads
Denver & Rio Grande Western Railroad 146
East TN & Western NC "Tweetsie" **136**
mining impetus 189
railroads **137, 147**
Southern Pacific Railroad 140, 145, 151
train robberies 150
Ramsey, Goodson 110
Rathbone, Sara 134
Ray, Edward W.
Anderson bond 89
character 86
claim jumper 88
escapes 93, 103, 106, 107
Malissa, wife 91, 189
Moonshine Wars (Dean) 189
murders 87, 93
surrenders 93
Ray, Garrett D. 37, 188
Ray Mica mine 179
Ray, Montraville "Mont"
Amos Ray, father 27, 30, 173

AWOL **28**, 174
  brothers 28, 33
  kills A. J. Brown 33
  Marshall card/ID 31
  photograph **28**
  State v. Montraville Ray 35
  wives 183
  years on the lam 34, 35
Ray, Sandy (Rev.) 110
Reconstruction 54, 70. *See also* votes; *See also* politics
Red Strings (Heroes of America) 53
Renfro, Marcus 37
Republicans. *See also* votes; *See also* politics
  biracial coalition 186
  Black voters 54
  elite 57
  James McGaha 56
  James M. Justice 59
  newspaper, *The Voice* 90
  Party meetings 142
  Reconstruction 54
revolvers. *See* firearms
rewards 15, 34, 93, 106, 155
Reynolds (Deputy) 111
Reynolds, Gus 105
Reynolds, Will 105
Richardson 152
Rich (Sheriff) 75, 102, 105, 107
rifles. *See* firearms
righteous retribution 8
Roaring Twenties 127
Ross, Delbert "Dell" 119
Rusher, Tom 188
Russell (Governor) 115, 118, 163
Rymer, Charley 110
Rymer, Will 110

S

saloons. *See also* alcohol
  cowboys **143**
  Exchange Saloon 142
  faro game **144**
  GEM Saloon **142**
  Oriental Saloon 149

Schwertner 151
salt as survival 20
Scales (Governor) 102, 105
Scoggins, Eli 98
Sevier, D. E. (Dr.) 110
Shelton, James 14
Shelton, John 25, 182
Shelton Laurel settlement 12, 20
Shelton, Roderick 13
Shipp (Judge) 69, 94
Shipp, Thomas **116**
shoes 35, 131
shotgun. *See* firearms
Shotwell, Randolph **45,** 47, 60, 184
Sierra Madre Mountains 145
Silver Lake Resort 140, **141**
Slaughter, John (Texas Ranger) **151**
slavery
   Amendments/Enforcement Acts 56
   cowhiding 5
   emancipation 31, 56, 117, 189
   Milt Penland 30
   Plato Durham 63
   Union Provost Marshal oath 31
Sluder, Philetus 103, 105
Smalley, George 150, **155**
Smith, Abram **116**
Smith, Will 110
Smoky Mountains x, 12, 13, 93, 120
smuggling 149
Southern elites 10
Southern Pacific Railroad 140, 145, 151. *See also* railroads
Sparks, Hardy 97, 191
Sparks, Reuben 102, 191
Stamey, M. G. (Attorney) 127
Starnes, Jesse R. 117
Stephens (Senator) 32
Stewart, Ike 97
Stiles, Billy 151, 152, 154, **155**, 196
Stoneman, George H. 19
Styles, Jane E. 182
Sullivan, Mike 141
Susan (N. Franklin attacks) 23
Swannanoa Valley 84, 115

T

T., Aunt 105
tax stamp 90
Taylor, Terrell (Sheriff) 51, 61, 185
Temperance Movement 70. *See also* alcohol
Tennessee 21, 24, 136, 137
Texas Rangers 151, 153
Thirteenth Amendment 56
trafficking 149
train robberies 150, **154**. *See also* railroads
turncoats 18, 23, 28
twenty-dollar rule 62

U

Unaka range 76
Union Provost Marshal oath 31
Until He Is Dead (Rusher) 197
"Up on Big Pigeon" (Rathbone) 134
US Deputy Marshals 70, 86, 144, **145**

V

Vandiver, Walter 113
Victims (Shaw) 181
violence. *See also* politics
    Boca Brewery and Sawmill Co. **138**
    Confederate Army 20
    familial 14, 53, 85, 121
    Ku Klux Klan 31, 32, 55, 61
    Yancey County 28, 174
votes 2, 31, 54, 56. *See also* politics
    biracial coalition 186
    free suffrage 2
    land ownership requirement 2

W

Walker (Sheriff) 47
Warner, Charles Dudley 96
warrants 35, 87, **148**
Watson (Dr.) 85
weapons. *See* firearms
Weaver, D. B. (Dr.) 110
Weaverville 111, 116

Webb, Leon "Corn" 69, 75
Weeks, M. E. 22, 25, 181
Welch (Sheriff) 77
Wells Fargo & Co. 146, **147**, 151
Western North Carolina—a History (Arthur) 183
Weston family murder 42, 48
Wheeler, Henry 36
Wheeler, Hiram 34
whiskey 40, 56, 65, 183. *See also* alcohol
White, H. A. (Captain) 181
White, Mims 127, 130, 131
White, Scott (Sheriff) 154
White supremacy. *See* Ku Klux Klan
Williams, Joshua 36
Williams, Mrs. 44
Williamson (Colonel) 105
Wilson, I. N. 98
Wilson, Mary (N. Franklin attacks) 23
Wilson, Richard "Dick" W. 67
witness, deathbed 16
Worley (Sheriff) 111, 114, 118

Y

Yoas, "Bravo Juan" Tom 153
York, Charles 84, 105, 191
York, D. D. **v**, x
York, Eveline "Vicey" Reese **85**, 192
York, John 84, 85, 192
York, William Samuel 192
Young, C. D. (Private) 183
Yuma Territorial Penitentiary 149

About the Author

Nadia Dean is the author of *A Demand of Blood: The Cherokee War of 1776*, and the writer/producer/director of the award-winning docudrama *Cameron*. She is currently at work on two books and a teleplay about North Carolina's nineteenth-century wild frontier. Nadia and her husband, an Eastern Band Cherokee, make their home in the Smoky Mountains.

Learn more about Nadia and her other work: nadiadean.com

Follow Nadia on Facebook: Nadia Dean, author

Made in the USA
Middletown, DE
08 November 2023

42222343R00137